**AA**

ILLUSTRATED GUIDE TO

# FRANCE

Illustrated Guide to France LEGEND 2002

Motorway, toll section (1),
Motorway, free section (2)

Toll gate (1), Service area (2),
Resting area (3)

Junction: complete (1),
Restricted (2), exit number

Connecting road between main
towns (green road sign) (1),
Trunk road (2)

Regional connecting road (1),
Other road (2)

Distances in kilometres (km),
Road numbering: motorway

Distances in kilometres on road,
Road numbering: other roads

Railway, Station,
Stopping place, Tunnel

Built-up area (1),
Industrial park (2), Woods (3)

International boundary (1),
Park boundary (2)

Cathedral (1), Abbey (2),
Church (3), Chapel (4)

Castle (1), Castle open to the
public (2), Museum (3)

Spa (1), Winter sports resort (2),
Viewpoint (3)

Place of interest (1),
Lighthouse (2)

Town of tourist interest

**LA ROCHELLE**
Baou-des-Blanc

For complete coverage of France please
refer to AA Road Atlas France at 1:250 000

# INTERNATIONAL DISTINGUISHING SIGNS

The following signs are used on the regional opener maps, which appear at the beginning of each section, to indicate adjacent countries.

| | | | | | | | |
|---|---|---|---|---|---|---|---|
| AND | Andorra | B | Belgium | CH | Switzerland | D | Germany |
| E | Spain | I | Italy | L | Luxembourg | NL | Netherlands |

Published by AA Publishing (a trading name of Automobile Association Developments Limited, whose registered office is Millstream, Maidenhead Road, Windsor, SL4 5GD. Registered number 1878835). A01080.

Road Atlas map extracts © Institut Géographique National (france).
Regional (chapter) opener maps © Automobile Association Developments Limited 2003.

ISBN s/b 0 7495 3493 1
ISBN h/b 0 7495 1277 6
Colour separation by Leo Reproduction
Printed & bound in China by Leo Paper Products

Additional research for the 2003 edition:
Jan Beart-Albrecht

Contributors:
Paul Atterbury (*The North, The Loire*)
Keith Howell (*Paris and the Ile de France*)
John Lloyd (*Burgundy, The Rhône Valley*)
Robin Neillands (*Brittany, Normandy*)
Tony Oliver (*Auvergne and Languedoc, Provence and the Côte d'Azur*)
Ian Powys (*Alsace and Lorraine, Franche-Comté*)
Mary Ratcliffe (*The Atlantic Coast, Périgord and Quercy*)
Kev Reynolds (*The Pyrenees*)
Richard Sale (*Auvergne and Languedoc, Provence and the Côte d'Azur*)
Melissa Shales (*Berry and Limousin*)
John White (*The Alps*)

# CONTENTS

# REGIONS AND *DÉPARTEMENTS*

I n this book France has been divided into 16 regions as numbered and colour-coded on the map opposite. Individual maps of these regions appear at the beginning of each section.

The maps also show the *départements* into which France is divided. Each *département* has a standard number, as shown on the map and in the key, which for postal purposes replaces its name. These numbers also form part of the registration number of French cars, thus indicating the *département* in which the car was registered. The *départements* are listed here alphabetically under the regional headings of the book.

## 1 BRITTANY
*(Bretagne)*
Côtes-du-Nord  22
Finistère  29
Ille-et-Vilaine  35
Morbihan  56

## 2 NORMANDY
*(Normandie)*
Calvados  14
Eure  27
Manche  50
Orne  61
Seine-Maritime  76

## 3 THE NORTH
*(Nord)*
Aisne  02
Ardennes  08
Aube  10
Marne  51
Marne (Haute-)  52
Nord  59
Oise  60
Pas-de-Calais  62
Somme  80

## 4 ALSACE AND LORRAINE
*(Alsace et Lorraine)*
Meurthe-et-Moselle  54
Meuse  55
Moselle  57
Rhin (Bas-)  67
Rhin (Haut-)  68
Vosges  88

## 5 THE LOIRE
*(Loire)*
Cher  18 (part)
Eure-et-Loir  28
Indre  36 (part)
Indre-et-Loire  37
Loir-et-Cher  41
Loire-Atlantique  44
Loiret  45
Maine-et-Loire  49
Mayenne  53
Sarthe  72
Sèvres (Deux-)  79 (part)
Vienne  86 (part)

## 6 PARIS AND THE ILE DE FRANCE
*(Paris et Ile de France)*
Essonne  91
Hauts-de-Seine  92
Paris  75
Seine-et-Marne  77
Yvelines  78
Seine-St-Denis  93
Val-de-Marne  94
Val-d'Oise  95

## 7 BURGUNDY
*(Bourgogne)*
Côte-d'Or  21
Nièvre  58
Saône-et-Loire  71
Yonne  89

## 8 FRANCHE-COMTÉ
*(Franche-Comté)*
Belfort (Territoire-de)  90
Doubs  25
Jura  39
Saône (Haute-)  70

## 9 THE ATLANTIC COAST
*(Côte Atlantique)*
Charente  16
Charente-Maritime  17
Gironde  33
Landes  40
Sèvres (Deux-)  79 (part)
Vendée  85
Vienne  86 (part)

## 10 BERRY AND LIMOUSIN
*(Berry et Limousin)*
Cher  18 (part)
Creuse  23
Indre  36 (part)
Vienne (Haute-)  87

## 11 AUVERGNE AND LANGUEDOC
*(Auvergne et Languedoc)*
Allier  03
Ardèche  07 (part)
Aveyron  12 (part)
Cantal  15
Gard  30 (part)
Hérault  34
Loire (Haute-)  43
Lozère  48
Puy-de-Dôme  63
Tarn  81

## 12 THE RHÔNE VALLEY
*(Vallée du Rhône)*
Ain  01 (part)
Ardèche  07 (part)
Drôme  26 (part)
Isère  38 (part)
Loire  42
Rhône  69

## 13 THE ALPS
*(Alpes)*
Ain  01 (part)
Alpes (Hautes-)  05
Drôme  26 (part)
Isère  38 (part)
Savoie  73
Savoie (Haut-)  74

## 14 PÉRIGORD AND QUERCY
*(Périgord et Quercy)*
Aveyron  12 (part)
Corrèze  19
Dordogne  24
Lot  46
Lot-et-Garonne  47
Tarn-et-Garonne  82

## 15 THE PYRENEES
*(Pyrénées)*
Ariège  09
Aude  11
Garonne (Haut-)  31
Gers  32
Pyrénées-Atlantiques  64
Pyrénées (Hautes-)  65
Pyrénées Orientales  66

## 16 PROVENCE AND THE CÔTE D'AZUR
*(Provence et Côte d'Azur)*
Alpes-de-Haute-Provence  04
Alpes Maritimes  06
Bouches-du-Rhône  13
Drôme  26 (part)
Gard  30 (part)
Var  83
Vaucluse  84

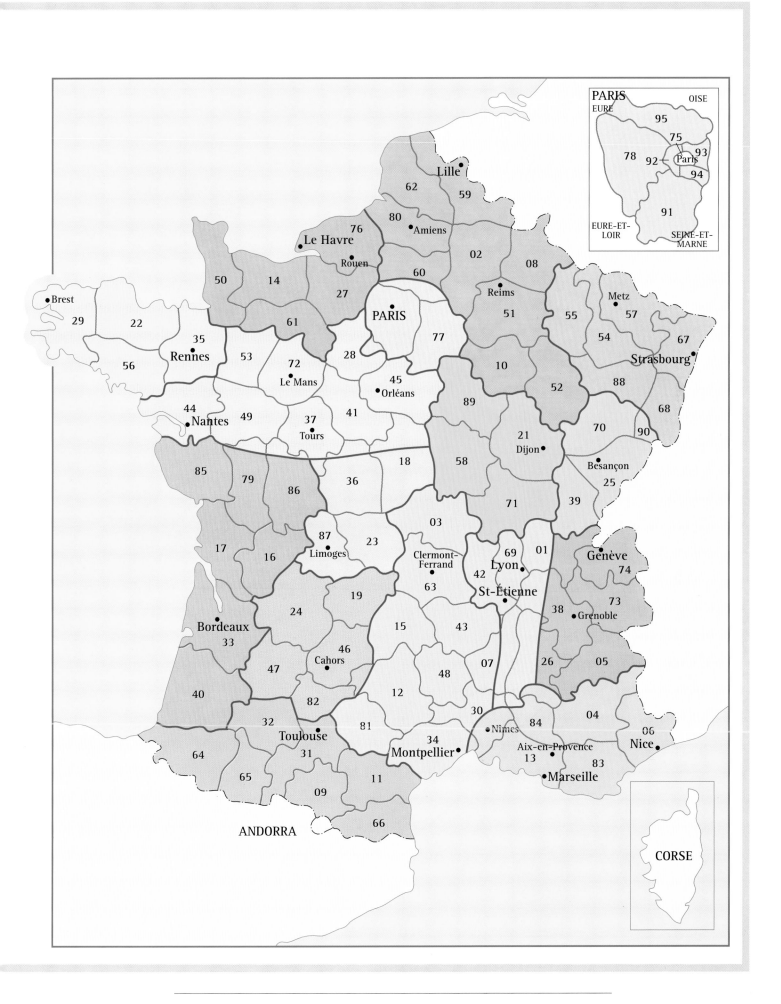

PARIS

OISE

EURE

95

75

78    92 — Paris    93

94

91

EURE-ET-LOIR

SEINE-ET-MARNE

Lille

62

59

80    •Amiens

76

Le Havre

•Rouen

02

08

50    14    27    60

•Reims

•Brest

29    22

35

Rennes

53

72

Le Mans

28

51

55

Metz•

57

54

67

Strasbourg•

PARIS

77

10

52

88

56

45

•Orléans

89

68

44    49    41

Nantes•

37

Tours•

21

Dijon•

70    90

•Besançon

85    79    86    36    18    58    25

71    39

03

87    •Limoges    23

Clermont-Ferrand•

69

Lyon•

01    Genève•

74

17    16

42

63

St-Étienne•

38    73

•Grenoble

24    19    15    43

26    05

Bordeaux•

33

46    Cahors•    12    07    04

47    48    30

40    82    •Nîmes    84

32    81    34    Aix-en-Provence    06    Nice•

Toulouse•    Montpellier•    13    83

31    Marseille•

64    65    09    11    66

ANDORRA

CORSE

# A JOURNEY THROUGH FRANCE

France is the heart of Europe, and in terms of its landscape, architecture, culture and history it is incomparable, without rival in the wealth and diversity of its appeal. Just across the Channel, and increasingly accessible, there is another world, full of secret delights waiting to be discovered and whose pleasures are a constant temptation to the senses. It is a world of space, light and colour, to be enjoyed in haste or at leisure, and made memorable by its contrasts. In France there is room still for both the traditional and the modern and for a way of life that reflects both the pace of change and the impact of centuries of civilisation.

This book is a guide to the best of France, a region by region exploration of the familiar and the unfamiliar by writers and photographers united by their love of the country, and by their intimate knowledge of their chosen areas. Together, they bring to life the distinctive qualities of a country remarkable for its variety in a book designed to please both the casual visitor and the dedicated traveller.

France is a country for all tastes and all times, always responsive to visitors' expectations and demands. This book will make easier the appreciation and enjoyment of a country whose essential differences are part of its widespread appeal.

PAUL ATTERBURY

# BRITTANY

Brittany is not like other parts of France. Brittany is Celtic, outward-looking, defiant, a wolf's head snapping and snarling at the green waves of the Atlantic. It is a place where the people sing their own songs, speak their own tongue and maintain their own ways.

That Brittany remains so different from other parts of France is hardly surprising because it became part of France late. The first dynastic link came in 1491 when the Duchess Anne – the same duchess who is commemorated in the names of restaurants and cafés all over Brittany – married Charles VIII of France. To maintain the link when he died in 1498 she then married his successor, Louis XII. Her daughter Claude married François I, finally ceding the Duchy to the French Crown in 1532.

Brittany is a place of magic and myth. King Arthur's wizard, Merlin, lives on in Brittany, trapped inside a stone in the Fôret de Brocéliande, which some call the Fôret de Paimpont. In times of drought locas go to the stone to pour water on it and magically, it usually rains. In a nearby castle Lancelot of the Lake was born.

Those who prefer a legendary character who actually lived need look no further than Dinan, home of the good knight and sometime constable of France, Bertrand du Guesclin. His body may lie with the kings in St-Denis, but his heart is safe in Dinan. For something rather more curious, visitors can splash across at low tide from St Malo to the Ile du Grand Bé, and visit the grave of the writer Chateaubriand, all alone on the rock, facing out to sea.

Brittany is full of such fabled characters and living legends. It boasts over 7,000 saints, most of whom no foreigner has ever heard of, though some, such as St Yves, are world-famous. To their shrines go the pilgrimage processions, the Breton *pardons*, to their glory and memory stand the great calvaries and the *enclos paroissiaux* (parish closes) of Finistère. Brittany has menhirs, including lines of these megaliths at Carnac, great castles such as Josselin and walled towns such as Vannes, Vitré and St Malo, the city of the Corsairs, and many more pretty places.

The coastline is long, rugged and full of sandy beaches and rocky coves, with offshore islands where seabirds gather. And for something different yet again, there is the Morbihan, the wonderful 'little sea' of Brittany (*Mor* meaning sea and *bihan*, small). The Bretons prize both the coast, Amorica, the Country of the Sea, and the Argoat, the Country of Wood, with its tracery of footpaths, canals and winding country roads. Brittany is not a place to rush around in, but one where wise visitors take their time, exploring this Celtic province at a gentle pace.

If there is a snag with Brittany – and every honest guidebook finds at least one – it is that this is not the place to visit if you hate seafood. Here it is excellent.

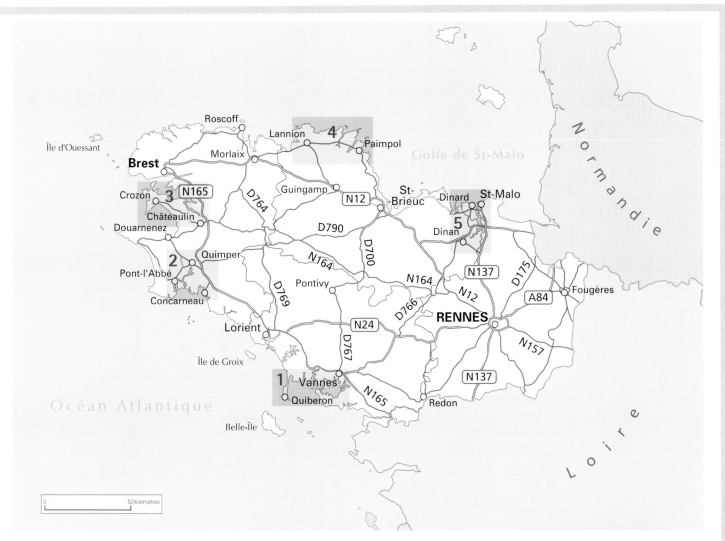

*Traditional Breton costumes (right)*

*Finistère, in the north-west, has a dramatic rocky coast (below right).*

*Pilgrimage processions, or pardons, take place throughout Brittany. Those saints who have a shrine – there are many in the region – are traditionally celebrated in these annual events.*

*Standing stones are a common sight in Brittany. Around Carnac (above) there are more than 5,000.*

# THE MORBIHAN GULF AND THE MEGALITHS OF CARNAC

The southern *département* of Brittany, Morbihan, is full of interest. It contains historic towns such as Vannes and Auray, the famous menhirs or standing stones of Carnac and the long Quiberon peninsula. All these places and many others worth visiting lie on or around the shores of the Morbihan. This great tidal gulf, crammed with islands, is a paradise for yachtsmen and sea birds.

*Standing stones such as these at Carnac may have indicated the direction of the sunrise at the solstices and the equinox, so playing a part in sun worship*

## Carnac

The standing stones of Carnac are said to form part of a prehistoric solar observatory arranged in long lines, one of which, the Alignements du Ménec, is nearly 1.5km long. The sight of these long lines of standing stones is curiously impressive. The story of what their purpose may be and how they were preserved is told in Carnac's Musée Miln-Le Rouzic.

## Locmariaquer

This village overlooks the narrow gap through which the Atlantic pours into the Morbihan gulf, and is another prehistoric sight, famous for the great dolmens and menhirs that lie in and around the village in considerable numbers. The largest and most impressive of all are the shattered Grand Menhir, which was over 20m tall, and the great flat Table des Marchands, which seals a huge tumulus. Boats of the Navix and Compagnie des Iles fleets stop here on their cruise around the gulf.

## Golfe du Morbihan

The Morbihan, or 'little sea', of Brittany, is one of the great attractions of the province. This is not simply because of the beauty of the gulf itself, a maze of sandbanks and green islands flooded twice daily by the Atlantic, but also because of the interesting places that lie around the shore.

The gulf is some 20km wide and about 15km in length, running inland from the narrow channel between Locmariaquer and

**Comité Départemental du Tourisme du Morbihan**
PIBS, Alée Nicolas-le-Blanc – BP 408
56010 Vannes Cedex
Tel: 02 97 54 06 56
www.morbihan.com

**Touring:**
AA Road Map France series 1: Bretagne

## MEGALITHS

Brittany is full of prehistoric sites, and menhirs, or standing stones, appear all over the province. There is a particularly splendid specimen at St Duzec, near Perros-Guirec, and more at St Pierre-Quiberon in the Morbihan, close to the large dolmens at Locmariaquer. These great flat stones cover grave-pits that date back to the early Celtic period, long before the coming of the Romans who invaded this part of Gaul in the 1st century BC. Splendid as these are, no megalithic site in Europe can rival the standing stones of Carnac. The word 'megalith' means 'large stone', and there are more than 5,000 megaliths around Carnac, most of them arranged in long lines – a feature that adds to the great mystery surrounding their transportation and erection. The manpower required must have been immense. But what are they for?

The Musée Miln-Le Rouzic in Carnac, founded by a Scot in 1881, gives a good account of the Carnac megaliths and their construction and contains a great number of prehistoric artefacts.

Port-Navalo to the walled city of Vannes. About 40 of the gulf's many islands are inhabited. The largest of these is the Ile aux Moines, which, as the name indicates, was once inhabited by a community of monks. The climate of this island is a certain attraction, for it is mild and mellow and permits palm trees and exotic flowers such as mimosa and camellias to flourish among the small walled gardens. The Ile aux Moines can be visited by taking one of the Navix or Compagnie des Iles ferries that ply around the gulf from Vannes.

The Ile d'Arz, just to the east of the Ile aux Moines, is somewhat smaller but still inhabited and noted for its megalithic tombs, which are common in and around the gulf.

## Quiberon

Set at the far end of a long peninsula, the town of Quiberon is a sardine fishing port and tourist resort, the point of departure for visitors sailing to Belle-Ile. The Quiberon peninsula is flanked by wide beaches popular with devotees of sand yachting, and the Côte Sauvage is the name given to the peninsula's wild west coast.

Places to visit here include the beautiful village of Port Maria at the southern end of the Côte Sauvage, and if time permits, Belle-Ile, an hour away by ferry. Belle-Ile once belonged to Nicholas Fouquet, finance minister to Louis XIV, and was captured briefly by the British in 1761. The main town, Le Palais, is most attractive. The island's west coast is, like that of the Quiberon peninsula, known as the Côte Sauvage.

## St Gildas-de-Rhuys

The village here grew up around the monastery founded by St Gildas-de-Rhuys in the 6th century, which became famous after Abélard, a noted scholar and the lover of Héloïse, became the abbot here at the end of the 11th century.

Visitors to St Gildas can see the much-restored abbey church, built in the 11th century, which still holds the tomb of St Gildas and a reliquary containing his arms and legs. The abbey is set in a beautiful spot near the sea and the great ducal castle of Suscinio, which was besieged and taken by Bertrand du Guesclin in 1373. The repairs he made to the breach can still be seen in the curtain wall. Close to Suscinio is the town of Sarzeau, now a resort and once the home of Lesage, the author of *Gil Blas*.

## Vannes

Walled Vannes is a splendid example of a medieval town, and with the walls still standing above formal gardens the setting is beautiful.

The streets of Vannes are narrow and winding, and lead to the Cathédrale St-Pierre, which holds the tomb of St Vincent Ferrier, who died in Vannes in 1419. The town has a great many old houses, one of which bears two gargoyles known locally as Vannes and his Wife; there are some further very fine examples to be seen in Rue de la Monnaie.

*Quiberon harbour is used by both sardine fishermen and pleasure boats since, like many fishing ports in Brittany, the town is also a popular tourist resort.*

*A good number of robust town houses, some of which have been turned into shops, survive in the old quarter of Vannes.*

# QUIMPER AND THE COAST OF CORNOUAILLE

The southern part of the *département* of Finistère, Cornouaille is the old heart of Brittany, a place of legend and folklore. Part of this area, around Pont-l'Abbé, is the Bigouden district, a place where the Breton language is still spoken and where visitors are most likely to see people wearing traditional costume.

## Bénodet

Bénodet is the archetypal modern seaside resort. It has beaches and a marina, a conference centre, a casino and many hotels, restaurants and discothèques, as well as a film festival, held every year in the last two weeks of June.

Essential sights include the lighthouse – the Phare de la Pyramide and there are various corniches that give fine views over the sea and the harbour. The church of St Thomas dates from the 13th century and is dedicated to the English martyr St Thomas à Becket. There is a bridge across the Odet and a ferry to the village of Ste Marine, and boats go upstream to Quimper.

## Concarneau

Concarneau is one of the major fishing ports of Brittany and a particularly attractive one, with a medieval quarter – the *ville close* – a colourful fishing fleet and an annual festival. This takes place on the third Sunday in August, when the blue nets of the fleet are hung up with bunting and most of the fishermen don traditional costume.

Sights to see in Concarneau include the daily fish auction, where a great number and variety of fish, especially tunny, are sold. The ville close occupies an island in the middle of the port and a walk around its ramparts is the best way to look at the new town on the mainland and the fishing fleet in the harbour.

## Fouesnant

This pretty village stands in rich farming country, surrounded by apple and cherry orchards, the former for production of Breton *cidre-bouché*, for which the village is famous. The villagers usually wear traditional dress and always do for the *pardon* of St Anne, which takes place on the nearest Sunday to the 26th July. Local costume is also worn by the figures depicted in the carvings on the monument outside the 12th-century church.

## Loctudy

The tiny seaport of Loctudy lies at the mouth of the Pont-l'Abbé estuary and was once one of the main fishing ports for the Bigouden district. The setting and the small houses and cottages around the harbour are the chief attractions, and the church is said to be the finest Romanesque church in all Brittany. From the harbour it is possible to take a boat to Ile-Tudy, a pretty fishing port well off the tourist track.

### COIFFES

Breton *coiffes*, attractive lace head-dresses, were once an everyday feature of Breton women's dress but are rarely seen today except at *pardons*, at weddings in Finistère and, from time to time, in church and at markets. The *coiffe* is the most distinctive item of traditional Breton apparel but the full costume includes a black dress and a fine lace apron, which, like the *coiffe*, varies in style from place to place. The men have their own costume – rather less distinctive, again in black but with an embroidered waistcoat and a beribboned felt hat – but it is usually the ladies' starched and lacey *coiffes* that steal the show.

Of the several different regional styles of Breton *coiffe*, the most famous is the tall 'Bigouden' *coiffe* from the country around Pont-l'Abbé. There is a good display of *coiffes* in the museum at Quimper.

*Built between the mid-13th and early 16th centuries, Quimper's most striking cathedral is considered to be the most complete Gothic cathedral in Brittany. Its twin spires were added much later, in 1856.*

## THE BRETON LANGUAGE

Breton is a Celtic tongue and those who speak Welsh, Cornish or Gaelic, especially Irish Gaelic, can understand it, at least to a certain degree. Undermined for many years by French, Breton is now undergoing a revival, and is taught again in many schools in Brittany, especially in Finistère, where visitors may sometimes hear it spoken in village markets. Visitors will soon pick up a few Breton words, realising that *ker* means place or village, *lann* means church, *plou* means parish and *aber* means estuary

## SEAWEED

Brittany is an agricultural and fishing province, the sea and land producing many valuable cash crops. Among the less familiar harvests is that of seaweed, which is dredged from estuaries, stacked in great piles in the fields and burnt to provide a rich fertiliser. A side benefit is that the constant dredging for seaweed helps to keep the estuaries open and small boats' propellers free of weed. Seaweed is also processed and used in a range of products, from cosmetics to iodine.

**Comité Départemental du Tourisme du Finistère**
11, Rue Théodore-le-Hars – BP 1419
29140 Quimper Cedex
Tel: 02 98 76 20 70
www.finisteretourisme.com

**Touring:**
AA Road Map France series 1: Bretagne

## Pont-l'Abbé

Pont-l'Abbé is the capital of the *pays Bigouden*, the part of Brittany that has most retained its old customs, costumes and traditions. It stands at the head of a wide estuary and takes its name from the bridge that was built here in the Middle Ages by monks from Loctudy. Sights to see include the good possibility of a lace *coiffe*, especially on Sunday outside the abbey church of Notre-Dames-des-Carmes. They are sure to be worn for the town *pardon*, which takes place on the first Sunday after 15 July. Alternatively, *coiffes* can be seen in the Bigouden museum in the castle.

## Quimper

Set astride the River Odet, Quimper is the capital of Cornouaille. The town hosts an annual international folk music festival, the Festival de Cornouaille, which attracts performers from all over the world but in particular from the Celtic fringes in Wales, Cornwall and Ireland.

The cathedral is dedicated to a Breton saint, St Corentin, and bears between the two towers the equestrian statue of King Gradlon, ruler of the legendary city of Y's. When Y's was destroyed in a flood, the king came to live in Quimper, where St Corentin looked after him. St Corentin lived on a miraculous fish: he ate half of it every day, throwing the other half into the Odet, where it regrew the missing half, ready to be caught and half-eaten again next day – a reliable if monotonous diet.

The Musée des Beaux-Arts in the town hall has an extensive collection, and the Musée Départemental Breton explains Breton life and the traditions of Finistère. The town has attractive public gardens and good walks along the Odet and up to Mont Frugy.

*Cornouaille's attachment to its roots can be seen in the manufacture and sale of traditional artefacts such as these plates.*

# THE WEST COAST AND THE CROZON PENINSULA

The Crozon peninsula rolls out westwards between the jaws of Brittany like a great lolling tongue lapping at the chill green waters of the Atlantic.

Although most of the peninsula is a summer resort, it is a place to visit out of season, when the great gales come booming in from the sea, pounding the coast until the air is full of salt spray. The hinterland is the Argoat, the old forested heart of Brittany.

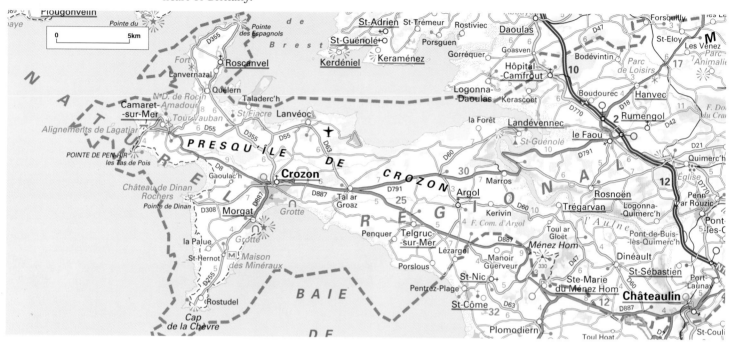

Comité Départemental du Tourisme du Finistère

11, Rue Théodore-le-Hars – BP 1419
29140 Quimper Cedex
Tel: 02 98 76 20 70
www.finisteretourisme.com

**Touring:**
AA Road Map France series 1: Bretagne

## Camaret-sur-Mer

Camaret is the foremost lobster port of France, but most of these succulent spiny delights vanish soon after landing *en route* for the restaurants of Paris, Nice, London or New York. Even so, the restaurants of Camaret can provide delicious meals and the port itself is pretty. So is the coast on either side, but particularly that to the north, up to the Pointe des Espagnols and the Brest Roads. The American inventor Robert Fulton used the waters off Camaret for the first experiments with his submarine in 1801, during the Napoleonic Wars. Propelled by oars and without a periscope, the submarine unsuccessfully attempted to sink a British frigate in the bay, but Fulton and his gallant crew eventually surfaced and survived.

Apart from fishing, Camaret is a seaside resort and local sights include the Château Vauban, built to protect Brest in the 17th century, and the chapel of Notre-Dame at the end of the Sillon dyke.

*The many opportunities to dine on delicious lobsters and langoustines do much to make Camaret-sur-Mer a popular tourist centre. But it is also a town with a history, for in 1694 the Château Vauban played a significant part in seeing off an attack on the port by a combined British and Dutch fleet.*

beneath a tomb in the churchyard in Minihy-Tréguier.

## Châteaulin

This little town on the River Aulne is noted in Brittany for its salmon fishing. Much of the river is tidal and Châteaulin has quays, but the tide subsides before getting this far inland. The best fishing takes place between Châteaulin and the village of Châteauneuf-du-Faou, some 25km upstream. The setting of Châteaulin, a wooded river valley, is most attractive and the town is a good excursion centre.

A little way to the west Ménez-Hom rises against the sky, a great bulk of moorland. At its foot is the small chapel of Ste-Marie-du-Ménez-Hom, from where a footpath leads up to the top of the hill. There is a statue of King Gradlon of Y's in the calvary at Argol, and 7km away, in the village of Cast, there is one to St Hubert, the patron saint of hunters.

## Crozon

Crozon is the small town that gave its name to the entire peninsula. It is a tourist centre crammed with visitors from Easter to October, although almost empty in winter. The church was built in 1900 and contains a tablet recording the fate of the Theban Legion, who underwent a mass conversion to Christianity and were crucified, all 10,000 of them, on Mount Ararat.

Places to visit around Crozon include the beaches at Kerloch and Cap de la Chèvre to the south. Another good excursion is to Pointe Dinan, to watch the waves coming in during a gale. The 'Dinan castle' referred to on maps is simply a large rock joined to the mainland by a natural rock bridge.

## Le Faou

This village at the head of the Faou estuary lies on the main road that leads round from Brest on to the Crozon peninsula. Apart from the old houses and the riverside church, it is chiefly notable as a tourist centre for Argoat and the area around the Brest Roads. A few kilometres to the north lies Daoulas, a small town with a very old *enclos paroissial* (parish close) and calvary. Another excursion from Le Faou is the ride round the Corniche de Térénez.

## Morgat

Morgat is the main seaside resort on the south shore of the Crozon peninsula, looking out to the bay of Douarnenez. Like most of the villages on the coast of Brittany, it is also a fishing port and a yachting centre with a large marina, harbour and good beach. The great attraction of Morgat is the caves that stud the surrounding cliffs. Some are of considerable size, while others are very colourful, with different kinds of rock. One, the Chambre du Diable, leads out to the cliff top. Some of the caves can be reached at high tide on boat trips from the mole in Morgat.

*There are many excellent viewpoints along the Crozon peninsula, but in places the combination of a rocky coastline and strong currents restricts bathing.*

# CASTLES AND FORTRESSES OF INLAND BRITTANY

Although Brittany has many coastal castles – notably at the Fort de la Latte and the Tour Solidor near St Malo, at Suscinio in the south, at Dinan above the Rance – the most splendid examples of medieval military architecture in the province are to be discovered further inland. Their purpose was both to defend the hinterland from ravaging armies and to protect Brittany's land frontiers from its most implacable foe, France.

Fortunately, these castles had to be maintained and repaired even after the advent of the cannon, and when the final conquest came, it was through marriage rather than the use of the ultimo ratio regis, 'the king's last argument' – artillery. As a result they survived the blast of war and even the hand of Cardinal Richelieu, who destroyed many strongholds of the turbulent, provincial French nobility. Many are still to be found in good condition.

## Josselin

The castle at Josselin was and remains the home of the dukes of Rohan, one of the oldest and proudest of the Breton noble families. 'King I am not, Prince I would not stoop to be, I am the Duke of Rohan', proclaims one of the family mottoes.

The present castle dates from the late 15th century, when it replaced the one dismantled by the Duke of Brittany. The original castle was the property of the Constable of France, Olivier de Clisson, husband of Marguerite de Rohan. It was from here that Beaumanoir led out the garrison to fight the mainly English garrison of Ploërmel at the Mi-Voie oak, in that murderous tournament of 1351 known as the Battle of the Thirty. The garrison of Josselin triumphed, though not without loss. This battle, fought in a time of truce between France and England, features in Froissart's *Chronicles of the Hundred Years War* and the surviving participants were greatly honoured in the years that followed. The site of the battle is still marked, 5km to the east of the castle, beside the road to Ploërmel.

The present castle has witch's-hat towers and crenellated walls, a small park, thousands of books and much fine furniture in the library, and shows every sign of constant care. The main building was restored as living quarters in the 19th century and is covered with extremely elaborate carvings and

tracery. The castle is open to visitors and one tower can be climbed, the top offering great views over the town and the valley of the Oust.

Apart from the castle, visitors to Josselin can also explore the small and delightful town that surrounds it and visit the Basilique de Notre-Dame-du-Roncier – Our Lady of the Brambles – a much-venerated local shrine. This is the site of a great annual *pardon* on 8 September. It is also famous as the place where the knights of Josselin prayed before marching out to give battle at the Mi-Voie oak.

## Vitré

Over in the east, in the *département* of Ille-et-Vilaine, the visitor will come to a fine frontier castle at Vitré. Essentially a fortified town, Vitré is probably the best preserved medieval town in Brittany, with lots of old houses set about narrow streets and small squares on the way up to the castle.

The castle was the seat of the La Trémoille family, who feature frequently in the medieval chronicles and who rebuilt and expanded the castle constantly during the Middle Ages and the Wars of Religion. The present building, triangular with turrets at each corner and curtain walls between, is set behind a large, cobbled forecourt, and overlooks the River Vilaine. The castle is now owned by the municipality and contains the council offices and

a fine museum that records the troubled history of this frontier town and has, among other treasures, Aubusson tapestries and fine furniture.

The best view from the castle is either from the forecourt, Place du Château, or from the road north of the town. Vitré itself is well worth exploring, with its many picturesque corners, especially along Rue d'Embas and Rue Poterie.

## Fougères

North of Vitré, the traveller will soon come to another frontier town and castle, at Fougères. This is a very fine castle with all the traditional accoutrements: towers, battlement, a moat and three lines of curtain walls. Furthermore, it has been very well preserved. The castle occupies a loop in the River Nançon, which serves it in the office of a moat, and can be viewed either close to the walls or from the Jardin Public in the town.

Five towers stud the outer curtain wall, which has musket loops as well as arrow slits, and gun platforms for cannon. The Tour Mélusine is the most splendid of these towers, with walls 3.5m thick. The castle is open to visitors and gives a great feeling of the Middle Ages, in a setting of considerable beauty.

Fougères itself contains an interesting old quarter around Place du Marchix, and was the place where the Chouan rebellion of 1793–1804 began and

flourished until it was put down with great brutality by French troops. The town was noted for the skill of its cordwainers from the Middle Ages until the 1920s.

## Combourg

The final example from a wide choice is the castle of Combourg, just south of St Malo. This is a real medieval castle, built and rebuilt between the 11th and 15th centuries, and belonging for a time to Bertrand du Guesclin. It was refurbished in the 18th century by the Chateaubriand family, of whom the most famous scion is the 19th-century writer François-René de Chateaubriand, who spent part of his childhood here and whose writing seems to have been influenced by the gloomy atmosphere that still hangs about this grim fortress.

The building does not contribute to levity. The castle is a real *château-fort*, and parts of it are said to be haunted. Although there are pleasant views from the battlements, the castle interior is particularly sombre. Open to the public, it contains a museum devoted to Chateaubriand's life and work and the tour includes a visit to the Tour du Chat, where the author had his bedroom. Chateaubriand was born in St Malo and after his death in 1848 was buried on the small island of Grand Bé. The tower gets its name from the spectre of a former lord of Combourg who was said to haunt the tower in the guise of a black cat.

Vitré's castle (above) was rebuilt in the 14th and 15th centuries.

The castle at Combourg (below) has its origins in the 11th century.

The fortress of Fougères (left) was of great strategic importance, being near Brittany's border with Normandy.

Owned by the Rohan family since the 15th century, Josselin castle (above) holds some fine family portraits.

# THE ROSE GRANITE COAST

Brittany's jagged, rocky, island-littered north shore is one of the most beautiful and interesting parts of its coastline, Much of the attraction comes from the curious red rocks that give this region its popular and evocative name, the Rose Granite (Granit Rose) coast, for they are indeed red, very often large, and smoothly rounded by the relentless scouring action of the sea.

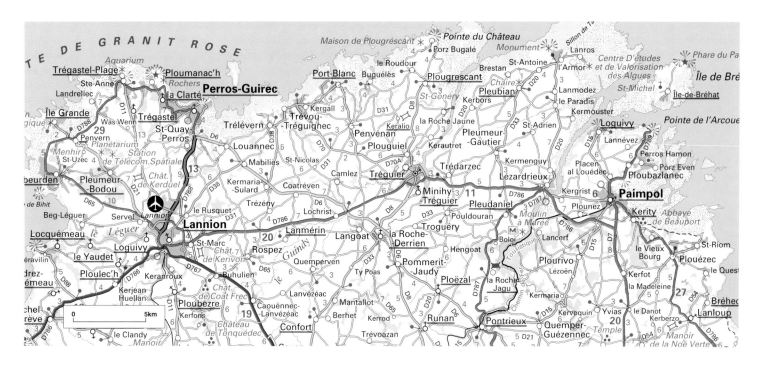

**Comité Départemental du Tourisme des Côtes-d'Armor**

7, Rue St Benoit – BP 4620
22406 St Brieuc Cedex 2
Tel: 02 96 62 72 00
www.cotesdarmor.com

**Touring:**
AA Road Map France series 1: Bretagne

*Lannion has many houses evoking the Brittany of the late Middle Ages. Some are half-timbered, others are slate-faced and all have slate roofs.*

## Lannion

Set on either side of the River Léguer some way inland from the sea, Lannion is a typical Breton town. This is a place to park the car and walk along the river and around the town centre. The church that dominates the town, the Église de Brélévenez, was built in the 12th century by the Knights Templars, but was rebuilt after the Order was suppressed in the 14th century.

There are good views of the town and river from the bridges, but Lannion is also a good excursion centre. Places to visit locally include the château at Kergrist, which displays architecture from every period of the Middle Ages to the 18th century; the Chapelle des Sept-Saintes, with a crypt dedicated to the Seven Sleepers of Ephesus, 10km to the south of Lannion; the chapel at Kerfons; and to the west of Lannion the village of Trédrez, where St Yves, one of the few Breton saints to win an international reputation, as the patron saint of lawyers, was the rector.

## Lézardrieux

This small town is the gateway to a part of the Rose Granite Coast known as the Presqu'île Sauvage. This runs west to the town of Tréguier and north to the real peninsula of the Sillon de Talbert, a dyke that juts out into the sea. Lézardrieux has an old mill and lots of pretty houses around

an 18th-century church, but is best known as a touring centre for the Presqu'île Sauvage.

## Paimpol

The harbour at Paimpol was once full of trawlers that made a good if hard living off the Newfoundland Banks, but that trade has almost entirely fallen away. Fortunately, Paimpol has the compensation of beauty and a good location. These have given it a fresh lease of life as a yachting centre, a market town for local farmers and a tourist resort.

Places to visit include the Musée de la Mer, which has interesting displays on the port's colourful past, Pointe de Guilben, and Place du Martray in the town centre, with its beautiful houses, one of them the home of Loti when he was writing his novel *Pêcheur d'Islande*. Like most Breton ports, Paimpol has a *pardon*, in December.

Paimpol is close to the Goëlo country, with its yellow gorse, and various other interesting excursions are possible. The ruins of the 13th-century Abbaye de Beauport, destroyed after the Revolution, are very evocative, as is the Croix des Veuves, near Perros-Hamon, where the fishermen's wives waited to catch their first sight of the returning fleet.

## Perros-Guirec

If the Rose Granite Coast can be said to have a first-rate tourist resort it is probably Perros-Guirec, which has the prime advantage of a delightful setting between two fine sandy beaches on a headland overlooking a magnificent, sheltered harbour. The harbour still has fishing boats and many yachts, while the town, apart from an abundance of agreeable houses, has a part Romanesque, part Gothic church.

Three kilometres to the west of the town lies the Chapelle de Notre-Dame-de-la-Clarté, built in fulfilment of a vow in the 16th century. East of Perros-Guirec, travellers should visit the little village of Port-Blanc, which has a tiny chapel perched on a rock just offshore – a most unusual sight. There are boat trips to the Sept Iles, now a nature reserve famous for gannets, kittiwakes and puffins. Most boats also stop at the Ile aux Moines, Monk's Island.

## Tréguier

A fine little town on the banks of the Rivers Guindy and Jaudy, Tréguier is famous as the home of famous men. The writer Ernest Renan (1823–92), who is little known outside France and perhaps not as well known as he deserves to be within it, was born in Tréguier and the town celebrates the fact with a statue and by preserving his house. The other famous son, St Yves, is celebrated not only as the cause of the largest of all the Breton *pardons* but also as the patron saint of lawyers.

Yves Hélori was born near Tréguier in 1253, studied law in Paris and took holy orders. He was soon regarded as a saint because, when arguing cases in the local courts, he refused all bribes, demanded the truth and declined to favour the rich.

Tréguier has a magnificent medieval gateway by the river and several half-timbered buildings. The Cathédrale St-Tugdual is held to be one of the finest in Brittany, part Romanesque, part Gothic, with lots of memorials, including the Chapelle du Duc Jean V and votive offerings to St Yves, plus a good treasury.

There are a number of good excursions and these should include a visit to the nearby castle of La Roche-Jagu and to Minihy-Tréguier, less than 1km from Tréguier. St Yves was born in this village and here his *pardon* takes place on the third Sunday in May each year.

*In the little fishing village of Port-Blanc, east of Perros-Guirec, you can see the unusual sight of a tiny chapel perched on a rock by the shore.*

*The timbers of some of Tréguier's well-preserved medieval houses are picked out in strong colours.*

# THREE HISTORIC TOWNS ON THE RIVER RANCE

The River Rance and its estuary connect three of the most historic, varied and interesting towns in Brittany. St Malo, a walled town, is a major port, yachting centre and holiday resort. Dinard, just across the estuary, is quite different: evoking the early 20th century, full of hotels, a pleasure ground for the idle rich, while Dinan, which lies up river, is purely medieval.

## Dinan

A fortress, a stronghold for the medieval dukes of Brittany, Dinan remains medieval, full of sloping, cobbled streets and leaning half-timbered buildings, many of them hung with painted shop signs. The Rue du Jerzual is one of the most photographed streets in Brittany, cobbled and sloping down steeply to the banks of the Rance, which almost encircles the hill on which the town stands. There is a late-medieval clock tower, donated to the town by the Duchess Anne. It can be climbed and the view from the top extends far beyond the river and over the surrounding countryside. There are some well-preserved timber-framed buildings, set in the narrow ways around the old centre, Place des Merciers.

Like many medieval towns, Dinan is a place to explore on foot, well supplied with parks, little squares and gardens. Set above the Rance is a small park known as the Jardin Anglais, behind which lies the Basilique St-Sauveur, which contains the tomb chest holding the heart of Dinan's favourite and most famous son, the good knight of Charles V, Bertrand du Geusclin.

Other sights to see in Dinan include the Hôtel Keratry in the Rue de Lèhon. A town walk, for which the tourist office (near the castle) can provide a map, takes in all the main sights. These include the school where Chateaubriand was educated, the Basilique St-Sauveur and the ducal castle, which was thrown up hurriedly between 1382 and 1387. The Duchess Anne sheltered here in 1507, and the Tour de l'Horloge was presented to the townspeople in gratitude for their hospitality. Parts of the castle are open to visitors and contain a museum of Breton life and furnishings, while the former quarters of du Guesclin are devoted to displays illustrating the town's history.

*Dinan's position on the River Rance and near the coast gave it strategic value during the Middle Ages. Today much of the town's medieval heart remains intact.*

### THE RANCE DAM

The road from St Malo to Dinan follows the course of the River Rance and crosses the top of the great Rance dam, the Usine Marémotrice. This is a large construction, 800m long, cleverly built to exploit the great tides of the Brittany coast, which surge up the narrow Rance valley and drive turbines at the installation. The dam then contains the sea water and lets it out gradually, back through the turbines at low tide, to maintain a continuous flow of power into the national electricity grid. There is a good view over the valley from a viewing platform on the dam, and a lock enables small vessels to travel from St Malo to Dinan.

Comité Départemental du Tourisme d'Ile-et-Villaine

4, Rue Jean-Jaurès – BP 6046
35001 Remes Cedex 3
Tel: 02 99 78 47 47
www.bretagne35.com

**Touring:**
AA Road Map France series 1: Bretagne

The resort has a number of fine hotels and good beaches as well as a selection of promenades and parks where the rich folk could mix and mingle while enjoying the crisp Channel air.

Modern attractions include a combined natural history and marine museum, with an assortment of Channel fish, and the Pointe de la Vicomté, which offers great views across the harbour to the walls of St Malo. Also recommended is a cruise up the Rance to inspect the tidal dam and power plant.

## St Malo

Many visitors enter Brittany by St Malo, an ancient and very fine seaport still enjoying a thriving trade as a yachting centre and port for Channel ferries as well as cargo ships and fishing boats.

The great interest for visitors is the old town, which lies inside the walls – the Intra-Muros. This is the site of old St Malo, but what we see today is largely a reconstruction, for the original city was severely shelled and bombed when it was beseiged in 1944. Fortunately, the people of St Malo not only rebuilt but also restored the town. It has been marvellously recreated and stands again as a great memorial and credit to the Malouins.

Just offshore and in reach at low tide lies the Ile du Grand Bé, where the writer François-René de Chateaubriand (1768–1848) elected to be buried. St Malo is also protected by a castle, now the town hall and museum. There are many hotels and restaurants and the town as a whole is well worth at least a day's visit.

Outside the Intra-Muros lie the town beaches, great swathes of sand at low tide, and the modern resorts of Rothéneuf and Paramé, which are now suburbs of St Malo. Other places to visit close to St Malo include the great castle at Fort la Latte, which lies on Cap Fréhel to the west, and the oyster port at Cancale to the east, which has restaurants famous for their seafood.

### TRAGIC LOVERS

The tale of Abélard and Hélöise is one of the world's great tragic love stories. Abélard was a Breton, born at La Palet near Nantes, and the most famous teacher of his day. Canon Fulbert of Notre-Dame invited Abélard to give lessons to his daughter Hélöise. When he discovered that his daughter had become pregnant by Abélard he hired thugs to beat and castrate Abélard, and sent Hélöise to a nunnery after she had given birth to a son.

Following his unhappy time at St Gildas-de-Rhuys, where he spent some months in fear of his life from the enmity of the monks, Abélard retired to Cluny to the protection of the Cluniac Order. He corresponded with Hélöise for the rest of his life, though they never met again.

*At the height of its elegance in the 1920s and 30s, Dinard is nowadays a busy tourist resort blessed with a mild climate.*

## Dinard

Dinard, in contrast, is a fairly modern town and resort, developed over the course of the 19th century on the site of the old fishing harbour. It is an international rather than a French or Breton resort, and attracted the smart set in droves between the wars.

*St Malo's mainly 14th- and 15th-century castle protected the coastal town from sea and land attack during Brittany's turbulent history.*

# NORMANDY

A gift to the Vikings from the King of France, later the vigorous heart of the Norman empire, then the great dukedom of the English kings and now a lush and prosperous modern province, Normandy is one of the most historic and interesting parts of France.

Because they are already well known and must be visited in the course of travel, certain famous places, such as Rouen, Caen and Falaise, are not covered in detail, though they appear when the castles, abbeys and history of Normandy are dealt with. Many of the places covered are no less worth visiting for being less famous: the Vexin, the hills of the Suisse Normande and the chalk plateau of the Caux. These are all worth exploring and have sights no traveller should miss. Besides, as the visitor travels from one to the other, the whole marvellous panoply of Normandy will unfold.

That Normandy has remained so beautiful and unspoiled is itself a minor marvel. This part of France has many times felt the heavy hand of war since Charles the Simple met Rollo the Viking on the banks of the River Epte in AD 911 and gave all the land between the Vexin and the sea to this fierce sea-rover in return for his allegiance and in hope of peace. So the Northmen gained their richest prize. Conflict continued: throughout the Middle Ages and the 16th-century Wars of Religion, right down to recent times.

It is a great tribute to the determination of the Norman people that the province today bears few marks of that terrible time apart from a great number of cemeteries and a coast and hinterland studded with memorials. The towns were rebuilt, the scars were painted over, and the Normans returned to their traditional pursuits of farming and fishing.

Apart from a long coast, a green hinterland and a good number of fine towns and cities, all offering much to see and do, Normandy can boast one of the great cuisines of France. This reputation is based on that superb fresh produce that both the sea and land of Normandy provide in such profusion: the sole of Dieppe, the cream and butter of the Auge and the Cotentin, a score of local dishes, and the cheeses, Livarot, Pont-l'Évêque or, perhaps best known of all, the Camembert of Vimoutiers. In addition to all these the area prides itself on its cider and calvados, the two great drinks of Normandy.

Normandy can also offer something for the mind and soul, for this is a province beloved of artists and writers. Courbet, Flaubert, Monet, Bonington, de Tocqueville – these and a score more found a home and inspiration here and a visitor would have to be lacking in soul indeed not to discover something worth seeing in this fascinating corner of France.

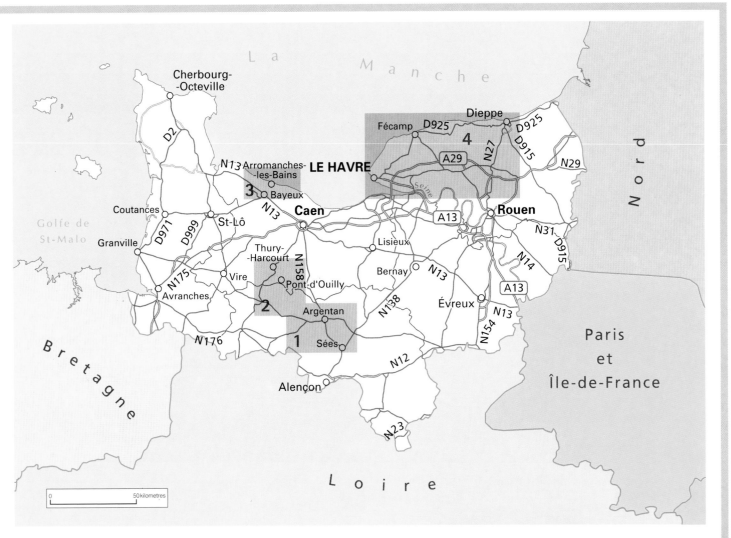

*Shellfish (right) are one of the gastronomic delights of Normandy. Other local fruits of the sea include sole, turbot and sea perch. Agriculture, the area's other major industry, is sustained by farmers like this (far right).*

*Honfleur, with its medieval quarter, is among the most attractive of Normandy's coastal towns. The port, where yachts have now largely replaced small fishing boats, was in the 18th century the principal port for the fur trade between France and Canada.*

# MONT ST MICHEL

Mont St Michel is said to be the most beautiful and spectacular tourist site in France. No one who has seen it rearing out of the golden sand in the vast bay of Mont St Michel, a cone of rock topped by a great Gothic church, is likely to disagree. Beautiful as it is, visitors will enjoy and appreciate Mont St Michel far more if they visit it outside the summer months, and in particular not in July or August, when the narrow main street is solid with tourists.

The first church, an oratory, was built on this 82-m rock as long ago as ad 708, when the Archangel Michael appeared to Aubert, Bishop of Avranches. The Archangel gave his name to the rock before striding on to fight the Devil on the top of Mont Dol, just south of the bay. This oratory was succeeded in turn by a Carolingian church, parts of which still remain in the abbey crypt, and then by a Romanesque building that was finished at the end of the 11th century, only to be destroyed by fire in 1203.

## Fortified Site

Most of the present building dates from the Gothic period, being built between the 13th and 16th centuries, a time of almost continual conflict in France, which accounts for the fact that that much of the site is fortified. The shrine of St Michel, which lies in the small chapel of St Pierre, to the left of the Grande Rue, drew pilgrims from all over Europe, even at the height of the Hundred Years War (1337–1453). Pilgrim badges can still be purchased from the tourist office just inside the main gate. This, the Porte du Roi, was the strong point in the lower bastion, and was guarded by cannon. These came into use towards the end of the 14th century, and Mont St Michel possesses some early and very rare examples of the 'hooped' cannon, which are set on plinths and can be viewed just inside the outer walls.

## Grande Rue

The Grande Rue is the main thoroughfare of Mont St Michel, and the first notable sight inside the gate is the Mère Poulard restaurant, famous in France for the production of large, feathery omelettes, the great gastronomic attraction of Mont St Michel.

After that, small restaurants and tourist shops filled with souvenirs and postcards and suchlike follow one another in relentless succession up the steep hill.

The first building worthy of attention as you climb the hill is the parish church, which, though dedicated to St Peter, contains a statue of St Michael, covered with silver. Pilgrim banners hang from the roof and votive offerings cover the walls. This church is an early foundation dating from the 11th century, and the apse spans the narrow side street. Near here is a medieval house said to have been built by Bertrand du Guesclin for his wife, Tiphaine, when she was sheltering on the Mont and Bertrand was soldiering in Spain. Bertrand was Captain of the Mont in the mid-1360s and much of the furniture is said to have belonged to him. Another old building is notable for its curious name: La Maison de la Truie-qui-file, the House of the Spinning Sow.

## La Merveille

Everything described above is a prelude to the great attraction of Mont St Michel: La Merveille, the Marvel, the great Gothic church and abbey buildings that occupy much of the top of the Mont. These were built between 1211 and 1229 and are a mixture of religious and military buildings but in a harmonious and pleasing style. The eastern half was the monks' quarters and contains the refectory, the guest hall and the almonry. The western half contains the garrison's quarters and Salle des Chevaliers, the Knight's Hall,

which was built for the Military Order of St Michael by King Louis XI in 1469. The cloisters, are in exemplary Gothic style, and open to the sky.

What makes La Merveille so marvellous is the purity of line in the architecture, probably because the buildings went up so quickly, in under 18 years, and therefore retain a continuity of

construction not spoiled by later alteration and repair.

Always a great church, the abbey has also been a fortress and, in the early years of the 19th century, a prison. One relic of this last function is a huge wheel, rather like a treadmill, which half a dozen prisoners operated to haul provisions up to the cell level. After the abbey had been decades in decline from the 1660s, the last monks were driven out at the Revolution, and the abbey, by now in urgent need of restoration, came into the hands of the state in 1874.

## Secular Architecture

Apart from the great church and the abbey buildings, the other great attraction of the Mont is that it is a treasure house of secular architecture, especially of buildings from the medieval period. Space is too precious to permit the establishment of large modern hotels. Most of the buildings that cram the rock date from the 15th and 16th centuries, still lived in and cared for by local families, who exist by catering in various ways for the million or so visitors who come here each year. Apart from the church and abbey there is an historical museum, a maritime museum, and the multi-media Archéoscope, which will appeal to children.

It would be easy to spend a full day exploring the Mont and the buildings of La Merveille, finding something new to enjoy around every quiet corner. But surprisingly few tourists ever go all the way to the top, or stay long if they get there, and visitors in the winter months may have the place almost to themselves. This is the time to climb to the top platform and watch the tide come booming in across the sands. The tide around the Mont is one of the highest in Europe, at over 13m, and with the wind behind it is said to come in at the speed of a galloping horse. Walkers on the sand should be aware of this fact and exercise care, especially when the tide is on the turn.

Once down from the heights of the Mont and back across the causeway connecting it to the mainland, visitors should look back for another view of this remarkable and beautiful sight, and take note also of the River Cousenon, which flows into the sea beside the causeway and has played its part in the long history of the Mont. By long tradition the Cousenon marks the boundary between Normandy and Brittany, and when a violent storm and flood switched the river's flow from east of the Mont to west of it, the ownership of the Mont transferred from Brittany to Normandy where, storms notwithstanding, it looks set to remain.

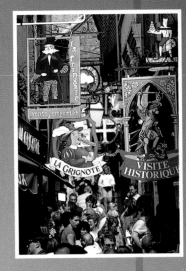

*Proud on its rock surrounded by sea, Mont St Michel is one of the finest sights in France.*

*Above, Mont St Michel is busy all summer.*

*The cloisters of Mont St Michel's abbey (above) and the abbey church (below)*

# THE PERCHE COUNTRY AND THE ÉCOUVES FOREST

The southern frontier of Normandy is marked by two great forests, the Forêt des Andaines and the Forêt d'Écouves. Large parts of these are contained within the boundaries of the great Parc Régional Normandie-Maine, which straddles the province from Mortain as far east as Alençon. This rolling landscape is horse-breeding country where the famous Haras du Pin, the French national stud, can be seen.

## Argentan

Argentan stands on a small hill above the Orne, a commanding site that inevitably attracted attention in the fighting of 1944, when much of the town was severely damaged by shell fire. The Église St-Germain was hit but, like the rest of the town, has now been carefully repaired and stands intact. The lacemaking industry here was established in the 17th century by Colbert and the famous Argentan lace, the *point d'Argentan*, is still made in the Benedictine abbey, which is actually a nunnery, the nuns owning the exclusive right to this intricate stitch. This and other types of lace can be seen in the town's Maison de la Dentelle museum.

Other historic sights include the castle from where Thomas à Becket's four assassins set out for Canterbury and the stained glass in the Église St-Martin which dates from the 15th and 16th centuries.

## Carrouges

The centre of Carrouges is set around a small square, a maze of little streets and leaning buildings – a typical small town of the French countryside. The great attraction lies just outside the town, at the gatehouse and château. This is now in the hands of the state, and part of it contains the Maison du Parc, a visitors' centre for the Parc Régional Normandie-Maine.

The gardens contain a splendid selection of apple and pear trees, and many of the varieties are no longer grown commercially. The brick gatehouse with its slender, witch's-hat towers is particularly fine, while the château contains interesting furniture, including the bed in which Louis XI slept when he visited Carrouges in 1473.

## Écouché

The first sight to greet the visitor to Écouché is a World War II tank mounted on a plinth, a memorial to the men of the French 2nd Armoured Division, which marched across here in 1944 and took the town of Alençon from the Germans after a stiff fight in Écouché . The rest of this otherwise pleasant little town has a somewhat unfinished air. The late-Gothic church was never completed, even after two centuries of effort, and the 13th-century nave has never been restored since being damaged in 1944.

## Haras du Pin

Set in splendid buildings amid lush green fields the national stud-farm (*haras*) at Le Pin, east of Argentan, has a long history. It was established in 1665 by Colbert, finance minister to Louis XIV, to improve the stock of French horses and in particular to provide breeding stallions for the cavalry. Even the gardens and buildings here are splendid, the former the

*The moated brick-built château near Carrouges dates mainly from the 15th and 17th centuries, but the gatehouse was constructed in the 16th.*

*A gilt horse's head looks down on visitors to the national stud-farm at Le Pin. Apart from its breeding role, Haras du Pin offers courses in all aspects of equestrianism and trains grooms and stable lads.*

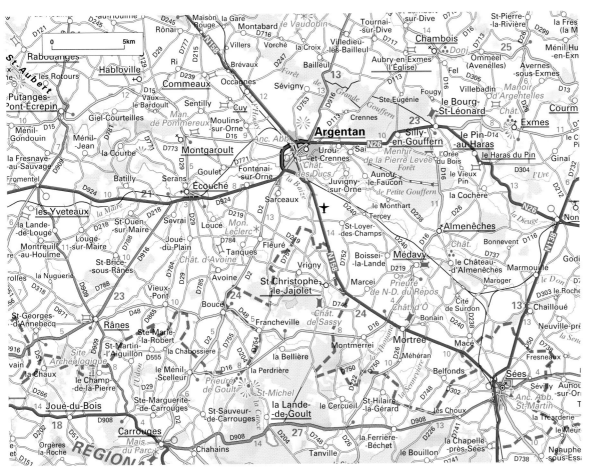

**Comité Départemental du Tourisme de l'Orne**
88, Rue Sainte-Blaise –
BP 50
61002 Alençon Cedex
www.le-perche.org
Tel: 02 33 28 88 71

**Touring:**
AA Road Map France
series 2: Normandie

work of Le Nôtre, the latter attributed to Hardouin-Mansart, and in this setting the work of breeding horses and teaching horsemanship continues.

A little to the north of Le Pin stands another magnificent pile, the 17th-century château of Le Bourg-St-Léonard. This is a most elegant building and contains the original Louis XV tapestries and woodwork as well as much 18th-century furniture.

## St Christophe-le-Jajolet

The church in this little village in the Orne is dedicated to St Christopher, the patron saint of travellers, and celebrates the fact in uncompromising fashion. The church door shows St Christopher standing guard over an aircraft, a car and the passengers, and there is an imposing statue of the saint in the grounds.

This church has become a pilgrimage centre for modern travellers, especially on the feast days of St Christopher. These are the last Sunday in July and the first Sunday in October. A visit should also be made to the nearby Château de Sassy, which is surrounded by beautiful gardens.

## Sées

Sées is an appealing market town, with a fine Norman-Gothic cathedral that contains the venerated statue of Notre Dame de Sées. Visitors should also note the column at the south end of the choir, which is carved with over 30 heads, some of them grimacing at the congregation, and the fine 13th-century stained-glass windows. Not far away, on the far side of the River Orne, which runs through the town, stands the market hall.

### NORMAN DUKES

Normandy is the land of the Northmen, the Vikings, who started ravaging the coast of France in AD 800, coming south from Denmark, or Frisia, in their longships. By 820 they had made their way up the Seine valley and started to settle, and by 885 they had laid siege to Paris. Finally, in 911, Charles the Simple, King of France, met the leader of the Northmen, Rollo the Viking, and concluded the Treaty of St-Clair-sur-Epte, by which Rollo became a Christian and a vassal of the French Crown. Thus began the dukedom of Normandy, which was to exercise great power in Europe over the following three centuries.

*The handsome Château d'O stands near Sées. It has three pavilions, each in a different style: Gothic, Renaissance and 18th-century.*

# THE ORNE VALLEY AND THE SUISSE NORMANDE

The River Orne is one of the great rivers of Normandy, flowing across the province to empty into the sea at Ouistreham, north of Caen. Caen, ancient capital of the Norman dukes, is the true gateway to the Orne valley, which lies to the south of the city – a fine place for walking and water sports, well supplied with good small hotels, a delightful area to wander in, on foot or by car.

## CALVADOS

The bright red cider apples that glow in the Norman orchards supply the juice for the two great native drinks of Normandy, cider and calvados (apple brandy). These two drinks form a part of any traditional Norman meal. The cider apples produce a potent, fermented apple juice, which wise visitors and many Normans prefer to dilute with water. Calvados is drunk as an aperitif or a digestive, 'un calva', or as 'le trou normand', between courses to create space for more of that rich Norman food. Those who do not care for strong liquor between courses may prefer to take their calva in a sorbet. A good calvados, kept in the cask for 10 or 12 years, is the perfect digestive. Pommeau is another local liqueur. People interested in distilling should visit the Maison de la Pomme et de la Poire at Barenton near Mortain.

*A couple of kilometres south-east of Clécy the impressive La Lande viaduct bridges the Orne. The stretch of river below the viaduct is particularly well suited to water sports.*

## Clécy

A small town that claims to be the 'capital of the Suisse Normande', Clécy clings to the side of the Orne valley in the very heart of the Suisse Normande. Lying at the heart of this region of hills and rivers, Clécy has long been a favourite centre for walkers and water-sports enthusiasts. Canoeists test their skill in the fast water by the Vey bridge and in the waters below the La Lande viaduct, overlooked by the towering rock face of the Rochers des Parcs, a favourite place for rock climbers.

Clécy lies on the GR36, one of the great footpaths of the Grande Randonnée, which runs from Ouistreham to the Pyrenees, but there are many short walks around Clécy, to the Pain de Sucre and over the Rochers de la Houle, and many of these walks have been waymarked by the local tourist board.

The town has several good hotels, and a museum containing Impressionist paintings, the Musée Hardy, as well as a model railway museum. Clécy is also an excellent base for visitors to the Suisse Normande, Falaise, Caen and the D-Day Coast.

## Pont-d'Ouilly

This little riverside town, situated at the confluence of the Orne and the Noireau, is a good touring centre, very popular with day-walkers, who can ramble out from here along the river to the great viewpoint of the Roche d'Oëtre, which overlooks the River Rouvre. The path from Pont-d'Ouilly follows the route of the GR36, and is therefore waymarked with the red-and-white GR signs, cutting round the great loop made by the Orne, the Méandre de Rouvrou, before climbing up to the high belvedere of the Roche d'Oëtr. *Do not let small children run about here, for the drop to the Rouvre valley is both steep and unguarded.*

*The impressive Roche d'Oëtre is the closest thing the Suisse Normande has to a mountain.*

Comité Départemental
du Tourisme du
Calvados
Place du Canada
14000 Caen
Tel: 02 31 27 90 30
www.normandy-
tourism.org

Touring:
AA Road Map France
series 2: Normandie

The hills of the Suisse Normande give drama to the countryside, even though they are not very high: the Rochers de la Houle rise to 258m and the Pain de Sucre near Clécy to 205m. Although close to several large towns and cities – Caen, Bayeux, Mortain and Falaise – the Suisse Normande remains rural and unspoiled, with only a few villages providing accommodation and refreshment for the thousands of visitors who pass through here every year.

## Thury-Harcourt

Known as 'the gate to the Suisse Normande', Thury-Harcourt stands at the northern end of the Orne valley, a few kilometres south of Caen. At one time this was mining country – the last mine closed in 1967 – and the scars left by the old iron workings can still be seen on the hillsides.

Thury-Harcourt was severely damaged in 1944, the château of the dukes of Harcourt being burned by the Germans on the night before they left the town. The park of the château is now open to visitors and offers good, gentle strolls to the banks of the Orne. Thury-Harcourt also has plenty of hotels and some very agreeable restaurants. There is a pleasant, early medieval church, with a 13th-century façade, and several hotels that cater in particular for walkers and fishermen.

From Thury-Harcourt there are good walks in all directions. Slightly longer tours by car will take the visitor to William the Conqueror's birthplace at Falaise, to the heights of Mont Pinçon, a moorland much fought over in 1944, and the Chapelle St-Joseph, where a viewing platform offers sweeping views over the Orne valley and the surrounding hills.

*The sad state of the ruined château at Thury-Harcourt is compensated to some extent by its park, which offers 4km of attractive walks along the tree-lined banks of the Orne.*

## Putanges-Pont-Écrepin

Like most other small towns of the Suisse Normande, Putanges-Pont-Écrepin is best regarded as an excursion centre. It stands at the southern end of the Suisse Normande, and straddles the river, the last place of any size before the hills give way to the flatter country of southern Normandy and the Sarthe.

## Suisse Normande

The Suisse Normande is a surprising area to find in Normandy, set as it is within a few minutes' drive of the *bocage* (open woodland country) and the Caen plain. A jumble of forested hills, streams and rivers, it is very beautiful, especially in the late spring and autumn, when the yellow gorse and broom are flaring on the hills. The region is small, some 60km from north to south, between Thury-Harcourt and Putanges-Pont-Écrepin, and about 24km from west to east.

### FOOTPATHS

Normandy is great walking country, seamed with footpaths. Every town, and nearly every village, boasts a waymarked network of local trails, details of which can be obtained from the local tourist office. Some of the best walking in Normandy can be found in the north of the Cotentin, in the Suisse Normande and in the forests of Orne and Seine-Maritime.

# THE D-DAY COAST AND THE BESSIN

The Calvados Coast of Normandy is a place where wide, sandy beaches, studded with small seaside resorts, fade away west of the River Orne into tall chalk cliffs. Behind the beaches lies open farming country, pleasant rather than striking, which soon gives way to the fields of the Normandy *bocage*.

*In June 1944, off Arromanches, the British created a huge artificial harbour. By August, having briefly been of great strategic importance, the harbour was no longer needed, largely because Cherbourg was once more in use. The full story of the Normandy Landing is told in the town's Musée du Débarquement.*

*Notre-Dame in Bayeux (right) is an outstanding example of the Norman Gothic cathedral. The tower and the crypt remain of an 11th-century building, but most of the rest dates from the 13th century.*

## Arromanches-les-Bains

Until 6 June 1944, Arromanches-les-Bains was a small, undistinguished seaside resort with a short promenade and a few hotels. Then came the Invasion. Arromanches was the site of the British artificial harbour, codenamed 'Mulberry', used by the Allies until a major port could be captured and made serviceable. When fully operational, this Mulberry – there was another in the Cotentin – could land 9,000 tons of military stores every day. The caissons of the Mulberry harbour still lie offshore.

## Bayeux

Bayeux is a very old town with roots predating the Normans and the Franks. Captured on the evening of D-Day by troops of the British 50th Division, it was spared the bombardment and street fighting that wrecked so many Norman cities in 1944. The city also contains what is arguably the most interesting relic in France: the famous *Tapisserie de la Reine Mathilde*, also known as the Bayeux Tapestry.

Housed in the Centre Guillaume le Conquérant, close to the cathedral, the tapestry – actually an embroidery – recounts in muted colours all the events of 1066 and the Battle of Hastings. King Harold is depicted with the arrow in his eye. The work, 70m in length, is Saxon and was probably commissioned in England soon after Hastings by Bishop Odon of Bayeux.

The old parts of Bayeux around the cathedral are well worth exploring, and there are many fine medieval houses along Rue St Malo and Rue Franche, and especially along the Quai de l'Aure, from where there is a photogenic view of the old watermill. There are several museums, including the Musée Baron Gérard in Place de la Liberté, which contains Italian and Flemish paintings of the 16th and 17th

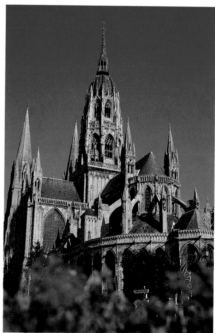

centuries as well as displays of local crafts and porcelain.

The Hôtel du Doyen houses the Bayeux lace workshop, where this local craft is being revived, and a museum of religious art, while on the outskirts of the town lies the Musée de la Bataille de Normandie, which commemorates the fighting that took place around here. Across the road is a movingly understated British war cemetery.

### D-DAY

The D-Day Invasion of 5–6 June 1944 took place along an 80-km front around the bay of the Seine, between what is now Utah Beach in the eastern Cotentin, and the Caen canal, east of what is now Sword Beach. American, British, Canadian and French soldiers took part, and they were opposed by strong and well-entrenched German forces. The invasion began shortly after midnight on 5 June, when parachute and glider forces of the American 88th and 101st Airborne Division landed in the Cotentin and astride the Orne at Bénouville to seal the flanks for the seaborne assault.

The latter began at dawn, when the troops of the American 4th Division landed on Utah Beach and continued to the east as the tide rose. The American 1st Infantry was checked and badly mauled, losing 3,000 men on the beach, before getting ashore at Omaha. Further east the Canadian and British Infantry, supported by tanks and Commando units, went ashore and seized all the objectives by the end of the day. The 6th Airborne and 1st Commando Brigade held Ranville, the British 50th Division took Bayeux, the Commandos and Americans seized all the vital objectives, and by nightfall on D-Day the 4th US Infantry had

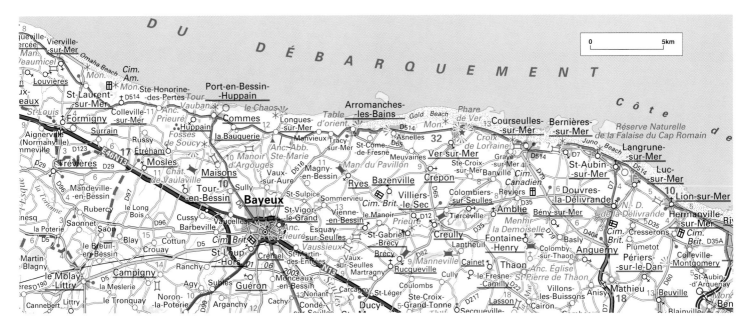

## Courseulles-sur-Mer

A seaside resort and yachting centre, the
little port of Courseulles is best known
locally for the quality of its oysters and as a
place where local fishermen come to buy
their boats. Courseulles has a thriving boat-
building industry, specialising in trawlers.

The D-Day landings are commemorated
by one of the rare D-D (duplex-drive)
swimming tanks, dredged from the sea
years after the war and now mounted in the
town centre as a memorial to the Canadian
troops who captured this town in 1944.

## Creully

Creully is a small, engaging town in the
valley of the meandering River Seulles. A
straggling place with a long main street, the
town is dominated by the walls and towers
of a very fine 12th-century castle. This
contains an exhibition of radio equipment
dating from World War II (open in the
summer only). Also notable is the Grange
aux Dîmes, a huge tithe barn just outside
Creully.

## Plages du Débarquement
### (D-Day Beaches)

There are five D-Day beaches around the
bay of the Seine, each remembered by its
codename. Apart from Utah, an American
beach in the Cotentin, this area contains,
from west to east, first Omaha, where the
American infantry divisions lost over 3,000
men before midday. Many of the fallen of
Omaha lie in the American military
cemetery at St Laurent-sur-Mer, just above
the beach. East of here, after Port-en-Bessin,
is Gold Beach, where the British 50th

Division came ashore and moved swiftly to
take Bayeux. Then comes Juno, the
Canadian beach around St Aubin, where 48
(Royal Marine) Commando had a very
rough reception before capturing the strong
point at Langrune, and finally, just west of
Ouistreham, the British Sword Beach.

Though most of the Atlantic Wall
fortifications have gone, the D-Day Coast is
littered with memorials to the fighting.

## Port-en-Bessin

Tucked into a niche in the cliffs, this little
fishing port of the Bessin had a brief
moment of fame in 1944 when it marked
the line between the invading American
and British forces, and was the landing
point for the cross-Channel petrol pipeline
code-named PLUTO (Pipe Line Under The
Ocean), which delivered much-
needed petrol to the Allied
tanks and trucks. As well as a
good beach, the town has a
large fishing fleet and therefore
a fascinating harbour, full of
life, especially when the boats
come in with their catch.

## St Laurent-sur-Mer

St Laurent was captured by the
US 1st Infantry Division on the
night of 6-7 June 1944. It's a
small village near Colleville, set above and
behind the low cliffs and sand dunes that
mark out the wide strand of bloody Omaha
beach, Here they brought in their dead and
here many of them still lie, in this vast but
beautiful plot above the sea. Other
memorials, to 1st Infantry ('The Big Red
One'), 29th Infantry and other American
units, can be found on the beach below.

Comité Départemental
du Tourisme du
Calvados
Place du Canada
14000 Caen
Tel: 02 31 27 90 30
www.normandy-
tourism.org

**Touring:**
AA Road Map France
series 2: Normandie

*A long-abandoned gun
emplacement speaks
eloquently of the conflict
witnessed by Utah Beach,
north-east of Carentan,
during the Allied invasion of
June 1944.*

# THE CÔTE D'ALBÂTRE AND THE CAUX COUNTRY

The *département* of Seine-Maritime, which runs from north of the Seine up the Channel Coast, offers a variety of scenery, from the high chalk cliffs along the Channel Coast to great forests, including those in the Parc Régional de la Brotonne. All this area, which marks the northern frontier with Picardy, is threaded with streams and rivers and dotted with small towns, the most beautiful of which are a string of resorts between Fécamp and Dieppe.

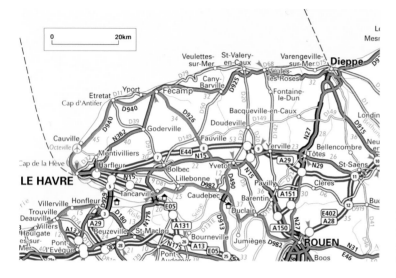

**Comité Départemental du Tourisme de Seine-Maritime**
Rue du Coeur Couronné
76460 Bihorel
Tel: 02 35 12 10 10
www.seine-maritime-tourisme.com

**Touring:**
AA Road Map France series 2: Normandie

## Cany-Barville

Set stride the River Durdent, this little town has several churches and a splendid late-16th-century château surrounded by a moat fed by the river. The setting is extremely picturesque: a quiet, green valley off the usual tourist track.

## Caudebec-en-Caux

One of the main towns along the lower Seine, between Rouen and the sea, Caudebec dates back to the 11th century, when it was founded by monks from the monastery at St Wandrille. Many medieval buildings remain, notably the Église Notre-Dame, which was built from 1425, and around Place du Marché, where the Saturday market dates back to 1390. The so-called Maison des Templiers is certainly 13th-century, but there is no record that the Knights Templars ever had a *commanderie* in Caudebec. Various sections of the ramparts remain, including two towers, the town prison and two chapels. Equally interesting and of more recent date is the Musée de la Marine de Seine, which describes river trade and navigation over the past three centuries. Caudebec is also a good touring centre, the south bank being served by two imposing bridges, the 1977 Pont de Brotonne, which lies just to the east, and further downstream the great Pont de Tancarville, opened by de Gaulle in 1959.

*Étretat is flanked by dramatic chalk cliffs: to the east by the Falaise d'Amont and to the west by the Falaise d'Aval, seen here. Steps at the western end of the promenade lead to a path that runs along the top of this cliff. For an excellent view that takes in the Falaise d'Amont, follow the path to the Porte d'Aval.*

## Dieppe

This busy, pretty port, set in the high cliffs of the Côte d'Albâtre, the Alabaster Coast, is the oldest seaside resort in France. Dieppe is also a major fishing port and has a new ferry terminal on the coast, completed in 1994 and offering faster berthing ferries, as well as easing congestion in the inner harbour. Near the harbour, children will enjoy the Cité de la Mer museum, which explores many aspects of seafaring life, including aquariums.

The seafront of Dieppe is set behind a long shingle beach, site of the famous Dieppe Raid of August 1942, when Canadian troops and British Commandos attempted a surprise attack on the town and were driven off with great loss, over 5,000 men being killed or taken prisoner on the beaches.

**IVORY CARVING**

Scrimshaw, the carving of ivory by seamen, has a tradition that goes back to the earliest days of seafaring. Given the great numbers of seafarers who lived in or sailed from the port, it is not surprising that Dieppe became a centre for the ivory trade. However, the quality of the work far exceeds that produced out of boredom by simple sailor folk.

Dieppe's ivory carvers were artists, and their work was profitable enough to support over 300 of them in the middle to late years of the 17th century. The Musée de Dieppe, in the château above the seafront, has an extensive collection of Dieppe ivory carving and a reproduction of a carver's workshop.

## Étretat

Although Étretat is a pleasant resort, full of good hotels and seafood restaurants, the great attraction here is not the town or the pebble beach, but the high chalk cliffs flanking it. These have been worn into curious shapes by the constant action of the sea, and here and there great holes have been worn in the chalk to create arches. The most striking is the pierced Falaise d'Aval, to the west of the town. Just out to sea stands a solitary pillar of chalk, L'Aiguille, Needle Rock, which rises 70m out of the water. A good view of these chalk formations can be had from the cliffs to the south of the town. For a look at the resort, go the other way, to the seaman's chapel of Notre-Dame-de-la-Garde, and the museum and monument to two French transatlantic flyers, Nungesser and Coli.

Sights in the town include the covered market and parts of the church of Notre Dame.

## Fécamp

A thriving fishing port, Fécamp is best known to visitors for two historic reasons. The first is as a shrine that has held, since the 7th century, the Precious Blood. This relic led to the creation of the Benedictine monastery by Count Richard at the start of the 11th century. The monastery provided the town's second claim to fame when, in

1510, a monk of the abbey used the aromatic herbs of the Pays de Caux to create a liqueur that is still known as Benedictine. Only parts of the abbey remain but the Benedictine distillery is still in working order and can be visited. So, too, can the Precious Blood, which is kept in La Trinité church. Other attractions include the Musée des Arts de l'Enfance, dedicated to childhood, and the new Musée du Chocolat.

There are good restaurants overlooking the harbour, and a large marina. Six kilometres to the south lies the Château de Bailleul, a splendid 16th-century château.

## Yvetot

Set in a breezy corner of the Caux plateau, Yvetot is a market town for the surrounding countryside, and a good touring centre. In the town itself the great attraction is the stained glass by Ingrand in the modern Église St-Pierre. This church was built in 1956 and is a very interesting example of contemporary religious architecture. Other sights worth seeing locally are the Musée de la Nature set in an old Caux farmhouse with displays of local wildlife, and the great oak outside the church at Allouville-Bellefosse southwest of Yvetot, which is said to be one of the oldest trees in France. Two chapels have been built inside the trunk.

*The fishing port of Dieppe remains active, for commercial fishing plays an important part in the local economy. Dieppe is also a major Channel ferry port, with the benefit of a deep-water harbour.*

*A famous liqueur, enjoyed all over the world, is produced in Fécamp. Visitors to the town should see both the distillery and the Musée de la Bénédictine.*

# THE NORTH

Many people simply hurry through the North of France on their way to other parts of the country, yet there are few regions that are so rich in history and architecture, or possess so varied a landscape. The coastline to the west is marked by dramatic cliffs and miles of sandy beaches, while inland the open countryside is broken by pockets of woodland and pleasant hidden river valleys. It is a well-developed landscape largely given over to the cultivation of cereals, sugar beet, hops and root vegetables, and in the south-east to the extensive vineyards of the Champagne region. To the west, on the low-lying estuarine marshlands that were formerly part of the sea, there are large flocks of the famous *pré-salé*, or salt-marsh sheep.

Composed largely of the old kingdoms of Artois, Picardy, Flanders and Champagne, the North retains a strong feeling of independence. Because the frontiers of France were established only relatively recently in the regions external influences remain strong. Since the Middle Ages the English, Dutch, Flemish, Spanish and Germans have fought with the French for possession of these territories, and have all left their mark on a landscape that has long been a battleground. Elements as diverse as Flemish architecture, beer, windmills and a distinctive regional folklore reflect the lasting impact of these cultures.

The Romans were the first to invade, and were followed by many others, the most recent being the Germans in 1940. The slaughter at Crécy (1346) and Agincourt (1415) was echoed centuries later on the Somme and the Marne, World War I having a major impact on the region, with vast areas being totally destroyed. The sombre legacy can be seen in the hundreds of military cemeteries and war memorials that litter this area. The best of these are masterpieces of 20th-century architecture, continuing a strong tradition of fine building in the region.

The North was the cradle of the Gothic style, which attained its peak in the great cathedrals of Amiens, Beauvais and Reims. After the Gothic came the northern Renaissance, with its emphasis on decorative brickwork, followed by the classical style of the 17th and 18th centuries. Abbeys and cathedrals apart, a number of buildings emerged to characterise the North: notably the towering belfries, the great town halls and the châteaux and citadels designed by Vauban in the late 17th century. In the 20th century art deco and Modernism made their impact.

The eastern part of the region has long been industrial, with a textile trade important since Roman times. Later came coal, and related chemical and heavy industries. The landscape is divided by a complex network of canals and navigable rivers whose leisure potential in the post-industrial age is just being realised. Even in the heart of the industrial region there are pretty villages, remarkable buildings and attractive countryside just waiting to be discovered.

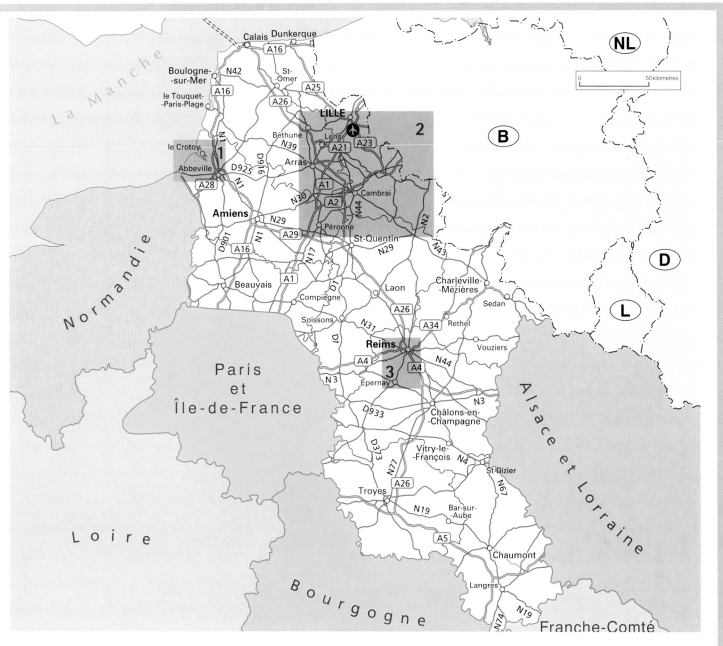

Coal mining (right above) and the production of steel, textiles and chemicals make a major contribution to the regional and national economies. Smaller but established since the 18th century is the North's ceramics industry (right below).

Rodin's imposing Burghers of Calais stands in front of that city's early-20th-century town hall.

# THE BAY OF THE SOMME

The Bay of the Somme is a distinctive region of low-lying salt-marsh and remote coastal scenery, famous throughout Europe for its bird life. Today, it is an area of old-fashioned towns and quiet resorts, yet within it are great cathedrals and abbeys, among other echoes of past glories and medieval might.

**Comité Départemental du Tourisme de la Somme**
21, Rue Ernest-Cauvin
80000 Amiens
Tel: 03 22 71 22 71
www.somme-tourisme.com

**Touring:**
AA Road Map France series 7: Le Nord & Ile-de-France

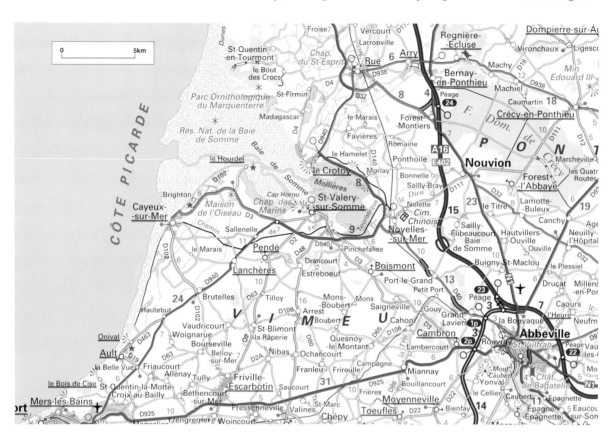

## BIRDS

The bay of the Somme is internationally famous for its bird life, and over three-quarters of all Europe's known species are recorded here. Large areas of the remote salt-marsh of the tidal estuary have been turned into wildlife reserves, and species that formerly fell in thousands to the guns of sportsmen are now carefully protected. A mecca for serious ornithologists, the region also caters excellently today for the less specialised tastes of the casual visitor. To the south is the Maison de l'Oiseau, a living museum that celebrates the bird life and the distinctive environment of the region, while to the north is the huge expanse of the Parc de Marquenterre, a reserve where both local and migratory birds can be observed from a range of carefully planned trails. Both have cafeterias and souvenir shops with ample parking, and there is a picnic area in the Parc de Marquenterre.

*The neo-Gothic railway station at Abbeville, a town that suffered massive destruction during World War II*

## Abbeville

The English owned Abbeville for two centuries from 1272, and in 1514 Henry VIII's sister Mary Tudor was married here to Louis XII. The great Gothic cathedral of St-Vulfran, begun in 1488 and left unfinished 50 years later, once towered over a network of narrow streets of timber-framed houses, but much of the medieval old town was destroyed by the Germans in one devastating air raid in May 1940. Notable survivors are the 17th- and 18th-century mansions with their grand gateways, built by the local textile barons of that era, splendid houses that ornament the streets of the town's compact centre. Abbeville's long history of manufacturing textiles continues, and this is still the town's most important industry. Also striking are the 13th-century belfry, now part of the local museum, and the decorative façade of the 1912 Flemish-style railway station, a period piece of great charm. The canalised Somme runs through Abbeville, and its quiet old quays and locks add a distinctly Dutch flavour.

## Ault-Onival

This small resort with its decidedly old-fashioned atmosphere is best known for the dramatic views of the cliffs that stretch westwards towards Le Tréport and the Normandy borders, perspectives familiar to painters as diverse as Cotman and Delacroix. At the town's centre is the large 15th-century church, with its unusual chequer-board flint and pebble decoration. Notable also are the tile panels and ceramic house name plaques with their strong *fin de siècle* flavour. These are a feature of the many holiday and retirement homes built in this area during the years that preceded and followed those of World War I.

In the Middle Ages Le Crotoy was rather more grand, boasting a château that guarded the Somme estuary. Here, in 1430, Joan of Arc was briefly held prisoner on her way to her trial in Rouen.

## Chemin de Fer de la Baie de Somme

A memorable way to travel either from St Valery-sur-Somme to the resort of Cayeux, or from St Valery round the bay of the Somme to Le Crotoy, is on the narrow-gauge steam railway, a rare survivor from the time when little lines such as this were the backbone of rural France. Elderly, panting locomotives haul iron-verandahed wooden carriages on a slow, rocking journey across the salt-marshes, giving wonderful views over the distinctive landscape of the bay. A short walk from the intermediate station at Noyelles-sur-Mer (a village in fact now well inland) leads to a remarkable World War I Chinese cemetery, set in empty fields. Trains run at weekends and on some weekdays during the holiday season, and the journey starts on St Valery's old quay.

## Crécy-en-Ponthieu

In 1346 a small English army under the command of Edward III defeated a much larger French force in a muddy field near Crécy, thanks largely to the devastating fire of the English archers. Over 20,000 French soldiers, 1,300 knights and 11 princes died that day, and English dominance over a large part of France was assured.

During the battle Edward used a windmill as his lookout, and the site of this, long since disappeared, is marked by a viewing platform with descriptive panels. There is a large car park near by, just off the D111.

Scenic trips by steam train to Cayeux and Le Crotoy begin at St Valery's old quay

## Le Crotoy

Isolated from the salt-marshes with wonderful views over the estuary of the Somme, Le Crotoy claims to have the only south-facing beach on the north coast. A popular resort since the 19th century and famous for its seafood, which helped attract writers and artists such as Jules Verne, Colette, Toulouse-Lautrec and Seurat, the town is still popular among holidaymakers and second-home owners. In the Middle Ages it was rather more, boasting a grand château to guard the Somme's entry. Here, in 1430, Joan of Arc was held prisoner on her way to trial at Rouen. She is commemorated by the square that bears her name.

## Rue

Centuries ago Rue was a busy seaport, but today this appealing little town is 8km from the sea. Unexpectedly grand buildings contrast with the quiet shops and cafés on the market square. The best of these is the extravagant Flamboyant Gothic Chapelle du St-Esprit, built originally to celebrate a wooden crucifix, perhaps the True Cross, which was washed up on a nearby shore in the 12th century, having been thrown into the sea by Crusaders in the Holy Land. Much simpler is the wooden roof of the chapel of the 16th-century hospice close by, carved with hunting scenes. Also worth a visit is the belfry with its four grand turrets. This now houses a small museum devoted to the local pioneers of aviation, the Caudron brothers.

## St Valery-sur-Somme

It was from St Valery that William set off in 1066 with his 400 ships to conquer England. Nothing remains from that eventful time, but today St Valery is a jolly little seaport at the mouth of the Somme, with brightly painted old houses lining the quay and looking over fishing boats and yachts to Le Crotoy, far away across the sandbanks and marshlands of the bay. The Écomusée Picarvie has an interesting collection of tools and artefacts relating to vanished trades and ways of life.

Fortified walls and gateways reflect the former strategic importance of medieval St Valery.

# THE HEART OF THE NORTH

This region of varied landscape has been marked by centuries of exploitation. Well watered by the Lys, the Escaut and the Scarpe, the area is a major producer of cereals, sugar beet and hops. The underground coal seams have encouraged industry for many centuries but the wealth of the region came initially from textiles. Directly attributable to this wealth are a number of fine towns with excellent Renaissance and 17th- and 18th-century architecture.

## Arras

Famed in the Middle Ages for its tapestries, which carried the town's name far and wide, Arras is a remarkable monument to the influence of the Flemish style in the North of France. At its heart are two great arcaded squares framed by handsome 17th-century town houses. In one is the town hall, marked by its 80m belfry, and richly ornamented in 15th-century Flemish

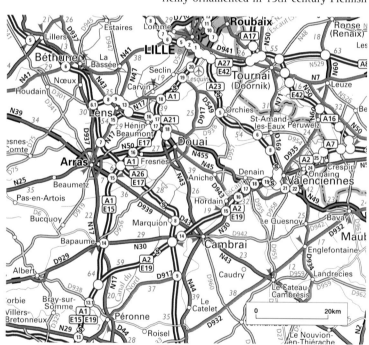

**Comité Départemental du Tourisme du Nord**
6, Rue Gauthier de Chatillon – BP 1232
59013 Lille Cedex
Tel: 03 20 57 59 59
www.cdt-nord.fr

**Touring:**
AA Road Map France series 7: Le Nord & Ile-de-France

Gothic style, a precise replica of the original which was destroyed during World War I.

These magnificent squares, seen at their best on market days and without equal in France, set the tone for a fine town, the capital of Artois, whose assets include the excellent Musée des Beaux-Arts, a grand late-18th-century cathedral built on the site of a former Benedictine abbey and a wealth of other interesting 18th-century buildings. Away from the centre is Vauban's massive citadel of 1670, still in military use and with its moats partly filled with water. Nearby is the British military cemetery and memorial, designed by Sir Edwin Lutyens. Arras is a town full of tradition and history,

with a compact centre that is easy to explore on foot.

## Cambrai

A famous name in the annals of World War I, Cambrai is a traditional Flemish town long associated with the textile trade. The fine linen known as cambric takes its name from the town. Despite wartime destruction, Cambrai still has great character, with old cobbled streets lined with 17th- and 18th-century houses, pleasantly old-world shops, handsome squares and a huge public garden filled with sculpture and laid out around Vauban's 17th-century citadel.

The town is notable for its churches, which include the 18th-century cathedral, a fine example of northern classicism containing a striking memorial by David d'Angers to the local writer Fénelon, the Jesuit chapel of 1694 and, best of all, St-Géry with its high tower, built between 1698 and 1745. Inside is a splendidly lively Baroque rood-screen in contrasting marbles, sculpted by the locally born Marsy brothers. Another building in the classical style, but more restrained, is the town hall, with its tall belfry, whose animated figures, Martin and Martine, strike the hours.

## Douai

Despite the proximity of the coalfields Douai is still an elegant, predominantly 18th-century town. There are plenty of fine façades and terraces in the old streets; particularly attractive are those flanking the old quays of the Scarpe on its course through the town centre. At the heart of Douai is the large main square, dominated by the town hall, the latter dating in part from the 15th century, and the famous

*The belfry of Cambrai's classical town hall, built in 1768, has the unusual feature of a pair of bronze figures from about 1510. Two metres tall and dressed in Moorish style, they announce the time by striking the bell with their mallets.*

*Canada's national war memorial honours the 60,000 Canadian soldiers killed in the battle for Vimy Ridge in 1917.*

## WAR MEMORIALS

Traditionally a battleground since Roman times, the North of France is marked, above all, by the scars of World War I – and by monuments to that conflict. Among the many memorials designed by the British architect Sir Edwin Lutyens, that at Thiépval stands out. It is a magnificent and powerfully complex composition of pierced arches carrying the names of 73,357 soldiers killed in the Somme who have no known grave. Also impressive are the huge American cemetery and memorial at Bony and Bellicourt, and Sir Herbert Baker's South African memorial at Delville Wood. Set high on a crest across the valley from Vimy Ridge is the French national memorial and cemetery, commemorating the dead of the battles of 1915. The cemetery, which mixes traditional and revivalist architectural styles, is immense. There are literally hundreds of lesser memorials and cemeteries, many of which have some artistic or architectural quality.

belfry with its carillon of 62 bells that plays tunes every quarter of an hour.

Douai is the centre of the French legal profession, maintaining the tradition established by Louis XIV when he made the town the seat of the local Flemish government that held power through much of the 18th century. The Palais de Justice is a handsome building of 1762. The painter Jean Bellegambe was born in Douai in 1470 and work by him is included in the collections in the Musée de la Chartreuse, together with Dutch and Flemish old masters (Rubens, Van Dyck) and French Impressionists (Rodin, Renoir, Sisley).

## Lille

A massive urban conglomeration devoted to the production of textiles, chemicals, beer and machinery, Lille is nonetheless a city of considerable style and elegance, with much to appeal to the visitor. It is a lively city that has preserved its links with its proud past while meeting very successfully the demands of modern urban life. A new underground railway network and new motorways have left intact the old heart of the city, where it is still a pleasure to explore streets lined with 17th- and 18th-century houses and an enticing variety of traditional shops and cafés. The city has its

own opera house and its own orchestra, numerous theatres, one of the best provincial museums in France, a contemporary arts museum and France's largest bookshop.

Lille's first great period of expansion was in the 17th-century, and dating from this time are the Flemish Baroque Vieille Bourse, on the main square in the city centre, and the huge Citadelle, the finest and best preserved of Vauban's fortifications. Other buildings echo the city's growth in the 18th and 19th centuries, but it was in the 20th century that some of Lille's most exciting buildings were put up. These include the new Bourse, with its tall belfry, the opera house, the eccentric art nouveau Maison Coilliot with its tiled façade, designed by Guimard, the architect of the Paris Métro and, above all, the art deco town hall with its 104m tower. Another definite architectural success is the Lille-Europe TGV and Eurostar station, which has transformed the city into the transport hub of northern Europe. The huge new shopping centre opposite the station is also worth a visit.

*A comic figure entrusted with an important role near the opera house in the heart of Lille.*

# NORTHERN GOTHIC

A battleground for centuries, the North of France has nonetheless preserved intact the prime examples of the region's greatest gift to the cultural development o Europe, the Gothic church. While the cradle of the style was certainly in the Ile de France, it was in the North, and above all in Picardy, that it reached its maturity. It was also in this region that the Gothic style achieved its aim of maximum lightness combined with a remarkable delicacy of structure, a final flowering of art and technology before the all-conquering classicism of the Renaissance replaced the Gothic as the Christian style *par excellence.*

The great abbeys, cathedrals and churches of the North give ample opportunity for visitors to explore and enjoy the style in all its diversity, by studying the buildings that echo the three main periods of Gothic.

The first of these was the transition in the 12th century from the Romanesque style of the Normans to the initial flowering of the Gothic, epitomised by Laon cathedral; the second was the 13th- and 14th-century development of mature Gothic, known in France as the Rayonnant style, and illustrated by Beauvais cathedral; and finally came the High Gothic, or Flamboyant, style of the 15th and 16th centuries, as at St Riquier.

## Transitional Gothic

Although the identities of the architects of many medieval buildings remain unknown to this day, some of the names of the master builders have been passed down by history. A key figure was Villard de Honnécourt, who was born near Cambrai and whose work at Laon, at the abbey of Vaucelles, at St Quentin and elsewhere was instrumental in marking the transition from the massive style and rounded arches of the Romanesque period to a far lighter and more daring structure based on the pointed arch,

*The 12th–13th-century Noyon cathedral (above)*

*Laon's Notre-Dame cathedral (above right and right)*

notably in the form of vaulting.

Laon's cathedral is the finest example of this style because its period of building was relatively short and it was not greatly altered during later ages. As a consequence, the primitive Gothic elements in its structure are still clearly apparent. The four-tier elevation of its nave walls, a major indication of the overriding desire for light and lightness, is also seen in Noyon cathedral, completed at the end of the 13th century. Similar in style is the cathedral at Soissons, whose nave and choir were built at the same time, yet both cathedrals still contain obvious Romanesque features.

The basilicas at St Omer and St Quentin also have interesting 12th- and 13th-century transitional work, but in both the impact has been lessened by later developments.

## Rayonnant Gothic

In the 13th and 14th centuries church builders were inspired by the pursuit of lightness. This was the great age of rose windows and walls pierced by soaring openings in delicate vertical Gothic, all intended to project light into the massive interiors. The primary monument to this period is Amiens cathedral, the largest, and to many eyes, the best

## Other Styles

While dominant for several centuries spiritually as well as architecturally, the Gothic style was often modified to suit local needs, or blended with types from other regions. In the north-east of France, where Flemish influence was strong, there are many examples of the Germanic *hallekirk*, a church with several naves of equal height side by side, designed to fulfil secular as well as religious functions. Even more distinctive are the fortified churches of the Thiérache region, powerful 12th- and 13th-century structures designed to give shelter to villagers in an area that was on the front line in the wars that swept across Europe in the Middle Ages. With towers that look like castles, and with an upper storey above the nave designed for defence, these churches were often equipped also with a well, an oven and a fireplace to withstand long sieges. Outstanding examples can be seen at Vervins, Burelles and in the surrounding villages of the Thiérache.

cathedral in France, a building whose finest qualities are its scale and its stylistic unity. Work on the cathedral started in 1220 and was virtually complete 50 years later, with only the towers and the west front belonging to a later period.

Even more ambitious was Beauvais, begun in 1247 but never taken beyond a choir and a transept. Yet the space inside is immense, a daring mass of delicate Gothic columns and vaulting, soaring to 50m. This building fulfilled the dreams of the Gothic architect, with walls reduced to a minimum and so pierced with tracery that the windows seem to float in space, and with stability maintained apparently by faith, but actually by flying buttresses on the exterior. Two further excellent examples of the Rayonnant Gothic style can be seen at St Omer and St Quentin.

## Flamboyant Gothic

The structural revolutions of the 13th and 14th centuries were exploited more decoratively during the Flamboyant period, with ornamentation in carved stone achieving the delicacy of lacework. The strong vertical emphasis of the Rayonnant

*The Cathédrale Notre-Dame at Amiens (above and left), largely completed in 50 years*

*St Riquier's abbey church (below), which was destroyed and rebuilt several times, is the finest example of Flamboyant Gothic.*

period was often lost in a mass of applied ornament and in many cases the aim seemed to be to achieve a decorative effect for its own sake. Typical examples of Flamboyant Gothic are the façade of St-Vulfran, in Abbeville, and the Chapelle du St-Esprit in Rue, but the most impressive in the region is the abbey church of St Riquier, which was almost entirely rebuilt in this style in the15th and 16th centuries. Flamboyant elements can often be found in lesser churches, in the details of façades and porches and applied to tombs.

# AROUND THE VINEYARDS OF CHAMPAGNE

The gentle hills of the Marne valley are dedicated entirely to the champagne industry. Vines stretch in regimented lines to the horizon, a sea of green and gold broken only by the sturdy towers of village churches. At the heart of the region is the dense natural woodland of the Montagne de Reims.

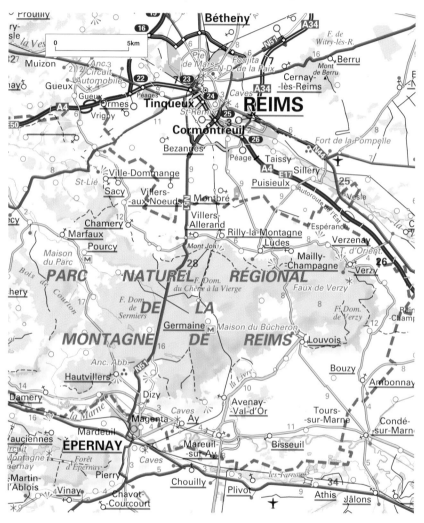

## SCHOOL OF REIMS

Ninth-century Reims was the centre of a thriving intellectual and artistic life that found its most lasting memorial in the style of manuscript illumination associated with the abbeys of the region. The creative centre for this new style was the abbey of Hautvillers, and between 820 and 830 the monks working in the scriptorium produced a series of revolutionary manuscripts. Supreme among them is the *Utrecht Psalter*, whose frenetic style of illumination was echoed by other manuscripts.

## Chapelle St-Lié

Hidden in a clearing that was once a Roman sacred wood and surrounded by trees is a simple stone chapel dedicated to St Lié, a 5th-century hermit. Dating largely from the 12th and 13th centuries, the chapel stands quite alone with its graveyard. Set into a niche is a statue of the Virgin and near by is a wrought-iron cross bearing the tools of the Passion and surmounted by a cockerel. From here there is a magnificent view over a landscape of vines and pockets of woodland punctuated by the towers of the 11th- and 12th-century churches of Ville-Dommange and Sacy.

## Épernay

After Reims, Épernay is the major centre for the production of champagne, and much of the town is devoted to this industry. It is a pleasant place without being in any way remarkable and the main feature of interest is the champagne houses, with most of the major names in grand mansions flanking the broad Avenue de la Champagne, which climbs away from the town centre. Behind these mansions, some of which date back to the 18th century, are the caves and cellars in which the wine is manufactured and stored. Among the leading names represented here are Moët et Chandon, Mercier and de Castellane, all of whose facilities can be visited. The architectural styles of the champagne houses are interestingly varied, ranging from 18th-century classical to 19th-century eccentric, and notable on some of the latter are decorative panels of richly coloured ceramic tiles.

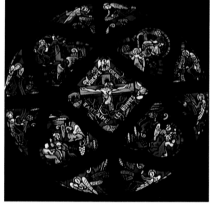

*Visitors to Épernay who want to see something of the town besides the champagne houses should visit the Église Notre-Dame and the Basilique St-Remi, both of which have some beautiful 16th-century stained-glass windows*

**Comité Départemental du Tourisme de la Marne**
13 bis Rue Carnot
51000 Chalons-en-Champagne
Tel: 03 26 68 37 52
www.tourisme-en-champagne.com

**Touring:**
AA Road Map France series 11: Champagnen–Ardennes

## Ay

Spread over the sheltered, south-facing slopes of the Marne valley, the vineyards of Ay have been famous since Roman times. The local wine found favour with such illustrious figures as François I and Henry VIII of England. Today this small town is still totally devoted to the production of wine. Best known among its many producers is Gosset, active in the town since 1584 and the oldest champagne house in the region. Another producer is based in the château at Mareuil, just to the east along the Marne valley, a fine 18th-century building overlooking the river.

## CHAMPAGNE

Reims, Épernay and the villages that surround the woods of the Montagne de Reims are encircled by vines that extend in every direction over the soft hills of the Marne valley. These vines grow the grapes used in the making of champagne, the sparkling wine that has changed the face, and the fame, of the region over the last two centuries.

The process of making sparkling wine was developed in the late 17th century by the monk Dom Pérignon, but the region had been known for its wines since before Roman times. Some of these wines had a natural effervescence, but it was the development of the double fermentation technique that inspired the creation of the true champagne.

The industry began in the 18th century but it was not until around the turn of that century that the manufacture of champagne achieved anything like its present significance. Many of the most famous champagne houses were established during this period, perfecting the complex techniques of blending and manufacture that have made champagne so famous throughout the world.

Much imitated but never equalled, the sparkling wines of the Champagne region have a unique quality that is jealously guarded by its manufacturers in order to preserve the integrity of a product vital to the local economy. Many leading champagne houses, in Reims and Épernay, can be visited and *dégustation* (sampling) is possible in many of the small villages.

## Fort de la Pompelle

Built in 1880 on a natural outcrop of rock, the Pompelle fort was designed to guard the eastern approaches to Reims. Although it was briefly captured by the Germans during their rapid advance in September 1914, it soon returned to French hands, to become a symbol of French resistance throughout the battles of Champagne and the Marne. Preserved much as it was at the end of the war, the fort is accessible to visitors and contains displays telling the history of World War I, and a collection of German helmets.

## Hautvillers

This pretty village on the south-facing slopes of the Marne is well known for its traditional houses with their decorative wrought-iron signs as well as for its vineyards, which, like those at neighbouring Ay and Avenay-Val-d'Or, produce the best wine of the region. At one end of the village is the abbey, founded in 660 by St Nivard, which reached its peak in the 9th century, although it is also famous as the place where Dom Pérignon served as a monk. It is privately owned, but the monk's grave in the village can be visited.

## Parc Régional de la Montagne de Reims

The Park is famous for its oaks, chestnuts, deer and wild boar. At the eastern edge are the famous Faux de Verzy, an extraordinary group of beech trees whose twisted and distorted trunks are the result of some local genetic variation. Near by, on one of the highest points of the Montagne de Reims, is the Mont Sinaï observation point, offering magnificent views westwards and northwards towards Reims.

To the north is Verzenay, one of several villages in a sea of vines. It is famous for its windmill, set dramatically on the crest of a ridge, an unexpected feature in a countryside devoted entirely to the vine, as well as for its lighthouse, the Phare de Verzenay, which contains a wine museum.

## Reims

The champagne capital of France, Reims has been a city of major importance since the Roman period, when it had a population of 80,000. However, the city was completely destroyed by the invading Vandals in 406. This pattern has been followed in subsequent centuries, most recently during World War I when over three-quarters of the centre was demolished. The textile trade remained important from Roman times until the 18th century, when champagne began to take over. Many of the great champagne houses are in the city, including Pommery, Tattinger, Veuve Cliquot, Mumm and Piper Heidsieck. Other attractions include museums devoted to painting, decorative arts, automobiles, and the Musée de la Reddition, where the German surrender was signed on 7 May 1945.

Even older than the cathedral is the 11th-century Basilique St-Remi, whose simple but powerful Romanesque style is in marked contrast to the cathedral's bold Gothic. Next door is the Musée St-Remi, the city's archaeological and historical museum.

*Vineyards dedicated to the production of champagne, such as these at Hautvillers, extend in every direction over the gentle hills of the Marne valley.*

*The greatest glory of Reims is the Cathédrale Notre-Dame. Planned as the largest church in Christendom, it was built largely in the 13th century and miraculously spared from destruction in World War I. The exterior is dazzling, the interior an eloquent expression of the Gothic desire for lightness. In front stands a statue of Joan of Arc.*

# ALSACE AND LORRAINE

A lsace-Lorraine does not exist. The linking of the two names reflects only the administration of the two regions as the German imperial territory of Elass-Lothringen, from 1871 to 1918. Each has its own varied landscapes, character, architecture and treasures.

This eastern flank of France has not always basked in the peace enjoyed by today's tourists. For a thousand years this was the frontier of the Holy Roman Empire. Its towns and villages still have their Porte de France, the start of the road leading west to whatever part of today's France was not at that time being disputed between Gauls, Romans, Englishmen, Burgundians, Swedes, Spaniards and others.

The constant passage of armies, bringing famine, plague and destruction, has, however, similarly tempered the inhabitants of both regions. The Alsatian dialect, still widely used every day in Alsace's two *départements*, Haut-Rhin and Bas-Rhin, and to a lesser extent in Lorraine, is the prime example of a determination that the individuality and character of both cultures should survive.

The fertile Plain of Alsace leads from the Rhine, through the vine-covered slopes with half-timbered houses and red sandstone churches, many still fortified, clustered together in medieval walled villages. Narrow streets, each a potential stage set for Faust, wrought-iron shop signs, *winstubs* (winebars), *flammekeuche* (pizza) and *kougelhopf* (cake), *choucroute* (sauerkraute) in the north, fried carp in the south – here the *gens de l'intérieur*, as French travellers from the rest of France are called, can go abroad without crossing any national border.

To the east the rounded summits of the Vosges rise to 1,424m at Grand Ballon. Cross-country skiers and summer walkers can follow well-signposted paths along hilltop or valley, and in spring the meadows are full of wild daffodils and orchids. Here the land slopes down to the plateau and the River Meuse, which for the most part marks the western limit of Lorraine.

Lorraine has as many attractions as Alsace, but is almost three times as big, so the tourist has to travel further to find them. Three *départements* – Meuse, Meurthe et Moselle and Vosges – never formed part of Elass-Lothringen and remain much more French than the rest of the province. There is Celtic Lorraine, its sacred springs and hilltops beloved of Roman and Christian. There is the Lorraine of Joan of Arc, of Stanislas, last Duke of Lorraine and inspirer of the magnificent architecture of Nancy and Lunéville. It was to Nancy that the inhabitants of Alsace, between 1871 and 1920, would make their annual visit to take part in Bastille Day festivities. A further attraction is the Parc Régional de Lorraine.

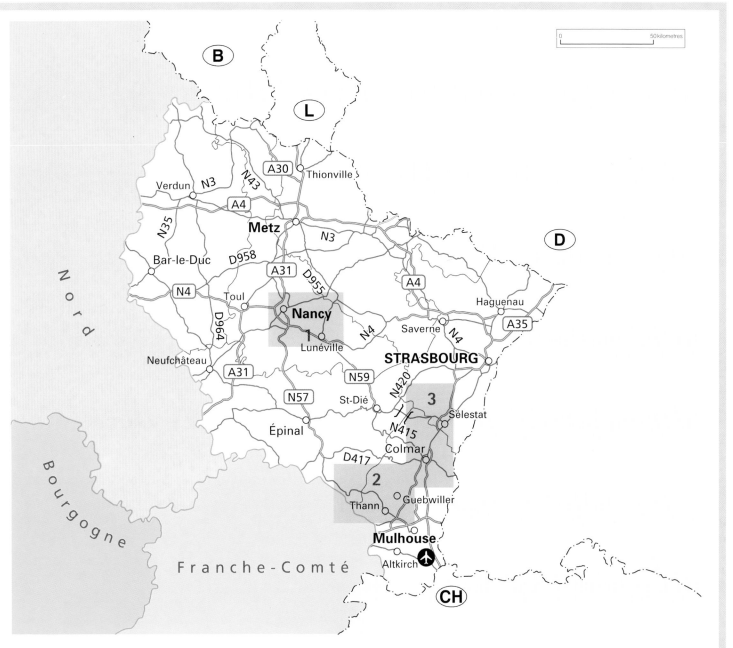

0    50 kilometres

B

L

Verdun  N3  N43  A30  Thionville

A4

N35  Metz  N3

Bar-le-Duc  D958  D955

D964  A31

N4  Toul  Nancy  D955

Neufchâteau  A31  **1**  Lunéville  N4  Saverne  N4  A35

N57  N59  St-Dié  N420  **3**  Sélestat

Épinal  N415  Colmar

D417  **2**  Guebwiller

Thann  Mulhouse  Altkirch

Haguenau

**STRASBOURG**

D

N o r d

B o u r g o g n e

F r a n c h e - C o m t é

CH

*Colmar (right) is a small town which retains a pleasingly human scale. Many of the houses have a friendly look, with their window-boxes and their extensive use of wood and coloured tiles.*

*Some local grapes (below) produce red wine*

*The wrought-iron shop signs in many of the medieval towns remind the visitor of the region's strong links with its past.*

# NANCY TO LUNÉVILLE

Although we are here concerned with the less well-known wonders to be discovered by the venturesome and enquiring traveller, no guide book should ignore the 18th-century architectural splendours of Nancy and Lunéville. In between, along a road and river both dedicated to industry and commerce, is the Gothic basilica of St Nicolas-de-Port. It is for these three gems, not for its natural beauties, that this area is best known.

## LIVERDUN

*Dun* was the Celtic word for a hilltop fort, and a bend in the Moselle encircles this hilltop village 4km north-west of Nancy. The road leads up past 13th-century walls and through the 16th-century 'Porte Haute'.

In the 13th-century church is the tomb of St Euchaire, martyred in nearby Pompey in 362. He is depicted lying in full episcopal robes, his crozier beneath his left arm, and his head, still wearing its mitre, cradled on his chest.

There are unusual 14th-century memorial inscriptions deeply carved into the pillars of the nave and chapels. Each inscription has a delicately wrought hand, in elegant ruffed sleeve, its finger pointing down towards the tomb in the floor.

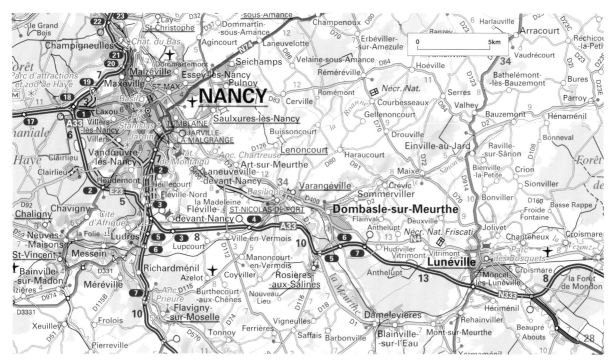

**Comité Départemental du Tourisme de Meurthe-et-Moselle**
48, Rue du Sergent Blandan
54000 Nancy
Tel: 03 83 94 51 90
www.cdt-meurthe-et-moselle.fr

**Touring:**
AA Road Map France series 12: Alsace et Lorraine

## Lunéville

Léopold, Duke of Lorraine, during the first quarter of the 18th century laid out and built much of the château. He laid out the park and planned the wide streets in respectful admiration for the Versailles of Louis XIV.

Stanislas Leszczynski, deposed King of Poland, was made Duke of Lorraine, placed here by his father-in-law, Louis XV. He acted as governor, to accustom the people to French rule, since the duchy would revert to France on his death. An easygoing man who loved good living and beauty, he was popular and attracted a dazzling court, both here and at Nancy. He chose good architects to enlarge the château and initiated the porcelain factory, many fine examples from which can be seen in the château's museum. Particularly splendid are the set of vessels made for the hospital pharmacy.

The life-size automata that Stanislas commissioned for the Parc des Bosquets were destroyed in the Revolution but the pools and parterres, fountains and statues are as they were. In the museum a painting shows the park as Stanislas knew it.

Also worth seeing in Lunéville is the Église St-Jaques. Built between 1730 and 1747, the church has impressive baroque woodwork and an ornate clock.

*The approach to the huge château at Lunéville, built between 1702 and 1712 and known at one time as 'Petit Versailles'*

*The Musée des Beaux-Arts, in Place Stanislas in the centre of Nancy, has a fine collection of paintings spanning seven centuries.*

*The heart of Nancy remains a virtually intact example of 18th-century urban planning. The driving force behind the town's redevelopment, among the most ambitious in France during that century, was Stanislas Leszczynski, Duke of Lorraine*

## Nancy

Nancy lay between Burgundy and Flanders and was coveted by the dukes of Burgundy. Before the walls of Nancy, on 5 January 1477, Charles le Téméraire, last of the Valois dukes of Burgundy, was slain. The victorious René II and later dukes of Lorraine made Nancy a worthy capital.

But it is 18th-century Nancy, Place Stanislas and its surroundings, that attracts today's tourists. Laid out by Stanislas Leszczynski, the centre of Nancy was ten years in the building and finished in 1760. Symmetry reigns supreme, with fountains, statues and nymphs and wondrous wrought-iron work. The nearby Musée des Beaux-Arts displays European painting dating from the 14th to 20th centuries.

In the Musée de l'École de Nancy are many of the extraordinary creations in glass of Émile Gallé. He founded the 'École de Nancy', leading the reaction against slavish copies of 'classical' art. In the Musée Lorrain, in Grande-Rue, can be seen the whole story of Lorraine from the Middle Ages to World War I. There are Books of Hours, sculpture, tapestries and in particular the work of Jacques Callot, who was an early 'war artist', recording, for Cardinal Richelieu, many sieges and battles. Next door is the Musée Régional des Arts et Traditions Populaires, where rural life in days gone by is illustrated.

## St Nicolas-de-Port

When Islam threatened the shrine of St Nicholas – patron saint of Russia, Greece and New York – Italian sailors took his body to Bari. Crusaders from the village of Port managed to acquire a finger joint, for which the earliest shrine was built. In 1429 Joan of Arc came here to pray for the success of her mission.

After his defeat of Charles le Téméraire, René II, ruler of an independent dukedom at last, decided on a fitting tribute. The first stone of this Gothic masterpiece was laid in 1481 and the towers were completed by 1560. The whole building was virtually destroyed by fire in 1635, during the Thirty Years War. These three dates are commemorated in the west window, where such stained glass as was saved has been incorporated under the vivid red rose design.

On entering the basilica, the immediate impression is of height and light. Newly cleaned pale stonework soars up 28m to the tallest vault in France. Old frescos on the pillars have been refurbished. In a niche of the centre doorway is a representation of the miracle of St Nicholas – the bringing back to life of three youngsters, pickled in brine as potential material for sausages by an unscrupulous butcher. This is believed to be by Claude, brother of the Lorraine sculptor Ligier Richier.

### SPAS OF LORRAINE

Vittel and Contrexéville are two names nowadays closely associated with slimming and healthy living. But they are only two of the many springs exploited since the days of the Romans and earlier. Plombières-les-Bains, with slightly radioactive waters, was appreciated by Roman gourmets, who came to treat their digestive problems and rheumatism. Bains-les-Bains could hardly have assumed a prouder name. Much of its charm lies in its peaceful setting on the banks of the Bagnerot amid beech and oak. The waters here help those suffering from typically 21st-century ailments: hypertension, heart disease and arthritis.

A hundred years ago Vittel was an agricultural village, with springs known to the Romans but abandoned after they left. Now it is the most important of the spas, with an airport at Mirecourt and road and rail bringing in over 7,000 'curistes' each year, seeking help with kidney and nutritional problems.

The waters of Contréxeville are used only for drinking today.

# THE STRONGHOLD OF THE VOSGES

Romanesque rather than the Flamboyant Gothic of the Alps, the Vosges rise up from the Lorraine plateau to the west, through green meadows and peaceful pastoral scenery. Viewed from the east, however, they are a bastion, crowned by hill forts and castles from which generations of sentinels have watched the Rhine and the Black Forest beyond, whence invaders came.

*Grand Ballon rises from the main chain of the Vosges and is the highest peak in the whole range.*

*The summit of Grand Ballon offers views of the southern Vosges and the Black Forest. On a clear day, the Jura and the Alps can be seen.*

## Ballons d'Alsace

As the crow flies, the three highest summits at the southern end of the Vosges lie within 15km of the central resort of Markstein. By road the circuit is considerably longer. The highest, Grand Ballon (1424m), is topped by an orientation table and the monument to the 'Blue Devils' – the Chasseurs Alpins. From both the Petit Ballon (1267m) and the Ballon d'Alsace to the south (1250m), there are equally breathtaking views.

## Guebwiller

At the entrance to the Lauch valley – known as Florival to its inhabitants – Guebwiller owes its existence and its walls to the monks who came here from Murbach. Cars are forbidden in many of the most picturesque spots in the local forest. Notre-Dame is one of the largest 18th-century churches in Alsace. The gradual transformation of style towards neo-classicism is well represented.

## Le Markstein and Jungfraukopf

In this centre for both downhill and cross-country skiing, many of the *pistes* serve also as summer rambles. By some of the ski lifts are wildly convoluted plastic channels, which when packed with snow become bob-sleigh runs. The enthusiast can hire mountain bikes and there are many signposted routes available for all levels of competence. All around are launching spots for hang-gliders, often seen to be sailing past below as you admire the view from one of the many belvederes.

From Le Markstein the D27 winds its way down to Lac Wildenstein and right around the lake, which has a ruined castle at one end. There are many spots at which to stop, admire the scenery, have a picnic, or watch local sub-aqua club members in action. Perhaps they should try Lac de la Lauch on the other side of the Route des Crêtes, for it is said that Attila lost a wagon load of treasure in the lake that was here before the present dam was built. The white bulls that pulled it are said to sometimes rise up from the lake at full moon, their horns hung with pearls and jewels.

## Murbach

The road up the valley effectively ends at nearby Belchenthal, but in a wooded valley, in the shadow of the Grand Ballon, the two towers of the abbey of Murbach rise impressively above the trees. Irish Benedictines founded the original abbey in 727. By 925 their work in clearing the forest, bringing prosperity and the word of God, had made the abbey so wealthy that Attila came to plunder its treasures. It attained its greatest influence in

## MUNSTER CHEESE

Tradition says that Munster cheese has been made in Alsace since the arrival of a group of Irish monks in the 7th century. True, cheese has long been made as a convenient way of preserving milk for consumption, and Munster can certainly trace its origins back 600 years.

By the 17th century, Lorraine herders had long been bringing their cattle up into the high pastures in Alsace in summer and they grazed them well down from the tops – in what was then the Holy Roman Empire and no longer the fief of the dukes of Lorraine. The consequent intricate legal disputes, beloved of the jurists of the day, took time to settle, but it was finally agreed that the rent should be the production of cheeses on 23 June.

Thus did the Holy Roman Empire collect its rent, and an annual fête has grown up

around this arrangement, at Gérardmer. There are many varieties of Munster, for milk is collected from over 5,000 farms, 500 of which make their own cheeses.

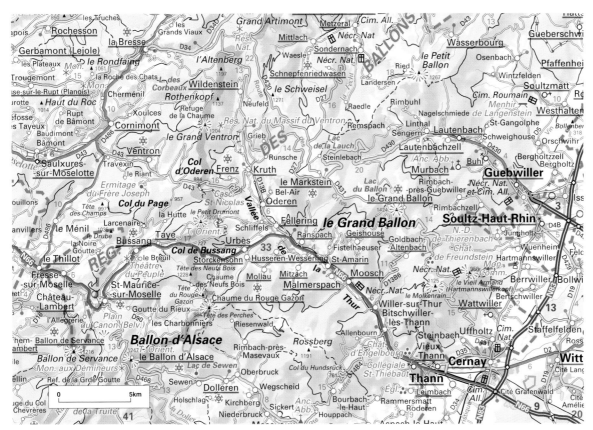

**Comité Départementale du Tourisme du Haut-Rhin**

1, Rue Schlumberger
68006 Colmar Cedex
Tel: 03 89 20 10 68
www.tourisme68.asso.fr

**Touring:**
AA Road Map France
series 12: Alsace et
Lorraine

the 11th and 12th centuries, when its library contained over 300 volumes, including copies of works by Charlemagne himself. Only the transept and choir remain of what was one of the flowers of Romanesque architecture in the Rhine Valley style. The abbey having been destroyed in 1444, and again during the Peasants' War (1524-5) and the Thirty Years War (1618-48), the community moved to nearby Guebwiller, where they founded a vast complex. This was sacked by the locals in 1789 and only the Notre-Dame church remains.

## Thann

*Thann, situated at the entrance to the Thur valley, was at one time on an important trade route between Italy and the Netherlands.*

Legend has it that Bishop Thiébaut, who died in Italy in 1160, had promised his ring to his servant. Trying to loosen the ring, the servant inadvertently pulled off the bishop's thumb. On his way back home with the relic, he stopped overnight by the river crossing at Thann. His pinewood staff took root and three bright lights hovered over the pine trees, attracting the attention of the Count of Ferrette in his castle of Engelbourg nearby. The count took them as a divine sign and promised to build a chapel on the site.

Thann is still surrounded by pine forests and on 30 June every year, the eve of the anniversary of the miracle, the town reaffirms the legend of its origins, burning three pine trees in the square in front of the church. By 1287 this Flamboyant Gothic church dedicated to St Thiébaut was attracting many pilgrims. The lace-like stone tracery of its 76-m spire makes it one of the most beautiful in Alsace. The church, finished around 1423, suffered badly during World War II, but the beauty of the original as been retained in the restoration.

The exquisite carved-oak stalls and misericords are incontestably the finest in Alsace. Among the figures and caricatures are a scholar and a fiddler and a quaint gentleman in 15th-century spectacles. Of the castle on the Engelbourg the most remarkable relic is the fine base of a tower, blown up by incompetent sappers in the 1670s. It stands, like a huge doughnut, overlooking the town.

## Viel Armand

The area around Thann, German territory at the start of World War I, was reclaimed by French forces on 7 August 1914. For months they battled against the Germans, well supplied by train from Mulhouse, to hold these commanding heights. After a year the sacrifices were finally seen as futile, but only after 30,000 men had died. The hilltop mausoleum, rows of crosses looking out over the plain with the tricolour for ever flying above, is a place for reflection.

*The main doors of Thann's Flamboyant Gothic church, built between the 14th century and the beginning of the 16th.*

# STORKS OVER THE WINE ROAD

Take the byways, enjoy the views, stop for a glass of wine at a roadside stall made from a huge wine barrel. On one side castles dot the hilltops and vines cover the lower slopes; on the other the fertile Alsatian plain stretches down to the Rhine. With luck, thanks to the rescue programme at Hunawihr, you will see storks flying again over the Route du Vin.

*The castle and church of Éguisheim (above)*

*Ribeauvillé (below)*

## Barr

Winding streets between the overhanging roofs of half-timbered houses make up characteristic Barr, a small town with tanneries and an excellent selection of good wines. The Folie Marco, built in 1763, now houses a collection of furniture, pottery and objects of local interest. Among the latter are the old man-hauled sledges on which felled timber was brought down log tracks from the forest.

## Dambach-la-Ville

All householders decorate their house fronts and window-boxes in the summer time, to maintain Dambach's reputation as the prettiest of the *villages fleuris* on the Route du Vin. But it could be that the excellence of the local wines has more than a little to do with the influx of visitors.

A forest road leads off the D203 up to the St-Sébastien chapel, with its Baroque carved wooden high altar. Further on – a couple of hours' return walk – the view from the Château de Bernstein on its granite spur amply repays the climb.

## Éguisheim

An octagonal basin, filled with lazy carp, surrounds the fountain in front of the castle where, in 1002, Bruno d'Éguisheim was born. He became the only Pope from Alsace, Léon IX. Here is a village in which the visitor can really walk around in circles, for at least seven of the narrow streets follow the concentric pattern employed for over 1,200 years, each time the village needed to grow. Walk around in circles, too, in the vineyards around Éguisheim. You will find Sylvaner, Pinot, Tokay, Muscat, Riesling and Gewürztraminer, apart from the rarer Auxerrois, as well as the whole range of Alsatian wines.

## Haut-Koenigsbourg

*'Ich habe es nicht gewollt'*. Do the Kaiser's words, on the fire-screen in the Great Hall, inscribed when he last visited, in April 1918, refer to his not having wished for World War I – or to the 'restoration' of this medieval castle? The subject of furious dispute among purists – 'pretentious', 'a pastiche', 'without soul' – the workmanship and quality of materials used are, however, above reproach. In ruins since the Thirty Years War, Haut-Koenigsbourg was presented to Wilhelm II by the deferential (but very hard up) citizens of Sélestat in 1900 and virtually rebuilt in 15th-century style.

On its 757-m crag, Haut-Koenigsbourg dominates the very heart of Alsace, and is the most visited tourist spot in the entire region.

**Association Départementale du Tourisme du Haut-Rhin**
1, Rue Schlumberger
68006 Colmar Cedex
Tel: 03 89 20 10 68
www.tourisme68.asso.fr

**Touring:**
AA Road Map France series 12: Alsace et Lorraine

*The resonant names of the wines of Alsace reflect the grapes from which they have been extracted.*

## WINES OF ALSACE

Unlike other French wines, those of Alsace tell you from which variety of grape they are pressed – Riesling, Muscat, Sylvaner, Gewürztraminer, Tokay and Pinot Blanc and Noir. A Tokay or a Riesling may come from anywhere along the 120-km Route du Vin, though individual villages have their own reputation for high-quality wine from particular grapes.

The vineyards are sheltered by the Vosges from westerly winds and enjoy a warm, dry climate with low rainfall. A wide range of soil types means there is always one best suited to a specific grape.

Sylvaner is the most widely grown *cépage*, doing best in the light, sandy soils around Barr and Rouffach. It produces a light, often slightly sparkling wine. Pinot Blanc, also known as Klevner, accounts for about 10 per cent of the area under vines. Only about one per cent of the area grows Pinot Noir, which gives the only rosé to light red wine in Alsace. Riesling is the favourite, growing best around Riquewihr, Ribeauvillé and Dambach. One of the older grape varieties grown here, it produces a wine well suited to *choucroute*. Muscat varieties grow in warmer southern vineyards. Tokay came, as its name suggests, from Hungary in the 16th century and produces a rich wine, excellently suited to *foie gras* and blue cheeses. Gewürztraminer has a splendid bouquet, well suited to both cheeses and some of the rich Alsatian desserts. Chasselas Blanc, grown principally in Haut-Rhin, is a pale, almost greenish-yellow wine, often the house wine in the grey and blue *pichets* of Betschdorf pottery.

## Hunawihr

Hunawihr has two assets not possessed by other equally picturesque villages along the Route du Vin: its fortified church and its stork-breeding centre. The 14th-century church tower is more castle keep than belfry. Its defensive wall, with six towers, dates from two centuries earlier.

## Kintzheim

The ruins of this 15th-century castle hold a collection of many different species of birds of prey, including condors and vultures. Demonstrations of their flying and hunting skills are a part of the visit.

## Ribeauvillé

Ribeauvillé is justly famous for its fine Riesling, but much of its attraction lies in its flower-decked houses, oriel windows, turrets, hidden courtyards and balconies.

The tradition of the Ribeauvillé 'Pfiffertag' draws large crowds to the town. A medieval seigneur tossed some coins to a piper who had broken his fife and had no way to earn his living. Tradition says 'a purse of gold', but then tradition often exaggerates! The piper and his friends paraded to the castle to thank their seigneur – and a parade is still held on the first Sunday in September each year. During the festival, the Renaissance fountain in front of the town hall runs with free wine all day.

Of the many ornately carved house façades, a particularly fine one is that of the 'Pfifferhüs', now a *winstub*, where the procession usually ends the day.

## Riquewihr

The Dolder and Obertor fortified gateways, a double row of ancient town walls, venerable cobbled streets, the Sinnbrunnen fountain, 16th- and 17th-century half-timbered houses with intricately carved corner posts, oriel windows and lintels, secretive courtyards hidden behind high doorways, old wine presses and a Renaissance château (rather incongruously now housing a postal museum) – all add up to what is frequently called 'the pearl of the vineyards'.

Riquewihr lives up to its reputation as a tourist attraction. In summer it can be crowded, but out of season it is a living open-air museum with a great deal to interest the visitor.

## STORKS

Symbol of Alsace for generations, the stork population had dropped from over 170 pairs in 1948 to just five pairs in 1976. It was decided to set up the Centre for the Reintroduction of Storks at Hunawihr. Here the eggs are incubated and the young storks raised, by hand and in semi-captivity for three years, until they lose all instinct to migrate. Storks did not fly to West Africa for the sunshine, they can withstand cold quite well. It was the lack of food, partly caused by the disappearance of the local wetlands, that drove them south each winter.

They suffered, also, from senseless slaughter, both in flight and in Africa. By 1988 there were over 60 pairs here, part hand-raised, part wild, breeding and remaining for the winters in the surrounding villages. The nest sites on many a house and church roof are

gradually being recolonised. In recent years a programme of otter breeding has also been introduced at the centre.

# STRASBOURG AND COLMAR

## Strasbourg

'City of the Crossroads' – Schweitzer, Gutenberg and Goethe, Maison Kammerzell and Vauban stonework, canals and cathedral, the Council of Europe, *winstubs* and *choucroute* – Strasbourg, part of France since 1648, has so much to offer and much is already well known. Petite France, all geraniums and tourists by day, is a different place in the dusk and dawn mists. Here, near water, lived the tanners, exercising their trade far away from – and hopefully downwind of – the houses of the good citizens.

Strasbourg and Colmar – two jewels in the crown of Alsace, both of equal brilliance, architecturally, culturally and historically. Each has its winding streets and multicoloured half-timbered houses, its river and its famous sons. Strasbourg now hosts the Council of Europe but Colmar has retained its quiet charm at the heart of the Route du Vin.

A good way to gain your own first impressions of Strasbourg is to climb the 365 steps to the top of the tower of Notre-Dame and see the city spread out 66m below. A less strenuous way is by boat. Strasbourg, with its canals and the River Ill, is ideally suited to such indolence. An hour's trip from the Palais Rohan will take you through 1,000 years of history: past the old mills, covered bridges and fortified towers of Petite France; along the line of the old ramparts to the Palais de l'Europe, former home of the Council of Europe and the European Parliament, and the

European Court of Human Rights, now in two brand new buildings opposite, passing the old harbour and the Krutenau before returning. Strasbourg has a proud history, but is also proud of the part it plays in today and tomorrow.

A Bronze Age trade centre became Roman Argentoratum, sacked by Attila the Hun in 451. A Frankish city was built along the Ill half a century later. When the wooden church that Clovis had built here in 510 burned down, Bishop Wernher began, in 1015, the construction of the magnificent cathedral that is so much a part of city life today.

For lovers of symmetry, it is perhaps a pity that Jean Hültz's steeple, completed in 1439, was not matched on the south tower, but the tracery is none the less magnificent standing on its own. Visit the Musée de l'Oeuvre Notre-Dame. Two gable ends, a courtyard and a hexagonal tower enclose a *courtil*, a tiny jewel of a garden such as can be seen in the background of so many medieval paintings of the Virgin. It was laid out between 1240 and 1268 by Albert le Grand, teacher of St Thomas Aquinas. This museum of medieval and Renaissance Alsatian art houses many of the original statues from the exterior of the cathedral, the replicas now in place being better able to withstand erosion and pollution.

There is nothing idealised here – these are the folk who were to be seen in Strasbourg's streets and alleyways: stolid, down-to-earth young women and the conniving Tempter with his apple – the serpents and toads crawling up the back of his robe being added for salutary effect. Perched on the western façade of the cathedral, a stork, symbol of Alsace, watches over the city.

*Petite France, the old quarter of Strasbourg (left), which surrounds the cathedral of Notre-Dame (inset), considered to be among the finest Gothic cathedrals in France.*

*An ornate clock on Strasbourg's Notre-Dame (above), which was begun in 1015 in the Romanesque style and completed in the Gothic around 1440*

*French and German influences meet in typically Alsatian Colmar (right)*

The pulpit, finished by Hans Hammer in 1486, is a masterpiece of intricate Flamboyant Gothic tracery. Followers of Geiler of Kaysersberg, already preaching sermons denouncing the iniquities of the Church, became so numerous that he was allowed to preach in the nave.

You should not miss St-Thomas, the 'Protestant Cathedral', with the magnificent tomb of Marshal Maurice de Saxe (1696–1750). Illegitimate son of a King of Poland, Marshal of France, Louis XV's Commander in Flanders, capturer of Prague, victor of Fontenoy, but 'bastard, a Protestant and a foreigner', he could not rest in the cathedral.

Strasbourg also has one of the oldest and most active universities in France, and is well endowed with museums to suit all tastes: Alsatian folk art; archaeology, decorative and fine arts (these three in the Palais Rohan); a zoological museum on the university campus; a prints and drawings museum, including work by Dürer and Daumier; a museum devoted to the work of native graphic artist Tomi Ungerer; and the major Museum of Modern and Contemporary Art, inaugurated in 1998, whose collection includes important 20th-century artists such as Arp, Kandinsky, Ernst, Picasso and Gustave Doré.

## Colmar

Colmar, a quarter of the size of Strasbourg, heart of the Route du Vin and the Alsace wine industry, has never lost its importance as a centre of art and culture. Its pattern of winding streets and multicoloured, half-timbered houses retains a warm, human dimension. Most of its historic

heart is now a pedestrian zone, adding greatly to its charm.

The Musée Unterlinden ranks second only in France to the Louvre in the number of visitors. Its greatest treasure is Grünewald's magnificent 'Issenheim' reredos. Curator of the museum until his death in 1951 was Jean-Jacques Waltz, better known as Hansi, the writer and caricaturist who kept alive the free spirit of France throughout two long occupations. His *Mon Village*, published in 1914, earned him a year in prison for making fun of the occupying power.

The Colmar-born sculptor Bartholdi, on his way to Paris in 1870, drew inspiration from the Unterlinden. He is famous for the statue which stands at the entrance to New York harbour. He also immortalised Schwendi, who brought back the Tokay grape to Alsace. Bartholdi was born in Rue des Marchands in 1834 and his house now contains a small museum.

Strasbourg's 'Ponts Couverts' (covered bridges), the Kammerzell, Notre-Dame cathedral and Petite France, are well matched – Colmariens say surpassed – by Colmar's Petite Venise along the Lauch, the Pfisterhaus and the Ancienne Douane, the church of St-Martin and the refurbished Quartier des Tanneurs. The church is notable for its 14th-century Crucifixion and the carvings on the Portal St-Nicholas.

Colmar is particularly worth visiting at the time of the Festival in June or the wine fair in August. Around Colmar not only is there the Route du Vin with its picturesque villages to discover, but towards Marckolsheim and Sélestat is the 'Ried', last remnant of the marshlands of the Rhine plain.

# THE LOIRE

Although it takes its name from the greatest river in France, the Loire is far more than just a river. It is a richly varied region stretching from the Atlantic coast to the country's very heart, and incorporating soft, green river valleys, rolling hills covered with fruit and vine, vast open plains planted with cereals and huge tracts of forest, woodland and heath.

The Loire is a landscape of small towns and villages, churches, abbey and châteaux marked by an instinctive feeling for architectural style and enriched with a wealth of ornament and detail that can be enjoyed in both grand buildings and ordinary houses. In all this stylistic diversity and flair an overriding sense of unity is achieved by the use of glowing white tufa stone and grey slate, both materials native to the region. The cities – Angers, Tours, Orléans – are also full of architecture and history. Any exploration of the River Loire and its main tributaries – the Indre, the Cher, the Loir, the Vienne and the Sarthe – will bring the visitor face to face with history, in the form of early Christianity, the Plantagenet and Valois kings, the wars of the Middle Ages and the 17th century, and the impact of the Renaissance, all of which have left their mark on the landscape. Notable above all are the châteaux, whose transition from medieval fortress to ornamental mansion echoes the change from feudal strife to a golden age of civilisation. Bound up with the architecture is the literary tradition of the Loire, for here more than anywhere else in France are the castles of legend and fairy story brought to life in the concept of courtly love as expressed in the *Romance of the Rose*. This literary style was continued by Ronsard and Rabelais, both men of the Loire, while later writers maintained the tradition, among them Balzac, Péguy and Alain-Fournier.

Well watered and blessed with plenty of sun, the varied landscape of the Loire has always been fertile. The region is famous for wine and fruit, cereals and mushrooms, vegetables and cheeses, and it has long been known as the Garden of France. It is also renowned for its gastronomic temptations, such as pike served with creamy sauces and locally produced pork sometimes cooked in white wine with prunes.

*The formal gardens at the beautiful Château de Chenonceau.*

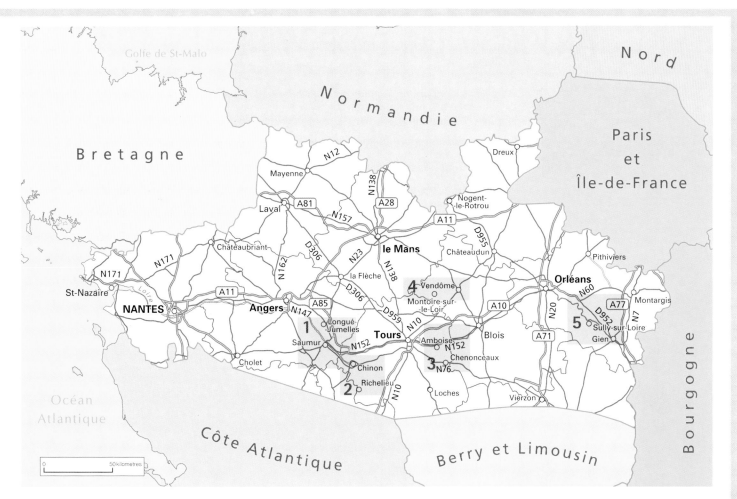

The Château de Chambord (below) is said to have inspired Versailles Sablé, a Loire shortbread (right).

As well as Chinon's regular street market (right) several fairs take place in the town. These include a medieval fair in August recreating the cookery, crafts, costumes and dancing and music of the Middle Ages.

The town of Château-Gontier, founded in the 11th century, has an attractive position on the banks of the Mayenne, north of the Loire.

# ANJOU — LAND OF WINE AND ROSES

The broad Loire flows lazily through the heart of Anjou, dividing the low-lying landscape of the northern shore from the wooded hills of the south. Anjou's fame today is based on wine, roses and mushrooms, but always present is a strong sense of history, conveyed by the Romanesque churches, the abbeys and the châteaux – the legacy of the dukes of Anjou and the Plantagenets.

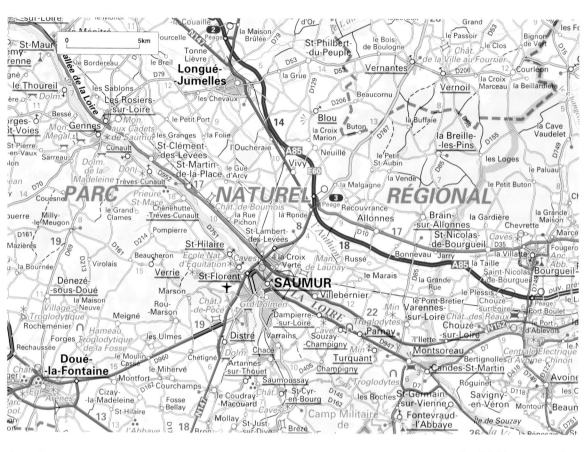

*Climb the path from Candes-St Martin for a panoramic view of the Loire valley*

## Candes-St Martin

This pleasantly old-fashioned and flowery village, climbing gently up from the river's edge, is remarkable for its church, Gothic rather than Romanesque, and built in the 12th and 13th centuries on the site of the monastic cell in which St Martin died in 397. A powerful, soaring structure, rich in carved decoration, it venerates St Martin, the first Bishop of Tours. Behind the church a well-signposted but rather steep walk winds up past old cottages and former stone quarries to a field high above the village. From here there is a wide panorama of the confluence of the Loire and the Vienne, a classic landscape of the Loire valley. Those requiring refreshment after the walk can visit the many establishments along the riverside road between Candes and Saumur that offer *dégustation*, tasting, of the local white wines.

## Château de Montsoreau

Montsoreau's château, a dramatic fortress towering above the Loire and the smart little village, was built in the middle of the 15th century. The grand but severe rooms were little used by the family that were responsible for the building of the château, and its recent restoration followed many decades of decay.

## Cunault

Most visitors to the Loire become familiar with the sight of Cunault's great abbey, rising above the stone walls and flowers of its tiny village. Yet far more memorable is the first view from the entrance along 70m of towering nave. Built over two centuries, and ranging in style from pure Romanesque to Angevin Gothic, the abbey is noted for its extraordinary carved capitals.

Comité Départemental du Tourisme d'Anjou
Place Kennedy - BP 2147
49021 Angers Cedex 02
Tel: 01 41 23 51 51
www.anjou-tourisme.com

**Touring:** AA Road Map France series 3: Pays de Loire

*The château at Saumur occupies a commanding position between the Loire and the Thouet.*

## MUSHROOMS

A legacy of the Loire region's white tufa stone mining industry was a mass of caves driven deep into the soft stone cliffs, cool, dark chambers that proved excellent for storing wine.

Even more significant for the economy of the region was the realisation that the tufa caves would be ideal for the cultivation of mushrooms, and many now support a major industry that has contributed greatly to the local cuisine. In a typical cave at St Hilaire-St Florent, north-west of Saumur, there is a museum that explains all about mushroom cultivation.

*The abbey at Fontevraud was richly endowed by the royal Plantagenet family.*

## Fontevraud-l'Abbaye

Set high in the wooded hills that flank the Loire's southern shore and surrounded by vineyards, this attractive village has inevitably become one of the region's most visited shrines. The reason is the great abbey, established by Robert d'Arbrissel early in the 11th century. It was a huge and remarkable establishment, and was chosen as the final resting place of the Plantagenet monarchs, including Eleanor of Aquitaine and Richard the Lionheart. Throughout its long life, until its final dissolution in 1789, the whole complex was always under the care of an abbess. Despite being used in later years as a prison, the abbey retains an atmosphere of peace and harmony, underlined by the fine Romanesque architecture.

## Gennes

A small town often overlooked on the south bank of the Loire, Gennes is linked to its better-known neighbour on the north bank, Les Rosiers, by a long suspension bridge whose delicate grace enhances this stretch of river. The predictable appeal of Les Rosiers is based on its famous restaurants, tree-lined streets and chunky Renaissance church tower that dominates the flat landscape. Gennes is very different, with much of the village hidden below the steep, wooded hills of the southern shore.

It is essential to take the path that winds up through the woods to St-Eusèbe, both for the views over the soft greens of the river valley and for the moving memorial to the cadets from the Saumur Cavalry School who died defending the bridge against the German invaders in June 1940. There are two ancient churches: that of St-Eusèbe, parts of which date back to the 8th century, is a ruin. A Roman aqueduct, baths and amphitheatre have been discovered near by.

## Saumur

Approached from the west along the Loire's northern bank, Saumur has a magical quality, the pinnacled skyline of its château looking like something from a 15th-century Book of Hours. Best entered by the old bridge that leads straight to its heart, Saumur is a small and compact town, easily explored on foot.

The château, built largely between the 14th and the 16th centuries by the dukes of Anjou, today houses two museums, one devoted to the decorative arts and the other to the horse. The latter has a fine collection of pictures, equipment and records of notable animals, telling the story of horsemanship through the ages. Saumur is further closely connected with the horse through its famous Cavalry School, and the annual military tattoo, with displays by the pre-eminent Cadré Noir, is a high point of the summer.

Finally, no visit to Saumur would be complete without a visit to one of the cellars where the famous sparkling wine is produced, such as Gratien et Meyer, Ackerman or Veuve Amiot.

## ROSES

Flowers, both wild and cultivated, add greatly to the pleasures of the Loire. At different seasons the yellow iris, the soft-pink valerian and multicoloured geraniums enrich the landscape and the villages. However, memorable above all else are the roses, filling the hedgerows and gardens and climbing freely over cottages and village terraces.

Rose growing is carried on throughout the region, but one town is particularly well known as a centre for their cultivation. In Doué-la-Fontaine there is a famous rose show, held in July in one of the old stone quarries that surround the town. Market gardens and garden centres that specialise in roses are all over the town, and there is a rose-water distillery. Just outside Doué is the public Jardin des Roses, a changing display whose colours and scents provide an enduring memory.

# THE VALLEY OF THE VIENNE

The Vienne is one of the most attractive of the Loire tributaries, and the area has been settled since before Roman times. It was from the massive military fortress of Chinon that Joan of Arc set forth on her mission to rescue France from English domination. Rabelais was born and brought up in the woodlands south of that city, while further south Cardinal Richelieu created a grand palace and a new town that still carries his name.

**Comité Départemental du Tourisme d'Indre-et-Loire**
9, Rue Buffon - BP 3217
37032 Tours Cedex
Tel: 02 47 31 47 48
www.tourism-touraine.com

**Touring:** AA Road Map France series 3: Pays de Loire

*Chinon's impressive château was a royal palace for a relatively short period, for the Court ceased to use it after the 15th century. The perspective of history reveals that Chinon was of far greater importance as a medieval military bastion, and it is an outstanding example of such architecture.*

## Champigny-sur-Veude

The Veude, a quiet but engaging tree-lined river, winds its way from the Vienne to Champigny, passing through the centre of the village, whose restful, old-world atmosphere is put completely in the shade by the decorative magnificence of the Sainte-Chapelle. Early in the 16th century a splendid château was built here, but it was demolished a century later on the orders of Cardinal Richelieu, who wanted no rival for his own new château at Richelieu to the south. Little was spared, except for a few outbuildings and the chapel, and so today a small provincial village is graced with one of the most glorious Renaissance buildings in the whole of France.

## Château du Rivau

Little known and rarely visited, le Rivau is undeservedly overshadowed by the more familiar châteaux of the Loire. Part fortress and part mansion, it dates from the 15th century and still has its moat and drawbridge, as well as other original late-medieval features. With its stern grey stone walls softened by the surrounding parkland and woods, le Rivau has a quality and an integrity often lacking in better-known but over-restored châteaux. The gardens have been re-created to a 15th-century design, using plants from Medieval times.

## Chinon

It is essential to approach Chinon from the south, to enjoy to the full the sight of the mighty fortress spread along its sheer cliff high above the town and the medieval bridge whose thirteen arches span the Vienne.

Lacking any domestic refinement or grace, the château is a powerful memorial to the centuries of bitter strife that characterised the Middle Ages. It is really a fort and two châteaux, linked by a bridge. The smaller Fort St-Georges, now a ruin, was built by the Plantagenet King Henry II, while the more substantial Châteaux du Coudray and du Milieu were added by King

*Joan of Arc, the 'Maid of Orléans', was cannonised in 1920, and her feast day is celebrated in May.*

## JOAN OF ARC

With the start of the English siege of Orléans in the autumn of 1428, the Loire had become the main battlefield in the long-running Anglo-French conflict. On 9 March 1429 Joan presented herself to the Dauphin in the Grande Salle of the Château du Milieu, successfully picking out his unobtrusive figure from the 300 people assembled in the room. She explained her dual mission, to raise the siege of Orléans and then to escort the Dauphin to Reims to be crowned king. Initially she was regarded with suspicion and was briefly held a virtual prisoner in Chinon and subjected to rigorous questioning at Poitiers. But eventually she was provided with armed men by the Dauphin, who was desperate to raise the siege. In May Orléans was relieved, and in June Joan's army twice defeated the English, at Jargeau and Patay. On 17 July she led the Dauphin from Chinon on the way to his coronation at Reims.

*Flowers, grain, grapes and other fruit from the surrounding countryside are sold at Chinon's long-established market.*

Philippe-Auguste. The Château du Coudray contains the royal apartments.

Below the château, huddled between the river and the cliff, is the town, a network of narrow streets lined with timber-framed houses often leaning at alarming angles. Hidden among the houses are little alleys and fine courtyards. Busy in summer, out of season Chinon is a delight. It offers a local museum in a fine 15th-century town house, a chapel cut from the solid rock of the cliff, a house with Rabelais associations, a barrel-making museum and, at various times of the year, an interesting variety of fairs and markets. Among these is the annual wine festival, held in April, which features the famous local red wines that are always available in the town's many restaurants and cafés.

### L'Ile Bouchard

Formerly a trading port on the Vienne, L'Ile Bouchard was originally built on an island in the river, clustered around a 9th-century fortress. Today little remains of this historic past and the town has spread away from the island on to both banks. Pleasantly provincial, it is at its best by the river. The real treasure is to be found to the south, approached along suburban streets around the railway station. Here, on its own and apparently in a farmyard, is the ruined

chancel of the former Prieuré de St-Léonard. A picturesque fragment, majestic in the open air, it is made memorable by its setting and by the ambitiously carved capitals on its broken columns, which feature New Testament scenes, foliage and sea monsters. The site can be visited every day, as the caretaker lives on the spot.

## Richelieu

Created from scratch in the 17th century at the instigation of Cardinal Richelieu, this is the perfect estate town. Built on a strict rectangular grid and surrounded by a moat and an enclosing wall pierced by elegant gateways, Richelieu is a delight in formal grey stone. Classical terraces cross the town, with grand houses in the centre for the courtiers, smaller ones on the edge for the artisans.

Richelieu's slightly faded elegance is very restful and its open squares seem to cope easily with the needs of modern traffic. Just beyond the southern gateway there is a statue of the cardinal, surveying the entrance to the great park that housed his château. This mighty building, a rival to Versailles, and the *raison d'être* for the new town, was demolished long ago and only the park and a few outbuildings remain today as a memorial to Cardinal Richelieu's worldly ambitions.

## SIGHT-SEEING BY RAIL

An enjoyable way to visit the pretty valley of the Veude is to take the steam train from Chinon to Richelieu. The line wanders along the river valley, passing close to the Château du Rivau and through Champigny-sur-Veude on the way to its terminus just outside Richelieu's enclosing wall. Old carriages and an ancient SNCF locomotive contribute to making the journey memorable, while the gentle speed ensures ample time for enjoyment of the view. The service operates on Saturdays and Sundays in July and August.

*Richelieu is a fine testimony to 17th-century urban planning, for an elegant uniformity is evident throughout the town.*

# THE CHÂTEAUX OF THE LOIRE

I n the Loire region as a whole there are probably 150 châteaux of some historical importance, and many more of lesser interest. They range in date from the 11th century to the 19th and reflect many of the architectural styles particularly associated with France. The habit of visiting châteaux was established in the 19th century, when the railways brought tourism to the Loire and its network of tributaries, and in more recent times the most famous examples – Angers, Saumur, Chinon, Azay-le-Rideau, Villandry, Amboise, Chenonceau, Chaumont, Blois, Chambord and Cheverny – have become household names. Every year many thousands of visitors come to see them, hoping perhaps to capture some hint of the spirit of creativity that brought them into being.

Many of the châteaux do stand beside the Loire, but others are on lesser rivers, the Cher, the Indre, the Vienne, the Loir and the Sarthe, or in woods or farmland well away from any river. Some are owned by the state, some by companies, some by private families, and their condition ranges from immaculate magnificence to a pile of broken stones. Yet all have played their part in the development of a region that has always been close to the heart of French history. There can be no river in the world with more historic associations than the Loire.

## A Witness to History

The history of the châteaux of the Loire is bound up closely with the history of France itself, fort the great river, in its 1020-km sweep from the south to the Atlantic coast, has always been a frontier, a battleground and a vital line of communication. The invading Roman army followed the Loire in its conquest of Gaul, meeting stiff resistance from the local tribes. Christianity spread into France along the same route, and then came the Huns and the Saracens, invading forces who were stopped at the Loire. The next aggressors were the Normans, who used the river to transport their troops for attacks on towns such as Nantes and Tours. The legacy of the Norman invasion was chaos, as feudal strife broke the region into small warring states.

By the 11th century Orléans, Touraine, Anjou and Maine were virtually separate kingdoms, and it was their rulers, semi-legendary figures such as Foulques Nerra, who built the first Loire châteaux, fortresses and strongholds to defend their frontiers.

With the emergence of the Plantagenets, Anjou became dominant, establishing by the middle of the 12th century an empire that stretched from the Pyrenees to the north of England. Dating from this period are the earliest of the châteaux that can still be enjoyed today, great fortresses such as Angers. The Plantagenets' great enemy were the French Capetian kings, whose base was at Orléans, and the rivalry between the two royal houses led directly to several centuries of strife between England and France. During this time the fortresses of the Loire region were constantly being rebuilt, attacked and rebuilt again as the armies battled for the key towns and strongholds, and defended crossing points.

When the Dauphin set up his court, first at Bourges and then at Chinon, the Loire became the front line and with the intervention of Joan of Arc, whose battles all took place around the Loire, the balance swung to the French. By the middle of the 15th century English rule in France was at an end, and for the first time in centuries peace came to this troubled region.

*The 17 towers of Angers' 13th-century fortress are built of red schist and white stone.*

*Azay-le-Rideau (far left) was erected between 1518 and 1527 by a wealthy financier. At this time châteaux were being built as homes rather than fortresses. The château at Blois (left) comprises elements ranging from medieval to the 17th-century. Among the most striking is the staircase built by François I.*
*It was Diane de Poitiers who extended Chenonceau (below) across the River Cher in a series of arches. The massive château at Chambord (bottom), begun by François I, is regarded by some as the finest Renaissance building in France*

## The Golden Age of the Loire

With the peace came the relative stability of the Valois kings, who turned the Loire from a battlefield into the centre of Court life. Towering fortresses, their military life at an end, began to be turned into domestic palaces, and so there emerged the most characteristic of all Loire château types, the fortress containing within its heart a handsome mansion. Early in the 16th century François I came to the throne and this cultured king launched the golden age of the Loire. He established a sophisticated and artistic court, with an enthusiasm for Italy that brought the Renaissance to France.

The new generation of royal palaces – Amboise, Blois, Chambord – launched a new style of domestic architecture in France, and the royal creations were soon being echoed all over the Loire region as artistocrats, courtiers and financiers vied with each other in stately magnificence. For the first time ladies played a part, with figures such as Diane de Poitiers and Catherine de Medici adding style and elegance to masculine architecture. In the case of these two powerful rivals for the attention of Henri II, it

was the château at Chenonceau that benefitted.

## Changing Fortunes

Peace was shattered by the violent religious wars of the end of the 16th century. These had a direct impact on the region, but château building continued

nonetheless through the 17th century, inspired by leading figures such as Cardinal Richelieu. By the 18th century the royal influence had moved away from the Loire, but the château tradition was maintained by the aristocracy and newly wealthy industrialists and bankers. The new rococo and

neoclassical styles came to the Loire, epitomised by Chanteloup, Ménars and Montgeoffroy, but the turmoil of the Revolution in 1789 brought an end to the Loire's powerful influence and prosperity.

## An Enduring Legacy

In the 19th century industry and modern transport took their place beside the traditional agriculture of the region, and the newly generated wealth encouraged the building of new châteaux and the restoration of many earlier ones.

All this came to an end with the outbreak of the Franco-Prussian War in 1870. However, the important contribution of the 19th century remained the appreciation of the architectural qualities of those châteaux built between the 12th and the 17th centuries, a legacy enjoyed by inhabitants of, and visitors to, the Loire today.

# CHÂTEAUX OF THE LOIRE AND CHER

In this region of forest and parkland, bounded in the north by the wide course of the Loire and in the south by the gentler Cher, the Renaissance brought about the replacement of the medieval fortress with something far lighter and more elegant. Châteaux such as the daring Chenonceau came to overshadow the more traditional style of Amboise and Chaumont.

## Amboise

Amboise is an attractive place, with narrow streets especially Clos-Lucé, a postal museum, and Leonardo da Vinci's house, with its displays of models made up from his drawings.

The town is best known to visitors for its *son et lumière* displays, the focal point of which is the château. For those with children there is plenty to see, including the mini-châteaux park, with miniature scale reproductions of the most famous of the Loire châteaux. On the same site is a donkey centre, comprising 50 or so different breeds, and nearby is the Aquarium de Touraine.

## Bléré

This small town, whose quiet streets and pleasant shops can be a relief after the turmoil of Amboise, grew up around a long-established crossing point on the Cher. Its former importance is reflected by several Renaissance buildings, the best of which is the Hôtel du Gouverneur.

## Château de Chaumont-sur-Loire

The little town of Chaumont, essentially one street running parallel to the river, is wholly dominated by the château. Thousands of visitors flock here each summer for the international garden festival in the castle grounds, where 30 landscape architects create original and exciting garden designs. There is also a permanent garden information centre.

## Château de Chenonceau

Visually the most exciting and, by its associations, the most romantic of the Loire châteaux, Chenonceau is in every way a remarkable building. Early in the 16th century Thomas Bohier, a Court financier, acquired the site of a medieval fortress beside the Cher and began the construction of a formal but highly decorative Renaissance mansion. In 1526 the château passed to François I to pay off some of Bohier's debts and became a royal palace. Some 20 years later Henri II gave

### ROYAL RIVALS

Considerably older than Henri II, Diane de Poitiers was far more than a mistress. Business manager, confidante and continual source of inspiration, Diane seems always to have outshone the queen, Catherine de Medici. The gift of Chenonceau to Diane, and her gardens and daring extension across the Cher, proved the final straw. When Henri died in 1559 Catherine took her revenge by forcing Diane to surrender Chenonceau for the gaunt walls of Chaumont. At Chenonceau Catherine flourished, expanding the building and linking the château's name with memorable masques and fêtes in the enlarged park. It was Catherine who fulfilled the promise of Chenonceau laid down by Diane, who spent the last seven years of her life in seclusion.

*Amboise (above) is a typical Loire town and attracts many tourists in summer. They come not only to see the château but also to visit the old quarter and to attend various festivals, including one in September that celebrates the melon.*

*Entry to the superb château at Chenonceau (right) is gained by passing through Bohier's original château.*

## WINE

Among the many distinctive wines of the Loire region are those of Touraine, dry whites and reds, and the notable rosés associated particularly with the Mesland area north of Amboise. Taking their names from the region as a whole, from towns and villages or local châteaux, the Loire wines come in all qualities, from Appellation contrôlée to ordinary table wines. A number of grape varieties are used, including Gamay, Cabernet Sauvignon and Chenin, and the changing soil conditions have resulted in a wide choice of wines.

Notable are the muscadets of the western Loire, the light rosés and whites of Anjou, the heavier sweet wines of the Coteaux du Layon, the light reds of the Angers region, the richer reds of Bourgueil and Chinon, the flinty-tasting white from Sancerre and, above all, the sparkling varieties from Saumur, Vouvray and Montlouis. Many of these wines are made and stored in the old tufa-stone caves and there are plenty of opportunities for dégustation, roadside tasting.

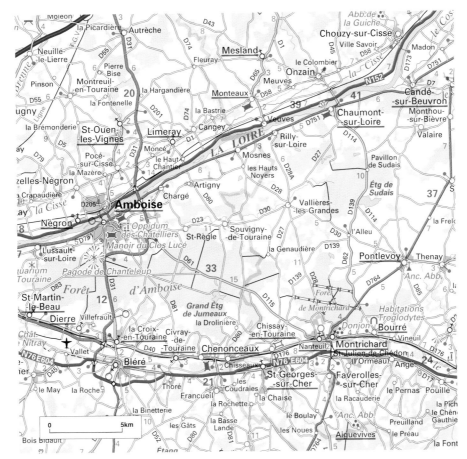

Chenonceau to his mistress, Diane de Poitiers, and it was she who extended it on a series of arches across the Cher. After Henri's death his widow Catherine took over the château and added two more storeys to the bridge.

In a separate domed-roofed building in the gardens, a waxworks museum re-creates the personalities who lived in the castle.

## Montrichard

The best way to see Montrichard is from the south, entering this attractive yet surprisingly little-known town via the 17th-century bridge across the Cher. This gives ample opportunity for the enjoyment of the splendid river front, with the ruined medieval fortress standing high above the town. Climb to the top for a superb view over the surrounding countryside, or go underground in the 15km-long passages of the Caves Monmousseau to learn how the local sparkling wine is made.

## Pagode de Chanteloup

Set on high ground at the edge of the Forêt d'Amboise, this entertaining fantasy is all that remains of an extensive château and park developed in the 18th century by the Duc de Choiseul. The château was actually much earlier and was bought by Choiseul when he was one of Louis XV's ministers. After falling foul of Madame du Barry, Choiseul was exiled from Court and spent four years confined to the Chanteloup estate. At the end of his exile, in 1762, he celebrated the loyalty of those friends who had made it bearable by commissioning the pagoda. Inspired by Sir William Chamber's structure in Kew Gardens, it was designed by the architect Le Camus, who turned it into something larger and more exotic. From the top of the pagoda the magnificent view of the sweep of the Loire from Tours to Blois makes the climb up the twisting staircase well worth the effort.

Some fragments of the vanished château's décor are in the museum in Tours, but these can only hint at the lifestyle enjoyed by Choiseul during his exile, when Chanteloup became a rival to Versailles.

## Pontlevoy

The main feature of this quiet town is the huge abbey. Founded in the 11th century, it was greatly expanded in later centuries, and much of what can be seen today dates from the 17th century. The town is famous as the birthplace of Auguste Poulain, the chocolate maker, and is decorated with old advertising posters and photographs.

**Comité Départemental du Tourisme d'Indre-et-Loire**
9, Rue Buffon - BP 3217
37032 Tours Cedex
Tel: 02 47 31 47 48
www.tourism-touraine.com

**Touring:**
AA Road Map France series 3: Pays de Loire, and 8: Centre

The impressive abbey at Pontlevoy is the town's principal attraction. Originally founded in the 11th century, it combines fine 18th-century buildings with an earlier former abbey church.

# ALONG THE VALLEY OF THE LOIR

Not to be confused with the Loire, its grander neighbour, the Loir is a delightfully rural river. A tributary of the Sarthe, and thus of the Mayenne, it has its own medieval fortresses, Renaissance châteaux, Romanesque churches and interesting villages and towns, as well as a history reaching back to before the Roman occupation of France.

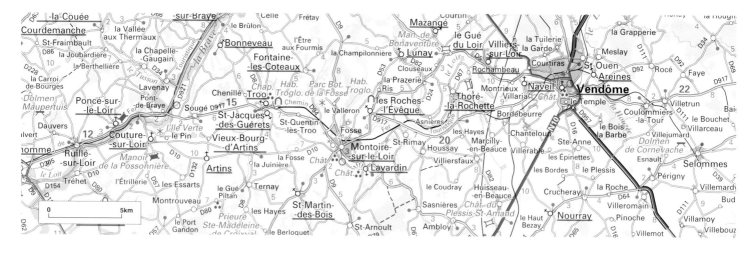

**Comité Départemental du Tourisme Loir-et-Cher**
5, Rue de la Voûte du Château de Blois
41005 Blois Cedex
Tel: 02 54 57 00 41
www.chambourdcountry.com

**Touring:**
AA Road Map France series 3: Pays de Loire, and series 8: Centre

*Montoire-sur-le-Loir's ruined château, with its 11th-century square keep*

## Lavardin

Set in a bend of the Loir, Lavardin is a remarkable little village, a cluster of old houses surrounding the hillside church, full of prettiness and picturesque detail and with only a hint of self-consciousness. Inside the church is a fine series of murals.

However, Lavardin's most spectacular feature is undoubtedly its ruined 11th- and 12th-century castle.

## Montoire-sur-le-Loir

In the Middle Ages the Loir formed a defensive barrier protected by a number of hilltop fortresses. Some have disappeared

while others survive as picturesque ruins. Notable among the latter is Montoire, whose battered keep and fortifications stand high above the south bank of the river and are well worth exploring for the views along the wooded valley. Close by the river on the château side is the Chapelle-St-Gilles, with its deservedly famous series of 12th-century murals.

## Poncé-sur-le-Loir

Almost out of place in the pastoral valley of the Loir is Poncé's fine château, a Renaissance building that owes more to the architecture of Chenonceaux and Azay-le-Rideu than any local tradition. Italianate and French design traditions come together, notably in the splendid coffered staircase that rises straight up for six flights. Poncé has the quality of a royal building, yet has no such associations.

To be seen in Poncé's church are good examples of the medieval wall paintings characteristic of this region. Painted in the late 12th century, the series includes a scene of a battle between crusaders and Muslims. Further examples of a similar date can be seen in the church at St Jacques-des-Guérets, which lies 10km to the east along the Loir.

Another attraction in Poncé is the arts and crafts centre in a former paper mill: ceramics, glassware, wrought ironwork, woodwork (open all year).

### CAVE DWELLINGS

A characteristic feature of the whole of the Loire region are the caves cut into steep riverside cliffs and hills during centuries of excavation of the soft, white tufa stone. Cool, dry, secure and often cut into huge caverns inside the hills, these caves have been adapted for domestic use since before Roman times. Many are used as stores, wine cellars or for the cultivation of mushrooms, but in a number of places there is an age-old tradition of troglodyte houses. The largest collection is cut into the hillside at Troo, but individual examples are to be seen in many other parts of the region. Some are quite clearly little more than inhabited caves, while others are on more than one storey and set behind a decorative architectural façade.

A variation to be found around Doué-la-Fontaine are the dwellings carved out underground rather than in caves in the riverside cliffs. At Rochemenier, for example, there is a subterranean village three times larger than the hamlet above ground, and dating back to the Middle Ages.

## THE SOLOGNE

The Sologne, a region of wild forest and heath broken by streams and innumerable lakes, was formed when the Loire changed its course to swing in a great curve south-west towards the Atlantic. Bounded by Blois, Orléans, Gien and Vierzon, the Sologne is a huge area where centuries of isolation have developed a particular way of life. Notable are the single-storey terraces in the little towns and villages, all built in simple styles from local brick.

The thick forests are full of deer, wild boar and other game, and the lakes are rich in carp and other fish. The whole region is a secret paradise for wildlife and insects, much of it accessible only on foot or horse.

*The village of Les Roches-l'Évêque lies in a wooded cleft between the Loir and sheer cliffs.*

*Houses built into the cliffs make cool dwellings.*

## Les Roches-l'Évêque

The setting of this little village is its main appeal. It is squeezed into the narrow strip of land that separates the Loir from the steep cliffs lining the river's north bank – squeezed so tightly that many of the houses are in the old tufa-stone caves. Some are actually not very old, for when demand outstripped supply the villagers simply carved out new cave homes, equipping them with all mod cons. Also partly in a cave is the church, decorated with 12th- and 13th-century frescos.

## Troo

This is one of the most curious villages in the whole of the Loire, and it reveals its curiosities layer by layer. At first sight it is a pleasant traditional village with houses ranged in rows along the minor road that follows the Loir's north bank. But set high on the hill above is another Troo, a much older settlement with battered fortifications, an impressive gateway and a castle mount.

A walk down the hillside towards the river uncovers Troo's third, and most surprising, aspect. Here is the most extensive cave town in the Loire, if not in the whole of France. A network of paths reveals a whole nest of cave houses set into the steep hillside, many still in use.

## Vendôme

The grandest town in this part of the Loire, Vendôme has been a settlement at least since the pre-Roman era and has subsequently had a colourful life. It was pillaged by the English, owned by the French royal family and the Bourbons, and attacked by the Germans in 1870 and 1940. It has associations with the 16th-century poet Ronsard and with Rochambeau, the leader of the French forces during the American War of Independence. High above Vendôme, and offering splendid views, is a huge, ruined medieval fortress, underlining the town's strategic importance in the Middle Ages.

This is a delightful town to explore, its centre spread over several branches of the Loir ensuring a proliferation of little bridges and pretty waterfronts. Near the central marketplace are two great towers: a 15th-century clock tower from the former parish church and a magnificent Romanesque campanile over 80m high, detached from its abbey church, La Trinité. The latter has fine sculpture on the Flamboyant Gothic west front.

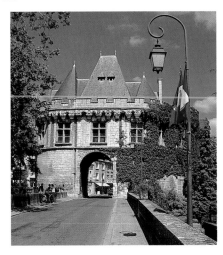

*Among Vendôme's several fine gateways is the Porte St-George.*

# THE LAST CHÂTEAUX OF THE LOIRE

The wide sweeps of the Loire separate the forests of Orléans from the empty heathland of the Sologne. The river itself is a band of civilisation and history flowing through this emptiness, its banks enriched with grand châteaux, with important associations with Joan of Arc and with sites vital to the development of Christianity.

## Château de Sully-sur-Loire

*In medieval times there was a rudimentary fortress at Sully, guarding the Loire, and part of the original structure still faces the river. Maximilien Béthune (later Duc de Sully) made extensive additions in the early 17th century, so that the château is a fusion of medieval and Renaissance elements.*

Badly damaged by bombing in World War II, the little town of Sully has never really recovered the style it must have enjoyed in the 17th century. The best approach is from the north, to enjoy the view of the château and the town while crossing the long bridge, preferably on foot. The château dominates the town completely, and there is really little else to Sully. It is a magnificent building, one of the most dramatic of all the Loire châteaux, wonderfully sited by the river and surrounded by a moat that reflects the glowing white stone to perfection. An excellent example of a Renaissance mansion inserted into an earlier medieval fortress, Sully is a harmonious mass.

The château enjoyed three distinct periods of history. The first was in the time of Joan of Arc, for it was from Sully that Joan set off in 1430 for her last battle, her capture by the English and ultimately her death. The second was in the 17th century when Henri IV's great minister the Duc de Sully rebuilt the château in its present form. The third was in the 18th century when the young Voltaire was exiled to Sully, bringing life and culture back to the old château. The interiors underline this varied history, but particularly impressive is the great hall with its massive chestnut roof of 1363, one of the greatest of all medieval timber roofs. However, best of all is the view of Sully from the Loire, with its parapets, towers and pepper-pot roofs.

## Châteauneuf-sur-Loire

This smart market town grew up to serve its château, originally a medieval fortress that was destroyed in the 16th century. In 1646 the estate was acquired by Louis de la Vrillière, and a new château was built, a small Versailles with magnificent gardens beside the Loire. This in turn was almost completely destroyed during the Revolution. In the 1820s the gardens were landscaped in the English style and are still a delight to explore, particularly when the rhododendrons are in flower. The château's creator is commemorated in the 13th-century church by a statue, which was hidden during the Revolution.

Châteauneuf-sur-Loire is a pleasant own with good shops and restaurants, and it is unusually blessed with two market halls, one wooden, dated 1854, and a later one in delicate cast iron. The château's former stables now house a museum of navigation on the Loire, bringing to life the boats, the boatmen and their families, the trade and the ports, of the once thriving river transport industry that died towards the middle of the 19th century.

**Comité Départemental du Tourisme du Loiret**
8, Rue d'Escures
45000 Orléans
Tel: 02 38 78 04 04
www.tourismloiret.com

**Touring:**
AA Road Map France
series 8: Centre

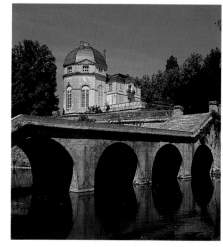

*Louis XIV's Secretary of State, Louis de la Vrillière, built a small-scale replica of Versailles at Châteauneuf-sur-Loire. All that remains of it are the domed rotunda, the pavilions in the forecourt and the outbuildings.*

## POTTERY

France's association with the manufacture of decorative pottery dates back to the 16th century, when the industry was greatly encouraged by the spirit of the Renaissance. In many parts of France where suitable materials could be found pottery making became a major activity. The most common form was faïence, an earthenware covered with a white tin glaze and then painted freehand with a wide range of designs based on oriental styles, Renaissance arabesques or natural forms. Production of faïence continued well into the 19th century.

Also popular was creamware, based on English models, and factories to produce this were established in Orléans in the late 18th century. However, the Loire was never a major pottery-producing region and until the 19th century the emphasis was on domestic wares and on bricks and tiles, particularly in the Sologne, where traditional factories still make a wide range of floor and roof tiling.

In the 1820s faïence and earthenware factories were established in Gien, and pottery making has remained the town's major industry and a tourist attraction.

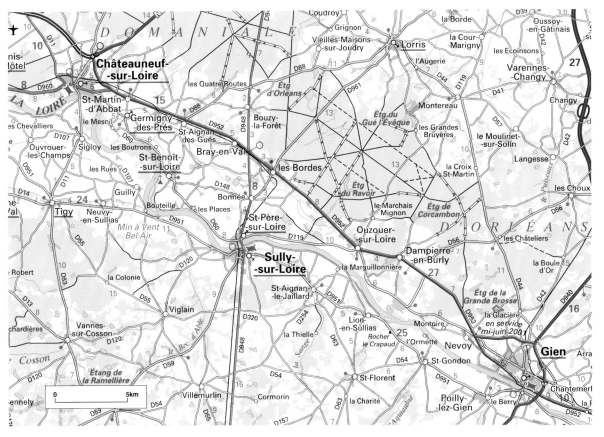

## Gien

Seen from the south bank of the Loire, Gien is a fine sight. The town's church and château stand together on a hill, high above the clustered riverside houses and the multi-arched bridge. The château, all in diaper-patterned brickwork and dating from the 14th century, is the key to the town's development, and is additionally important in that it is geographically the last, or the first, of the châteaux of the Loire. It played its part in the dramatic career of Joan of Arc, for it was here that she first reached the Loire, on 1 March 1429, on her way to see the Dauphin. She was to stay here again four months later with the Dauphin on the way to his coronation at Reims.

Today the château houses a museum devoted to hunting, telling the history of a sport so significant in the Loire region. Much of the church is modern, for the building that Joan of Arc knew was largely destroyed by bombing in June 1940 – raids that also flattened Gien's river front. Much of the heart of the town has been carefully rebuilt in a sensitive manner.

## St Benoît-sur-Loire

In this little village is the abbey of Fleury, built between the 9th and the 11th centuries. This is one of the foremost Romanesque buildings in France, notable for its early transept, choir and crypt and its multi-pillared porch.

A small road leads down to the old quays and cottages of St Benoît's long-disused port, which was a busy place in the 17th and 18th centuries, when Loire navigation was at its height.

*Gien's heart, including the church and the area by the river, was badly damaged by bombs in World War II. However, much of the town's character has been regained through careful rebuilding with local materials.*

# PARIS AND THE ILE DE FRANCE

The Ile de France, with Paris at its hub, remains the political, economic, artistic, cultural and tourist centre of France. First inhabited more than 5,000 years ago by Bronze Age tribes who established a settlement on the banks of the Seine, the region has played a vital role in the country's development throughout the centuries. It was the ancient heartland from which the French kings gradually extended their control.

Today the capital city stretches across some 100 square kilometres of the Paris Basin, and has more than two million inhabitants, with another seven million spread throughout the surrounding metropolitan area. Despite the fact that it is among the world's most densely populated cities, it retains a balance between spaciousness and human scale. The last decade has witnessed many remarkable changes and alterations to the city's glorious and historic architectural treasures, and in that period these have been joined by some equally striking modern buildings.

Inevitably the demands of modern society and in particular those of motor transport have wrought many changes. Every day three million cars enter Paris via the Périphérique and its associated motorways, producing severe air pollution and causing massive congestion and parking problems. Although there is an excellent subsidised public transport system, many of these vehicles continue to come from the surrounding commuter towns and villages.

Despite its remarkable population growth, the Ile de France has retained much of its original ancient forests, including those around Versailles and Fontainebleau, as well as the great royal palaces and châteaux of the 16th and 17th centuries. All of these lie within a few hours' drive of the centre of Paris, offering visitors an opportunity to view examples of a great variety of architectural styles. Development of the region continues, with the Ile de France providing the setting for the vast Euro Disney complex at Marne-la-Vallée, as well as a string of new towns spread around the capital.

*Pavement cafés are an essential part of daily life in this vibrant capital.*

*The arcades of the Place des Vosges (below) provide a shady spot for a break.*

*The Sun King's palace of Versailles (below, centre) beggared the treasury.*

*Gustav Eiffel's enduring icon (top) was not built to last. The dome of Les Invalides (above, centre) The steps of Sacré Coeur provide one of the best views over the city (above). Ancient and modern meet at the Louvre museum (left).*

# ESSENTIAL SIGHTS OF PARIS

The city of Paris, with a population of nearly 2.2 million, and the eight départements of the surrounding Ile de France, with over 10 million people, together provide France with a powerful engine – economic, political, administrative and cultural.

*Napoleon's triumphal arch is a major landmark on the busy Champs Elysées.*

*The distinctive white stone of Sacre Coeur was brought from Château Landon, which lies to the south of Paris.*

## Arc de Triomphe

This, the world's largest triumphal arch, 50m high and 45m wide, was commissioned by Napoleon in 1806 to celebrate his military victories.

The arch was designed by Chalgrin, and completed in 1836. Four years later Napoleon's body would be returned to Paris from St Helena to be transported on a chariot under the arch on its way to the Invalides. The main façades are adorned with colossal reliefs, of which the finest is *The Departure of the Volunteers*, which is better known as *The Marseillaise*, by Rude.

In 1854 Haussmann redesigned the square surrounding the Arc, now Place Charles de Gaulle, adding a further seven avenues to the existing five.

On Armistice Day 1920, the body of the Unknown Soldier was laid in state beneath the arch to symbolise the dead of World War I, and the Eternal Flame, rekindled in a brief ceremony each evening, has burned there continuously since 1923.

## Basilique du Sacré Coeur

The white domes of the Sacré Coeur and its 80m campanile rising from the peak of Montmartre are a familiar sight on the Parisian skyline. Initiated by the French government in 1873 as a reaction to the country's defeat in the Franco-Prussian War two years earlier, the basilica was built

as a symbol of contrition and atonement for the 58,000 who lost their lives in the struggle.

Although the Sacré Coeur was not consecrated until 1919, worshippers have maintained a constant day and night vigil of contrition before the altar since 1885, continuing even throughout the German occupation of the city. The more secular visit for the panoramic views from the steps and the dome.

## Centre Pompidou

Inaugurated in 1977, Richard Rogers' and Renzo Piano's controversial five-storey jumble of high-tech plumbing and glass still attracts six million visitors a year.

The revolutionary structure houses the Musée National d'Art Moderne, which is situated on the fourth floor. This is the largest art gallery of its kind in the world and features works by 20th-century artists as diverse as Picasso, Dali, Braque, Miró, Kandinsky, Matisse, Léger and Warhol in a comprehensive collection stretching from the Fauves up to the present day.

## Eiffel Tower

This 300-m tower was built in two years from 7000 tons of pig-iron and linked together by two and a half million rivets. Each of its 15,000 components is replaceable. But in spite of its overall size and weight, each of the four base pillars exerts a ground pressure no greater than that of a person sitting on a chair.

Originally intended to be a temporary structure and to be pulled down after 20 years, the tower was saved from demolition by the invention of wireless telegraphy, for which purpose it was used during World War I. It was declared a national monument in 1964, and is still one of the tallest man-made structures in the world. The two lower stages accommodate restaurants and souvenir shops, while the platform on the third, on a clear day, offers panoramic views of the city and surrounding countryside as far away as Chartres, 72km distant.

*The Centre Pompidou appears inside-out, with heating ducts, water pipes, electrical cables and air conditioning ducts proudly displayed on the exterior.*

*The Eiffel Tower was completed in time for the Paris Exposition of 1889.*

*The Église du Dôme was added to the Invalides comples in 1705.*

The top of the tower is now crowned with TV antennae, which add a further 20m to its height. On a hot day the metal structure grows by another 15cm. At night a new lighting system illuminates the entire tower from within to create a dramatic golden tracery against the sky, underlining the fact that the original objections to Eiffel's creation have faded with the years, and that it has come to be the best known and best loved landmark in Paris.

## Invalides

This monumental group of buildings was commissioned in 1674 by Louis XIV to provide a home for wounded veterans. Few soldiers now live here, but the military connection is retained in the form of the Musée de l'Armée, a magnificent collection of arms, armour, uniforms and banners from throughout the ages.

The impressive Église du Dôme is one of two adjoining churches in the complex. Its baroque interior houses the tomb of Napoleon Bonaparte. The Emperor's remains are contained in no fewer than six coffins, one inside the other.

## Louvre

This is Europe's largest royal palace, covering 18 hectares, the biggest single building in Paris and the largest museum in the Western world.

Begun by François I, with 12 paintings looted from Italy, and added to by succeeding monarchs and by Napoleon, the museum's greatest pride lies in its art collection. Leonardo da Vinci's *Mona Lisa* is a major attraction, and the collection includes works by pre-eminent artists of the Italian, Spanish, French, Flemish, Dutch, German and English schools. Famous sculptures on display include the *Venus de Milo* and the *Winged Victory of Samothrace*.

The Louvre's enormous wealth of material – more than 400,000 works of art – has meant that until recently only a small part could be exhibited at one time. However, a massive programme of building and redevelopment to mark the bicentenary of the museum in 1993 has added to the museum's facilities. The main courtyard is now graced by a 21.5m glass-walled pyramid, designed by architect I. M. Pei, which serves as the central entrance to the museum and leads to new galleries.

*Inside the Louvre, one of the biggest museums in the world*

*Garnier designed his Opéra as a 'monument to art, to luxury, to pleasure'.*

## Opéra

Designed by Charles Garnier, on completion in 1875 the Opéra was the world's largest theatre. The façade is ornately decorated with columns, friezes and busts of famous composers, while inside, gold caryatids clasp elaborate candelabra. Although the whole building covers more than a hectare, the auditorium, resplendent in red plush and gilt, is surprisingly small, seating only 2,158 people. The interior of the central dome was redecorated in 1964 by the Russian artist Chagall, producing an effect that many find inappropriate.

## Madeleine

*Corinthian columns mark out the façade of the Église de la Madaleine*

The foundation stone of this austere edifice, now dedicated to St Mary Magdalene (Marie Madeleine), was laid in 1764, but during the following 80 years the building was considered for use as a bank, banqueting hall, theatre, railway station and a temple to Napoleon's army, before finally being consecrated as a church. The façade of 52 soaring Corinthian columns is surmounted by Lemaire's relief of the Last Judgement, while the bronze doors carry bas-reliefs of the Ten Commandments by Triquetti.

## Montmartre

Until the middle of the last century Montmartre was still a country village, rising 100m above the city, bristling with windmills on the surface and undercut by gypsum mines. The district's picturesque charm and atmosphere, along with low rents, enticed artists, sculptors, writers and musicians to live and work here, and the heyday of bohemian Montmartre lasted until World War I.

Today the winding streets and peaceful, tree-lined squares retain much of their charm, but Place du Tertre, which is the hub of Montmartre, is now the preserve of tawdry souvenirs and street artists, and sadly Place Pigalle has descended from a racy vitality into outright sleaziness.

## Musée Marmottan

This is a specially created basement gallery containing a marvellous collection of Impressionist paintings, pastels and drawings by Claude Monet, as well as works by Sisley, Renoir, Gauguin and Pissarro. Originally the collection of the 19th-century industrialist Jules Marmottan, and enlarged by his son Paul, it was bequeathed to the Institut de France in 1971.

## Musée Rodin

Auguste Rodin lived and worked in a ground-floor studio of this elegant Regency mansion during the last nine years of his life. It now houses a superb collection of his work and plaster casts arranged in chronological order, as well as some of his personal art collection.

## Musée d'Orsay

This museum provides a chronological link between the Louvre collections and those at the Centre Pompidou.

More than 2,000 paintings, 1,500 sculptures, 13,000 photographs and other *objets d'art* span the years 1848 to 1914. Among these works is a remarkable collection of Impressionist masterpieces,

*Interior of the Musée Marmottan (above)*

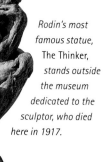

*Rodin's most famous statue, The Thinker, stands outside the museum dedicated to the sculptor, who died here in 1917.*

*The Musée d'Orsay makes full use of the lofty space of the former railway station.*

*The Musée Picasso lies behind the graceful façade of the 17th-century Hotel Sale.*

paintings by Romantic artists such as Ingres and Delacroix, and by Degas, and examples of Realism. The subsequent period is represented by outstanding works of Manet, Monet, Renoir, Sisley, Cézanne and Van Gogh. Also on display are paintings by post-Impressionists such as Seurat, Gauguin, Signac, and the Nabis.

## Musée Picasso

The 17th-century Hôtel Salé now provides a home for the world's largest collection of Picasso's work. Although few of his masterpieces are here, the 203 paintings, 158 sculptures and more than 1,500 drawings, along with his 30 sketchbooks, were acquired by the French government in lieu of inheritance taxes after Picasso's death in 1973.

The collection is exhibited in chronological order, with Picasso's early and late periods particularly well represented. Exhibits also include his personal art collection, with works by Matisse, Braque, Cézanne, Renoir and Rousseau.

## Notre Dame

One of the great masterpieces of Gothic architecture, the cathedral of Notre Dame stands on the site of an earlier Gallo-Roman temple, dominating the skyline of central Paris with its beautiful, richly decorated façade and twin 69m towers. Pope Alexander III laid the cathedral's foundation stone in 1163, but the building was not completed until 1330.

During the Revolution the statues around the portals were decapitated, orgies staged and the cathedral turned into a 'Temple of Reason'. By 1804, when Pope Pius VII was summoned from Rome to officiate at Napoleon's coronation, Notre Dame was a shambles but later in the century Viollet-le-Duc undertook its restoration. He replicated the carvings on the façade, as well as adding the bestiary of gargoyles and demons that adorn the flying buttresses.

Inside the echoing building, capable of holding nearly 10,000 worshippers, the majestic walls rise in three tiers to a ribbed, vaulted ceiling 35m high. Illumination is provided by the three stained-glass rose windows, of which only the northern window retains the original 13th-century glass. The massive organ, with more than 7000 pipes, is France's largest, and is used for regular Sunday afternoon recitals.

*The classic view of Notre Dame Cathedral is across the River Seine, near the Pont Tournelle.*

# OUTDOOR PARIS

Paris is a city in which you can enjoy open-air pleasures for much of the year, and is best explored on foot. You can stroll the wide, tree-lined boulevards, savouring the atmosphere of the city, perhaps pausing to study some otherwise unnoticed detail on a building's façade. Or you may prefer to sit with a coffee at a pavement café and just watch the world pass by.

*Walking the dog is a pleasure in the open woodland of the Bois de Boulogne.*

*The famous cemetery is laid out on a hillside in Menilmontant.*

## Bois de Boulogne

The 900 hectares of woodland and open space of the Bois also encompass the 18th-century white villa and English-style garden of the Bagatelle, the Pré Catelan and its magnificent copper beech, the Shakespeare Garden with plants mentioned in the plays and the amusement park and zoo of the Jardin d'Acclimatation. The Bois also has two racecourses: Longchamp for flat-racing and Auteuil for steeplechasing.

## Cimitière du Père Lachaise

Named after the Jesuit confessor of Louis XIV, whose house stood here, this is the largest and most select cemetery in Paris. The 47-hectare site was bought by the city in 1804 and the first interments were those of Molière and La Fontaine. The tomb of the country's most famous lovers, Abélard and Héloïse, was transferred here a few years later.

A detailed map showing the most famous graves is available from the custodian at the entrance. Among them are those of the writers Victor Hugo and Oscar Wilde, musicians Chopin and Bizet, singers Maria Callas and Edith Piaf, and American rock star Jim Morrison.

## Jardin des Plantes

Louis XIII initiated a medicinal herb plot here in 1626, but it now encompasses within its 28 hectares not only the botanical garden but also a zoo, a maze and the Muséum National d'Histoire Naturelle. The collections of wild and herbaceous plants are excellent, and in early summer the gardens make a magnificent display of colour. The zoo now contains large reptiles, birds and wild animals.

## Jardin des Tuileries

These 24 hectares of formal gardens, laid out by Louis XIV's gardener, Le Nôtre, are an oasis of calm, despite the nearby traffic. On raised terraces at the western end stand the museum buildings of the Jeu de Paume and the Orangerie. At the opposite end of the gardens, in the Pavillon de Marsan, are museums devoted to the decorative arts, fashion and advertising.

*Enjoying the boating lake in the Tuileries park*

## Jardin du Luxembourg

Situated in the heart of the Left Bank, these gardens were formally laid out in the Renaissance French style in 1612, but with Italian touches to please the owner of the adjoining palace, Marie de Médicis.

The Luxembourg is now one of the most popular open spaces in the city, a magnet for students from the nearby Sorbonne and for children, who sail their boats in the octagonal pond by the romantic Fontaine de Médicis. Tennis, *pétanque* and chess players have their own corners.

*An obelisk and fountains stand at the centre of the vast Place de la Concorde.*

## Place de la Concorde

In spite of the crush of traffic, this is one of the world's most impressive squares, spanning 8.5 hectares. It was originally designed to provide the setting for an equestrian statue of Louis XV, unveiled in 1763. A guillotine was set up here in 1793, close to the spot where Cortot's statue of Brest now stands, and more than 1,100 people were executed in the renamed Place de la Révolution over the next two years, including Louis XVI and Marie-Antoinette. Place de la Concorde was given its present name at the end of the Reign of Terror, and the 23-m high Obelisk of Luxor, a gift from the Viceroy of Egypt to Charles X, was erected at its centre in 1836.

## Place des Vosges

The oldest and possibly the most beautiful square in Paris was commissioned by Henri IV, and designed by Metezeau. On the square's completion in 1612 all the buildings were quickly acquired by leading courtiers and senior ministers, including Cardinal Richelieu and the dramatists Molière and Corneille, and it became the capital's most fashionable address.

The central garden was originally a gravelled area used for games and spectacles, which

the residents viewed from their balconies, but also for duels in which many aristocrats died.

## Place Vendôme

Conceived by Louis XIV and designed by Hardouin-Mansart, this opulent square, with its graceful two-storey buildings, and their Corinthian pilasters and sculpted Bacchanalian masks, originally provided the backdrop for an equestrian statue of the Sun King.

The gilt statue was destroyed during the Revolution, and the heads of victims of the guillotine mounted on spikes briefly took its place. The central column commemorates Napoleon's victories in Germany and is faced by 378 spiralling sheets of bronze made from cannons captured at the Battle of Austerlitz, Napoleon's greatest victory.

## Seine

The 11km stretch of the River Seine that passes through Paris is arguably the most beautiful length of urban waterfront in the world. The glass-topped *bateaux-mouches* that ply up and down the river are an ideal way to get a relaxed view of the city and its 33 graceful bridges. The Eiffel Tower, Louvre, Quai d'Orsay, Grand Palais, Institut de France, Conciergerie, and Notre Dame are among the many monuments given a fresh perspective from a waterborne viewpoint.

*Jousting once took place in the attractive Place des Vosges.*

*Trees line the leafy walkway beside the Seine.*

# AROUND PARIS

*A simple headstone marks the grave in Auvers-sur-Oise of one of the 20th century's greatest painters.*

### Auvers-sur-Oise

Dr Paul Gachet, an enthusiastic amateur painter, moved to this small village in 1872 and subsequently shared his house and studio with Paul Cézanne, who painted more than 100 works while staying here. In 1890 Vincent Van Gogh came to Auvers to place himself in Dr Gachet's care. He painted portraits of the doctor and the landlady of the Ravoux café, where he lodged, as well as local scenes of the church, town hall and a field with crows. In July that year, overwhelmed by his mental disorder, he committed suicide. His body lies in a simple grave in the local cemetery.

### Basilique St-Denis

This imposing Gothic cathedral dating from the 12th century houses the shrine of St Denis, the Apostle of France, as well as the tombs of royalty. According to legend, the saint was executed by the Romans around AD 250 on the slopes of Montmartre but, having picked up his severed head and washed it in a nearby fountain, he walked for several kilometres to this spot, where he finally died.

### Le Bourget

The Musée de l'Air et de l'Espace is installed in the former terminal building of this airport north-east of Paris, where Charles Lindburgh landed after the first successful transatlantic flight in 1927. The exhibits cover the history of manned flight from balloons and gliders to space capsules.

*The elegant horseshoe staircase was added to the palace at Fontainebleau in 1643.*

### Chartres

This masterpiece of medieval cathedral architecture dominates the surrounding plain of Beauce, and its non-matching spires can be seen from 20km away. The sixth church to stand on the site, it was built over 25 years from 1194, and the speed of its construction accounts for the harmonious composition of the whole structure.

The 12th- and 13th-century stained-glass windows are the outstanding glories of the cathedral, with a galaxy of more than 2,500 square metres of glass illuminating the interior of the building with its opalescent colours. The oldest example is *Notre Dame de la Belle Verrière* above the south choir. In a magnificent old tithe barn next to the cathedral is the International Stained Glass Centre.

### Fontainebleau

This beautiful Renaissance palace is largely the creation of François I. Inspired by the architecture he had seen during his Italian campaigns, in 1528 François replaced the medieval building with two main structures, decorated by pupils of Michelangelo and

*Chartres Cathedral is striking from the outside, but it is the glowing colours of the medieval stained glass which are its chief glory.*

Guilio Romano. The elegant frontage, with its sweeping horseshoe staircase, was the scene of Napoleon's emotional farewell to the members of his Imperial Guard after his abdication in 1814. The palace, surrounded by formal gardens laid out by Le Nôtre and a thickly wooded park, is set in the heart of the Forêt de Fontainebleau.

## Senlis

The whole of this ancient town, 45km north of Paris, is classified as an historic monument. Circled by the remains of Roman walls 8m high and 4m thick, it has preserved its character of an old cathedral city with cobbled streets that oblige the visitor to proceed on foot. The 12th-century Cathédrale Notre-Dame is contemporaneous with the Basilique St-Denis and was crowned in the mid-13th century with a slender 78-m spire.

## Vaux-le-Vicomte

This superb 17th-century château was created by the architect Le Vau for Louis XIV's finance minister, Nicolas Fouquet. Its construction entailed the razing of three villages and the employment of 18,000 workmen for five years. Standing on a raised terrace, and surrounded by a moat amid gardens landscaped by Le Nôtre, and with lavish interior decoration by Charles Le Brun, the imposing building makes an immediate and dramatic impact.

## Versailles

Originally the site of a hunting lodge, this grandiose structure, with its extensive park and adjoining town, stands as a permanent testament to Louis VIV's belief in the principles of absolute monarchy. The Sun King's monumental undertaking cost the treasury 60 million *livres* and impoverished the nation.

The building was begun in 1661, under architect Louis Le Vau. The ornately decorated interior was largely the work of Charles Le Brun. The landscaping of the spacious gardens and park, which still cover 800 hectares, was entrusted to André Le Nôtre. Work on the palace and its surroundings continued for 50 years, with 36,000 men and 6,000 horses still labouring hard when Louis XIV moved his court and the seat of government here in 1682. His successor, Louis XV added further embellishments in the form of the rococo private royal apartments, opera house and a country retreat, the Petit Trianon. Louis XVI and Marie-Antoinette later took refuge from court formalities and routine in this rural mansion.

Following the Revolution, most of the furnishings and contents of the palace complex were removed, and parts of the buildings and grounds were allowed to deteriorate. However, restoration during the 20th century has given back to Versailles much of its former glory.

*Finance minister Nicolas Fouquet died in prison after embezzling money to fund his grand designs for Vaux-le-Vicomte.*

*Versailles excels in splendour, from the Bassin d'Apollon fountain (left) to the glittering Galerie des Glaces (above).*

# BURGUNDY

Burgundy is one of the most underrated areas in France; thousands of travellers pass through but few take the trouble to explore it. This is a pity, for the region has much to offer. Not for nothing is it called the land of great art and good living. It offers varied scenery, picturesque towns and villages and a history as rich as that of any region in France.

It is also the home of some of the finest food and wines in the country. For those who choose to leave the A6, Burgundy becomes a land of discovery, recalling an earlier age, as if the rush of the 21st century did not exist. Life seems to be lived at the pace of the snails that play such a part in Burgundian cuisine. The passing landscapes take a shape and form: the green becomes a range of high, tree-clad hills, an expanse of vineyards, a thick forest or meadows where white Charollais cattle graze peacefully.

What soon strikes the visitor to Burgundy is its size. It consists of Yonne, Côte-d'Or, Nièvre, and Saône-et-Loire, four *départements* that meet at Burgundy's heart, the Morvan. There is so much to see that here we can only pick out a few jewels from its many treasures and leave you to discover more. We do, however, uncover the character of the place, the mysterious mountains of the Morvan, the wine-producing slopes of the Côte-d'Or, gentle pastoral scenery and sparkling rivers and canals.

Sadly there is not space for places such as Mâcon, the lively wine town that was the birthplace of one of France's greatest writers, Alphonse de Lamartine; for Auxerre, capital of lower Burgundy and starting place of many boat trips along the canals, a town built in terraces on a hill overlooking the River Yonne; for ancient Autun with its numerous reminders of Roman occupation; or for Nevers, famous for its fine pottery, ducal palace and St Bernadette, who, like Sleeping Beauty, lies in a glass tomb at the Couvent St-Gildard.

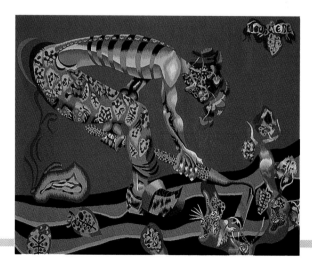

*Le Vigneron can be seen in Beaune's Musée du Vin*

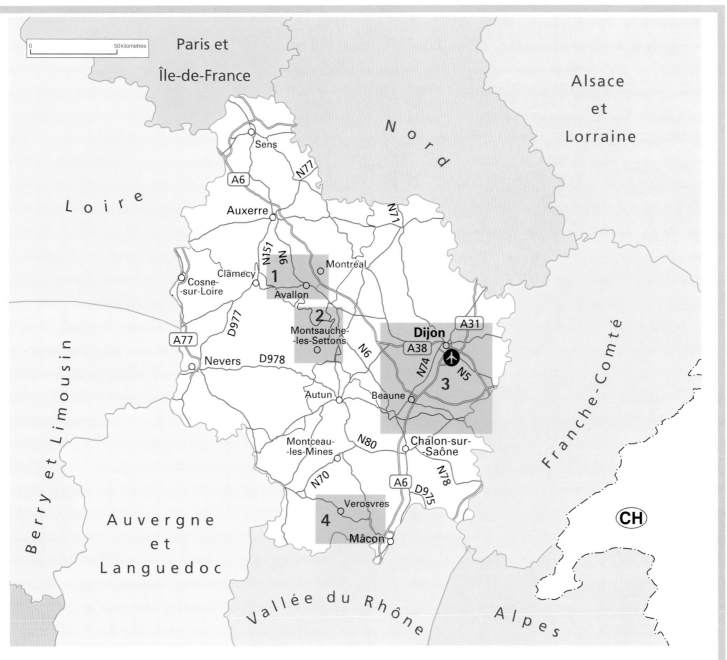

*A bookshop sign (right) adds charm to pretty Noyers*

*Sabot flowerpots (below) in St Amand-en-Puisaye, centre of the local pottery industry*

*A statue in Auxerre by François Brochet commemorates the poetess Marie Noël (1883-1967), who was born in the city.*

# PILGRIMAGE TO VÉZELAY

For more than 900 years pilgrims have flocked to the 'eternal hill' of Vézelay. They still come, but are now outnumbered by the tourists who want to see not just this remarkable sight but the surrounding landscape of rolling, wooded hills, fairy-tale valleys and delightful medieval towns.

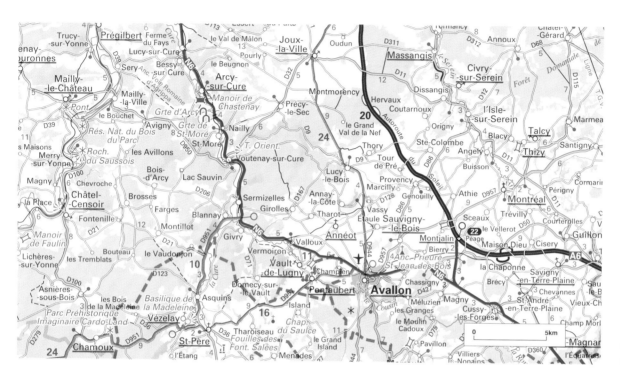

## CUISINE OF BURGUNDY

Burgundy has been described as a gastronomic paradise. Favourites such as *boeuf bourguignon*, a beef stew cooked in red wine, and *coq au vin*, chicken in red wine, are well known as main courses, but there are many other lesser known dishes that together make an attractive menu.

*Jambon persillé*, ham seasoned in parsley and a white-wine jelly, is a traditional starter, as are snails cooked in their shells. In winter, cabbage soup is a tasty warmer. Local cheeses are not well known outside Burgundy, but ones to look out for include Époisses, Cîteaux and St Florentin.

*The façade of St-Lazare in Avallon displays a wealth of carved detail.*

## Avallon

Occupying a picturesque position on a granite promontory overlooking the wooded Vallée du Cousin, Avallon is a charming town. The fact that the busy N6 passes through it is hardly noticed, for the town's main area of interest lies to the south of the road and is contained within the old fortifications, parts of which date back to the early 15th century.

The old town is divided into two by the main street, the Grande-Rue Aristide-Briand. This leads from the Place Vauban, with its statue of the famous local military engineer, the Marquis de Vauban, to the Promenade de la Petite Porte, a terrace of lime trees high above the Cousin, from where visitors can walk around the ramparts. The Grande-Rue, cobbled and lined by several 16th- and 17th-century mansions, some embellished with turrets, passes under the famous clock tower, a main feature of the town since 1456, and in front of the mainly 11th-century Église St-Lazare. Opposite the church is an interesting museum containing Gallo-Romano remains from archaeological sites in the area.

## Manoir du Chastenay

This manor house, dating from the mid-16th century, is almost hidden away in the pretty hamlet of Val-Sainte-Marie, just off the N6 in the Cure valley 3km north of St Moré. Behind high walls it displays a number of Renaissance features such as an hexagonal tower, mullioned windows, and a richly sculpted portal and dormers. Among the treasures inside is a 14th-century polyptych portraying the story of Joseph.

## Montréal

Like Avallon, Montréal shelters behind walls, perched on a hill. Narrow streets wind up from the lower gate and eventually pass through the upper gate, which also serves as a bell tower, to the 12th-century Église Notre-Dame.

Apart from the views from the terrace, the church is quite unremarkable from the outside, but it is well worth a look inside

**Comité Départemental du Tourisme de l'Yonne**
1/2, Quai de la Rèpublique
89000 Auxerre
Tel: 03 86 72 90 00
www.tourisme-yonne.com

**Touring:**
AA Road Map France series 13: Bourgogne Franche-Comté

*Vézelay is blessed with an attractive hillside setting overlooking vineyards.*

*The chief glory of Montréal's church is its 26 carved oak stalls*

for its oak stalls, elaborately carved in 1526 and depicting biblical scenes. The two brothers who carried out the work have also portrayed themselves enjoying some wine.

## St Père

Lying beneath the famous hill of Vézelay, the village of St Père has attractions of its own. Among them are the Église Notre-Dame with its graceful spire and delicately worked porch. Next to the church is the Musée Archéologique Régional, which includes exhibits unearthed at the excavations of the spring-fed Gallo-Romano baths at nearby Fontaines Salées.

## Vallée du Cousin

Skirting Avallon's rocky promontory on the south side the River Cousin has created a beautiful verdant valley between the villages of Méluzien and Pontaubert. The narrow D427 follows the river's winding course past a succession of pretty sights including several old water-mills, two of them now converted to comfortable hotels.

## Vézelay

A jewel of Burgundy, Vézelay sprawls up the side of a hill looking out over the hills and valleys of the Parc Naturel Régional du Morvan and surmounted by the Basilique Ste-Madeleine. One of the great pilgrimage churches of France and visible from some distance, Ste-Madeleine was one of the four departure points for the pilgrim trail to Santiago de Compostela in the Middle Ages and is still the scene of pilgrimage every 22 July. It is best to leave the car at the entrance to the village and then follow the route of the pilgrims on foot up the steep and winding Grande-Rue.

Built in the 12th century, the basilica fell into ruin after the Revolution of 1789, but was restored some 50 years later by the controversial architect Viollet-le-Duc. Unusual use has been made of alternative light and dark stones in the arches of the nave, and with its remarkable purity of line and lightness the basilica is a wonderful monument to Romanesque art.

### VIOLLET-LE-DUC

Eugène Viollet-le-Duc, the controversial 19th-century architect who carried out the restoration of the Basilique Ste-Madeleine in Vézelay, made quite a name for himself restoring medieval buildings. He worked on churches throughout Burgundy, notably at Auxerre, Beaune, Clamecy, Dijon, Semur-en-Auxois and St Père, as well as the Synodal Palace in Sens and the Gallo-Roman Porte St-André in Autun.

Vézelay was his greatest task, undertaken when he was less than 30 years old, but many people felt that his work there and elsewhere spoiled the original designs. Yet but for him, many of Burgundy's treasures would have fallen into ruin.

# THE MORVAN NATURE PARK

One of France's largest regional nature parks, the Morvan is a strange region of gentle wilderness, with lakes, hills and thick forests that conceal its scattered communities from the outside world. As such it served the local population well during the war and there are several reminders of the Resistance groups who operated here.

## Abbaye de la Pierre-qui-Vire

*The candid Latin inscription above the door of the Abbaye de la Pierre-qui-Vire reads, 'I am the entrance'.*

This abbey, hidden away among the woods and hills of the Morvan, was founded as recently as 1850 at the site of the Pierre-qui-Vire (Stone that Turns), a large granite dolmen that, according to legend, could be moved by one hand. The stone is still there in the woods, but is now surmounted by a statue of the Virgin.

In accordance with the strict Benedictine laws of the abbey, most of it is not open to the public, though its Gothic-style church, which has recently undergone renovation, is. An exhibition room gives the visitor an idea of how the monks live. There are pleasant walks through the woods around the abbey.

## Barrage Pannesière-Chaumard

This dam holds back the waters of the largest lake in the Morvan, the Lac de Pannesière, 7.5km long and 2.5km wide. Just below the dam a small hydroelectric power station operated by just two men produces 18 million kw per year. The lake, though less frequented than some of the other local waters, is in an attractive setting in wooded hills and is popular with anglers, especially fishing for pike and perch, and also lovers of sailing and canoeing. From the top of the dam there are fine views across the lake.

## Gouloux

This is a straggling village in an attractive area overlooking the valley formed by the Rivers Bridier, Caillot and Cure. A small family business makes clogs by hand from birch, beech or alder, for sale all over France, and a shop sells completed clogs to passers-by.

A short distance outside the village, close to where the D977 *bis* crosses the Cure, a footpath leads through woods to the Saut de Gouloux, a beautiful waterfall with a 10-m drop, seen at its best after rainfall. There are also the ruins of an old water-mill.

**Comité Départemental du Tourisme de la Nièvre**
3, Rue du Sort
58000 Nevers
Tel: 03 86 36 39 80
www.nievre58.com

**Touring:**
AA Road Map France series 13: Bourgogne Franche-Comté

*A secluded area in the heart of Burgundy, the Morvan is dotted with dairy farms set among dense, hilly woodland.*

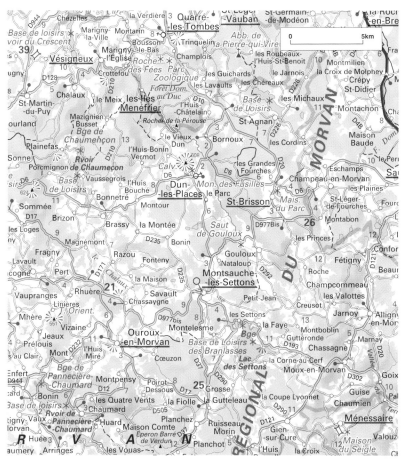

## Lac des Settons

Dating from 1861, this reservoir was originally built to improve logging operations on the River Cure and to keep the Cure and Yonne navigable in times of drought. It is now a popular beauty spot and holiday centre and several communities have sprung up around the wooded shores.

The biggest is Les Settons at the northern end, which consists mainly of hotels, restaurants, holiday homes and camp sites, but there are smaller centres at Les Branlasses and Chevigny. It is possible to drive right round the reservoir, and there are several waymarked footpaths through the pine woods. Fishing is a prime attraction and other water activities are well catered for too.

*The tranquillity of the Lac de Settons at sunset contrasts with the excitement generated by the regatta held here during summer.*

## Montsauche-les-Settons

Situated at an altitude of 650m, Montsauche is the highest village in the Morvan. During World War II its inhabitants provided aid and supplies for members of the Resistance living in the forest, until the Germans destroyed it in 1944. Rebuilt after the liberation, Montsauche is an ideal base for visiting the Morvan.

## Quarré-les-Tombes

There is an air of mystery about Quarré-les-Tombes. Named after the large number of stone sarcophagi in the area, the village is thought to have been involved in their construction in the late 7th to early 8th centuries. Another, less likely, theory is that the town was the site of an ancient necropolis. Only about 100 sarcophagi remain and these are laid out around the Église St-Georges, which looks across the village's vast square. At the far end of the square is a memorial to members of the Resistance.

## Roche de la Pérouse

Named after an 18th-century French explorer who, with his crew, was killed by Pacific islanders in 1788, this rocky promontory rises above the forest north of Dun-les-Places. It offers an extensive panorama south across the gorge of the River Cure.

## St Brisson

A small, quiet, grey village, St Brisson is better known as the home of the Maison du Parc, the visitor centre for the Parc Régional du Morvan. Located at the Château de St Brisson beside the Étang Toureau, a haven for wildfowl just outside the village, the centre offers, as well as details about the park, a herb garden, an arboretum, a deer park, and a picnic area.

This area was used by the Resistance in wartime, and the château is also home to the Musée de la Résistance en Morvan.

*Ancient sarcophagi are strewn around the church of St-Georges in Quarré-les-Tombes, their significance still not fully understood.*

**RESISTANCE GROUPS**

Because of its isolation and the difficult nature of the countryside, the Morvan became a stronghold of the Resistance during World War II. Between 1942 and 1944 some 15 groups operating from mountain refuges caused havoc among the occupying German forces, carrying out ambushes, capturing and destroying enemy equipment and aiding British agents parachuted in under cover of darkness.

The groups' success was such that towards the end of the war the increasingly frustrated Germans carried out reprisals in the region, including the destruction of villages. Numerous roadside memorials stand as witness to the high number of executions.

# ALONG THE CÔTE-D'OR

Extending along a ridge of hills from Dijon to Chagny, the Côte-d'Or is one of the most famous wine-producing areas in France. From the N74, sign after sign leads through seemingly never-ending vineyards to tiny villages with huge reputations for their wine. But along the way there are many other places to explore, as well as treasures from earlier times to discover.

*Winged angels guard the final resting place of Philip the Bold, Duke of Burgundy from 1364 to 1404, in Dijon's ducal palace.*

**Comité Départemental du Tourisme de la Côte-d'Or**
1, Rue de Soissons
21000 Dijon
Tel: 03 80 63 66 95
www.cotedor-tourisme.com

**Touring:**
AA Road Map France series 13: Bourgogne Franche-Comté

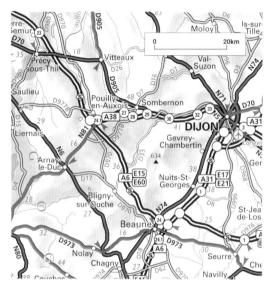

## Beaune

City of wine and tourism, Beaune is a must for any visitor to Burgundy. Still enclosed with medieval walls, it contains a wealth of treasures, the most outstanding of which is the Hôtel-Dieu.

Founded in 1443 by Nicolas Rolin, chancellor to the Duke of Burgundy, the Hôtel-Dieu was built as a hospital for the poor, a function it fulfilled for more than 500 years. Visitors can see the paupers' ward, the chapel, the dispensary and the museum where a 15th-century masterpiece is exhibited, a triptych by Roger van der Weyden depicting the Last Judgement. But best of all, and symbolising Burgundy for many, is the Cour d'Honneur, the cobbled inner courtyard overlooked by a timber gallery and roofs of colourful varnished tiles.

Beaune, whose connections with wine go back 2,000 years, is famous for its prestigious wine auctions held in November. Worth a visit is the Musée du Vin de Bourgogne in the former palace of the dukes of Burgundy, for it gives an insight into the history of wine production along the Côte-d'Or.

*Wine pitcher on show in Beaune's fascinating Musée du Vin de Bourgogne*

## Clos de Vougeot

The enclosed vineyard of Clos de Vougeot, 5km north of Nuits-St-Georges, has a history going back to the 12th century, when it was founded by monks from the abbey of Cîteaux. More recent is the picturesque château, which dates from the Renaissance and appears to float like a great ship on a sea of vines. The château is now owned by the Confrérie des Chevaliers du Tastevin, a society pledged to uphold the quality of Burgundian wine. There are regular guided tours of the splendid cellars and chambers, and among the sights are four huge medieval wine presses made of oak. The vineyard itself, which each year produces around 200,000 bottles of one of the finest red wines in the world, is divided among about 80 owners.

## Dijon

Burgundy's capital old and new, Dijon grew in importance once chosen by the early dukes as their seat. Today's lively city, famed for its gastronomy, centres on the former ducal palace, the Palais des Ducs et des États de Bourgogne, most of which was rebuilt in the 18th century and now houses the town hall and Musée des Beaux-Arts, one of the finest museums in France. It

### DUKES OF BURGUNDY

Created a duchy in the Middle Ages, Burgundy acquired great wealth and possessions during the reign of the Valois dukes between 1363 and 1477.

When Philip the Bold became the first Valois duke, the duchy was smaller than today's province, but by marrying Margaret of Flanders he took over large tracts of land, including Flanders and Artois. He also made use of his access to Flemish painters, and Dijon, the dukes' capital, became a magnificent city of art.

Philip's son John the Fearless was not so successful. He often quarrelled with the king and was murdered in 1419 by supporters of the Crown. The Hundred Years War was raging at the time, and John's death led his successor Philip the Good to side with the English. It was he who sold the captured Joan of Arc to them.

With the Treaty of Arras in 1435, Philip made his peace

*After five and a half centuries the Hôtel-Dieu in Beaune remains in excellent condition, a gem of Burgundian-Flemish architecture.*

with the king, as a result acquiring even more land. Burgundy now included much of Holland, Belgium, Luxembourg and northern France, and Philip lived like a king.

In 1467 this massive inheritance fell to Charles the Bold, who immediately set out to achieve even more. Successful at first, he later suffered a string of defeats in battle and was killed at Nancy in 1477. With his death the Valois dynasty ended and Burgundy returned to the Crown.

contains a wealth of paintings and sculptures and two dazzling tombs. The Musée Magnin specialises in lesser-known 16th–19th-century French artists.

In the pedestrian streets around the palace, notably the Rue des Forges, the Rue de la Chouette and the Place François Rude, are several fine medieval and Renaissance houses, while in the Place de la Libération is a crescent of elegant arcaded 17th-century houses. Among the churches worth seeing is Notre-Dame with its incredible rows of gargoyles and Jacquemart clock tower, St-Michel, a mixture of Gothic and Renaissance styles, and the cathedral, St-Bénigne, which was built in the Gothic style on the site of a Romanesque church. The crypt of the original church survives, full of pillars and superb sculptured capitals.

## Nolay

Situated at the southern end of the Côte-d'Or, Nolay is a charming little town of narrow streets and half-timbered houses radiating from an attractive central ensemble around the Place Monge. This comprises the much rebuilt Église St-Martin with its attractive bell tower, the half-timbered Auberge du Centre and the 14th-century chestnut-framed market hall.

## Nuits-St-Georges

The reputation of the wine of Nuits-St-Georges has been made over the last 1,000 years and was given special impetus in 1680 when Louis XIV's doctor advised the king to drink only Nuits-St-Georges to cure an ailment. As a result the whole court wanted to drink it.

The town itself, on the busy N74, is attractive, with its pedestrianised main street, ivy-covered bell tower and St-Symphorien, one of the Côte-d'Or's most beautiful churches. Although it was built towards the end of the 13th century, this church is nevertheless a perfect example of the Romanesque style. The museum contains finds from the Gallo-Romano site of Les Bolards, which lies to the south-east of the town.

## La Rochepot

A small village not far from Nolay, La Rochepot is best known for its château, whose pepper-pot towers and glistening Burgundian tiled roof rise from a wooded hill on a rocky promontory above the village. In a state of ruin after the Revolution, the château was restored in the early 20th century by Sadi Carnot, son of a former President of France. Tours of the interior take visitors to the dining room, guard-room, Captain's room, kitchen and chapel.

### DIJON MUSTARD

Dijon mustard goes back, like so much of Burgundy's history, to the 14th century, when Philip the Bold was given some by his wife Margaret as a gift from Flanders. Henceforth it became very fashionable and many tried their hand at making it.

However, the mustard's quality varied and in the 19th century the Dijon Academy laid down a standard. Even today the name Moutarde de Dijon is not protected by patent and producers in other parts of the world use it. The mustard's strong, spicy flavour comes from crushing the seed of black or brown mustard and emulsifying them in verjuice, an immature wine obtained from unripe grapes.

*The castle at La Rochepot was extensively restored in the last century*

# BETWEEN CHAROLLES AND MÂCON

This is an area of gentle and attractive scenery, with here and there a high point offering a panoramic view. Wine plays a significant role in the east, around the Mâconnais, although some outstanding natural features lend drama to the tranquil scene. But without a doubt it is the ancient religious centre of Cluny that takes centre stage.

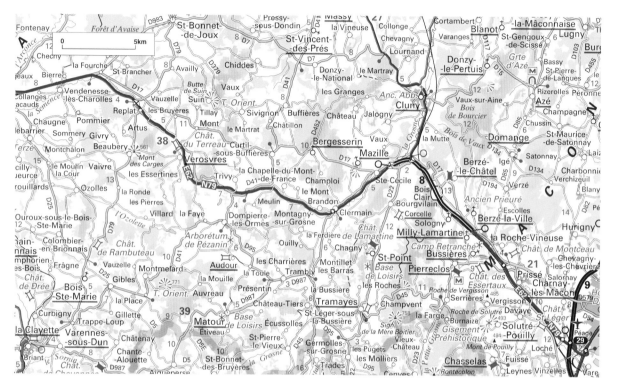

## CHAROLLAIS CATTLE

Very much a part of the Burgundy countryside are the distinctive white or cream Charollais cattle, first bred at the Château de Chaumont south of Oyé in the mid-18th century.

Several other distinctive features, including a wide muzzle, short neck and great strength, mark the Charollais, but it is best known for the quality and tenderness of its exceptionally lean meat. The top breed in France for beef production, the Charollais numbers over three million head. They are exported to 68 countries worldwide, including well-known beef-rearing areas in South America and the USA.

---

**Comité Départementale de Tourisme de la Saône-et-Loire**
389, Avenue de Lattre-de-Tassigny
71000 Mâcon
Tel: 03 85 21 02 20
www.bourgogne-tourisme.com

**Touring:**
AA Road Map France series 13: Bourgogne Franche-Comté

## Arborétum de Pezanin

Created in 1903 just outside the village of Dompierre-les-Ormes, this is one of the oldest arboretums in France. It suffered a severe set-back in 1982, and again in 1999, when bad storms caused extensive damage, but the efforts of the Office National des Forêts, which owns it, have ensured a swift recovery. More than 400 species of trees and shrubs from all over the world, including some exotic varieties rarely seen in Europe, have been planted in a peaceful setting around a small lake. A short forest drive winds through the arboretum, but there are also waymarked footpaths allowing more leisurely strolls of up to an hour and a half.

## Berzé-la-Ville

Once the site of a priory used as a country retreat by the monks of Cluny, Berzé-la-Ville is best known for its Romanesque Chapelle des Moines, which occupies a rocky spur above the village. Inside, its

walls are covered with remarkably well preserved and colourful 12th-century frescos, including a Christ in Majesty and some favourite saints of Cluny. Nearby Berzé-le-Châtel, an imposing feudal castle on vine-covered slopes, formerly played a major role in the history of Cluny, guarding the abbey's southern approaches.

*The mural paintings in the Chapelle des Moines at Berzé-la-Ville are a fine example of the art of the monks of Cluny.*

*A climb to the top of the Tour des Fromages at Cluny is recommended, from where there is a good view of the other parts of the abbey and of the town*

## Butte de Suin

Midway between Cluny and Charolles and reaching a height of 593m, this is one of several rocky hills in the area. Surmounted by a statue of the Virgin and an orientation table, the hill, once the site of an impregnable fortress, offers panoramic views to other local high points. On a clear day it is possible to pick out the steeples of over 50 churches. The hill is now a popular launching-point for hang-gliders.

## Cluny

Despite the ravages of the Wars of Religion (1562-98) and the Revolution of 1789, modest Cluny, once the greatest religious centre in Christendom, continues to attract large numbers of visitors. Of the abbey buildings that still stand, the finest is the Clocher de l'Eau Bénite, but five of the original 15 guard towers also remain. Tour des Fromages, once used to store cheese, houses the tourist office and from the top provides panoramic views of the town and the abbey's surviving buildings. A model of the abbey and details of its history can be seen at the art and archaeology museum in the town.

## Montagne de St Cyr

This mountain, about 6km north-west of Matour along the D211 is, at 792m, the highest in the area. Signs lead by way of a wooded road to a picnic area from where a track leads to the top. There are two viewing areas to choose from: the orientation table and a large crucifix mounted on rocks.

## Pouilly-Fuissé

Surrounded by gentle, vine-covered hills at the heart of the Mâconnais wine-producing area, Pouilly-Fuissé is in fact two villages that give their names to one of the best white wines in the world. A local saying goes, 'White is white, Pouilly-Fuissé is something else'. There are several *caves*, including the famous Château Fuissé, where tasting is possible.

## Solutré

Another village known for its Pouilly-Fuissé vineyards, Solutré has more to it than wine, for its name has been given to the Solutrian Era, a period of the Stone Age around 18,000 BC. This link with prehistory is connected with the spectacular Roche de Solutré, an enormous limestone outcrop just outside the village.

At the rock's foot the dramatic discovery was made in 1866 of the fossilised remains of some 100,000 horses, which are thought to have been led to their deaths by early man.

## Vergisson

Like Solutré, Vergisson occupies an attractive position beneath huge, golden cliffs, a fine limestone escarpment that is part of the same formation as its neighbour's famous rock. Surrounded by vineyards stretching up to the foot of the cliffs, Vergisson too produces Pouilly-Fuissé wine. This no doubt gives strength and courage to hunters of the fearsome P'teu de Vergisson, a mythical winged monster said to carry off farm animals in the area.

*At the foot of the Roche de Solutré there is a museum of prehistory that gives a fascinating insight into how early man lived in this area.*

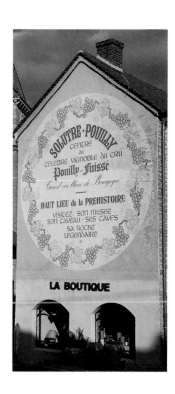

*For many visitors to Solutré the local wine is the main attraction, for this is Pouilly-Fuissé country.*

# FRANCHE-COMTÉ

To the south of Alsace the hills of the Sundgau lead into Franche-Comté and the Jura Mountains. From the top of sheer limestone cliffs you can look out over Switzerland and forests that still cover more than a third of this province, which comprises the four *départements* of Doubs, Jura, Haute-Saône and the Territoire-de-Belfort.

Multicoloured patterns of tiles, similar to those in Burgundy, cover the uniquely shaped church towers of Franche-Comté. This is a land of rivers and lakes, waterfalls and gorges, seducing the visitor into taking time just to watch the water ripple by. Many of the limestone cliffs hide grottos and caverns, carved out over millennia by subterranean rivers and rain. Many are open to the public but there are doubtless many others still to be discovered. Trout-filled rivers – the Doubs and the Loue are among the most picturesque – are confined for much of their length to steep-sided valleys, before finally seizing their chance to break through, over wide, shallow steps and spectacular cascades, to join the Rhône and Saône. The Ain, now dammed to form the long Lac de Vouglans, boasts spectacular gorges to the south of Nantua.

The Jura is also a pastoral land, known for its Comté cheese and its red and white Montbéliard cows grazing peacefully in verdant meadows. The Route du Vin runs from Beaufort, south of Lons-le-Saunier, to Arbois, near Salins-les-Bains. Salins, like Arc-et-Senans and Lons-le-Saunier, was once an important centre for the production of salt, a valuable commodity in the Middle Ages. The *gabelle* – a tax on salt not repealed in France until 1790 – provided as much as 40 per cent of the revenue of the rulers.

Franche-Comté can be enjoyed summer and winter. Light-green pastures and dark-green forests wear a glistening blanket of snow in winter. The blue of the sky is reflected in clear waters and there almost seem to be enough signposted paths to provide one for each summer rambler or winter cross-country skier.

*Franche-Comté, like many areas of France, loves pétanque*

Morteau (left) was rebuilt after being largely destroyed by fire in 1865. Like St Dizier (below), it still possesses some attractive architectural details.

The source of the River Lison, east of Salins-les-Bains, is a typically pretty sight in this region of tumbling rivers.

Colourful bread dolls are among the regional handicrafts to be seen in Franche-Comté.

Franche-Comté

# ORNANS — REFLECTIONS AND BELVEDERES

If staying at Besançon, see it first from the Citadelle and then from a bateau-mouche. On foot, see the old houses, the Porte Noire and the Cathédrale St-Jean. Around Ornans is a landscape of limestone cliffs, belvederes, caverns and waterfalls. The Loue has the loveliest river valley in France, unspoilt by the foundries, tanneries and distilleries of years past.

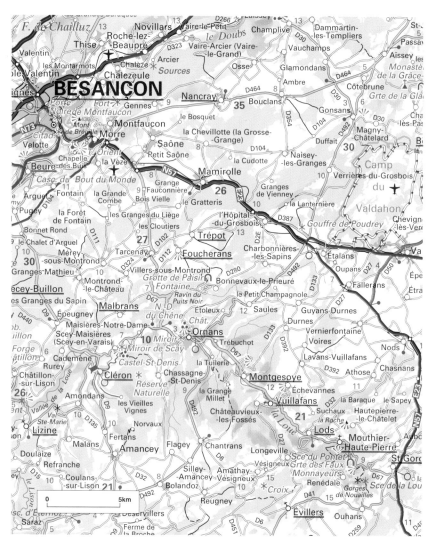

## Château de Cléron

The château is open only for visits by groups, by prior arrangment, in the summer. On a calm day, from the bridge a wonderful series of reflections can be seen in the river – château walls and church tower – with the occasional leaping trout blurring the image.

As the D103 climbs up towards Amondans there is a view across the weir of the mainly 14th- and 16th-century château. Several of the villages hereabouts have large copper cauldrons – big enough to boil missionaries – once used to heat the milk to make Comté cheese. They are now used to hold floral decorations outside churches and are often seen by the pump or fountain in village squares.

On the same stretch of road are three belvederes. From that at Gouille Noire there is a view down into a thickly wooded cleft, in which you can hear the water rushing through the trees far below. The cows grazing along the banks, under limestone cliffs, are a typical sight in this peaceful pastoral region.

## SOURCE OF THE LOUE

A stiff half-hour's walk from a small car park on the D67 out of Mouthier-Haute-Pierre brings you to the source. The narrow path runs halfway up a cliff and several hundred breathtaking metres above the bottom of the gorge. You can hear the river's noise rising from a sighing as of wind in the trees to a full-throated roar as you approach the dark cave from which it emerges, already 30m wide at birth.

Alternatively, you can take the D443 from Ouhans as far as it goes, park the car and walk along the bottom of the valley to the source. This takes only half an hour, there and back. Do not miss this chance to see a river plunging, full grown, from a dark cavern part of the way up a cliff. Afternoon light is best for photographs.

**Agence de Dévelopement Économique du Doubs**
Hôtel du Département
7, Avenue de la Gare d'Eau
25031 Besançon Cedex
Tel: 03 81 65 10 00
www.aded.org

**Touring:**
AA Road Map France series 13: Bourgogne Franche-Comté

*The Château de Cléron is in a good state of preservation and benefits from a picturesque setting on the banks of the Loue.*

## GUSTAVE COURBET

Born in Ornans in1819, in the riverside house now turned into a museum of his life and works, Courbet was an independent and self-assured character. He was one of the Realist school, which took over as the Romantic and neoclassical schools declined. When asked to include angels in a painting for a church, he said 'I have never seen one. Show me one and I will paint it.'

Courbet delighted in everyday scenes, two of which, *Enterrement à Ornans* and *L'Atelier du Peintre*, are in the Louvre. He loved to return each summer to Ornans, capturing the wild limestone landscapes and cliffs of the surrounding countryside. Many of these are in the Musée Courbet, as is the very 'realist' painting of the *Retour de la Conférence*. Happily inebriated clergy are returning home, among them the *curé* of Bonnevaux, easily recognisable on his little donkey. So recognisable was he that Courbet was never again invited to the presbytery wine cellars.

The house has been little modified since Courbet's family lived there, though it did serve as a brewery for a while.

Courbet's revolutionary leanings led him to take part in the destruction of the Colonne Vendôme in Paris in 1871. He was imprisoned but chose exile in Switzerland, where he died on New Year's Eve 1877.

## Gouffre de Poudrey

Situated on the north side of the N57, to the north-east of Ornans, the entrance to this cavern, one of the ten largest in Europe, is marked by a statue reminiscent of Mickey Mouse – it is in fact a bat – in the car park, alongside souvenir shops and a café. Do not let this deter you, for the 60-m high ceiling and the sheer size – it could swallow up Notre Dame de Paris – together with the stalactites and stalagmites, the latter in both blue and white, and the dramatic lighting effects, are very impressive.

## Lods

The River Loue, not far from its source, has escaped from the Gorges de Nouailles and tumbles over several small faults in its bed as it passes through the riverside village of Lods, which should not be confused with Nods, some 8km to the north-east. One single arch remains of an old medieval bridge across one of these 'weirs'. This, and the many old picturesque houses in the village, make it a pleasant spot in which to spend an idle hour.

## Mouthier-Haute-Pierre

Only the name remains of the Benedictine abbey founded here in the valley meadows. The Roche de Hautepierre, 882m above, affords a view across the whole plateau, with the river below and the Vosges, and on clear days, the Alps behind.

## Ornans

Ornans, on the banks of the Loue, is home to the Musée National de la Pêche, the National Museum of Fishing. It was also the birthplace of the Realist painter Gustave Courbet. On a sheer bluff overlooking town and river is the site of the château, destroyed on the orders of Louis XIV when the region was wrested from the Spanish in 1674. Now occupied by a few houses and unmade paths and gardens, the spot affords a magnificent view on a sunny evening. There is a tiny chapel to St George, founded in 1289 by Othon IV and rebuilt in 1500.

Another spectacular viewpoint overlooking the otwn is the Roche du Mont. The tourist office can supply a map showing walks in the surrounding area At the east end of the Église St-Laurent, in

Ornans itself, is a strange table tomb, its inscription illegible now. The church was reconstructed in the 16th century.

## Scey-en-Varais

In the little commune of Scey-en-Varais is the Miroir de Scey. A sweeping curve of the Loue reflects – in moods that vary according to the time of day and the skies overhead – a large rustic farmhouse on the far bank. It can also catch the jagged likeness of the Châtel St-Denis perched on the crag above.

*The medieval bridge and the series of little weirs that punctuate the Loue as it passes down through the attractive village lend charm to Lods (pronounced 'Lô').*

# THE RIVER DOUBS - A FRONTIER

The River Doubs is the undisputed star of this corner of France – and Switzerland – being assigned for part of its length the role of guardian of the frontier itself. The customs posts are not official but rather set up, tongue in cheek on 1 April, by the citizens of the Republic of Val du Saugeais, who have even elected their own President.

**Agence de Développement Économique du Doubs**
Hôtel du Département –
7, Avenue de la Gare d'Eau
25031 Besançon Cedex
Tel: 03 81 65 10 00
www.aded.org

**Touring:**
AA Road Map France series 13: Bourgogne Franche-Comté

*This stretch of the Doubs forms part of the border between France and Switzerland. The river's name derives from the Latin dubius, which means doubtful, since for much of its length it takes a hesitant, sinuous course.*

## Cirque de Consolation and Roche du Prêtre

Follow the signposted route up to the Belvédère de la Roche du Prêtre. From the car park there is a pleasant walk until suddenly you are on the edge of a sheer drop down into the wooded valley. Far below is the seminary of Notre-Dame de Consolation. Three hundred and fifty metres of fresh air right at your feet is certainly exhilarating.

## Défilé d'Entreroche

The D437 from Montbenoît towards Morteau certainly lives up to its name of 'Defile between Rocks'. Once out of the narrowest part of the defile, at Pont de la Roche, the valley broadens out considerably.

The Doubs, with its wide bed and lush water-meadows, can absorb a large volume of winter flood water without problems; if it could not the road itself could very easily become impassable.

## Grotte du Trésor and Notre-Dame de Remonot

These two caves in the base of the limestone cliff are close together and yet very different from each other. At the Grotte du Trésor, park alongside a broad, lazy sweep of the Doubs, cross the road, scramble down a culvert and up a dry watercourse, to the lip of a huge cavern with a rough, rocky floor that disappears into the gloom at the back.

Notre-Dame de Remonot is 2km along the road. A grotto once venerated by druids, it was claimed for Christianity by hermits in the 8th century. The same underground stream that feeds the recesses of the Grotte du Trésor also flows here, and there is a small footbridge just behind the altar. Mischievous water spirits from time to time flood the flagstone floor and float the chairs. For hundreds of years those afflicted with problems of sight have come here to bathe their eyes with the water running down the walls. Plaques on the walls give thanks for many a cure gratefully received.

*Smoked sausages are a speciality of Franche-Comté. The small ones known as 'Jésus' are used in a hotpot eaten in the Morteau area.*

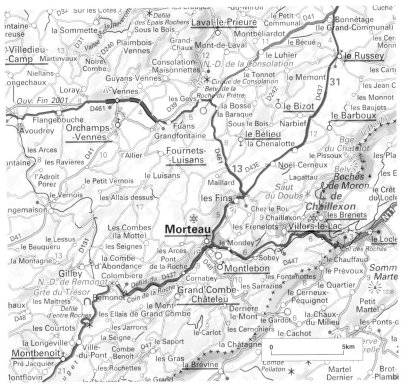

## Morteau

The town grew up in the 13th century around a Benedictine priory and became, in the 19th, a centre for clock making.

After the ravages of 17th-century wars and a disastrous fire in 1865, a few older buildings survive. The Hôtel Fauché, built in 1590, is now the town hall. The former Pertusier family home, dating from 1575, with its stone façade, mullioned windows, columns and colonnades, is one of the few such Renaissance buildings in the region.

The gastronomic speciality of Morteau is its little smoked sausage, locally known as 'Jésus'.

## VAL DU SAUGEAIS

At an altitude of over 800m, where the houses begin to look distinctly Alpine, is the Val du Saugeais, south of Montbenoît. Devastated and depopulated during wars four centuries ago, when France regained the Comté, this region was largely resettled from Haute-Savoie and elsewhere. The locals have their own dialect and customs, and in 1947, with the accord of the local prefect, proclaimed their region the Republic of Saugeais, with their own elected President. For over 30 years the position has been held by the energetic Madame Gabrielle Pourchet, now in her nineties.

## Lac de Chaillexon

Formed by rockfalls, this lake, only exceptionally more than 200m wide, first winds its way between wooded slopes, its blue waters full of trout and other sport fish, before running between steeper cliffs. The short 3km boat trip past the varied scenery feels like a much longer expedition.

## Montbenoît

A clapper bridge crosses a bend of the Doubs in front of the abbey church of Montbenoît. Hidden at the end of its small valley, Montbenoît, 'capital' of the Val du Saugeais, is different, in patois and customs, from the other upland communities. In 1150 the local Sire de Joux offered land to the monks from Valais. The abbey remained a feudal possession and many different architectural styles are represented. There are lovely carved choir-stalls, some depicting subjects unusually sensual for a church. The pillars of the tiny 15th-century cloister are carved with the monks' interpretations in stone of local animals and flowers. As secular interest in the wealth of the abbey increased, so discipline and religious observance declined. Soon it was said to be 'gaining each year in gold what it lost in wisdom'.

*The choir-stalls in Montbenoît's abbey church depict some surprisingly worldly scenes.*

## Saut du Doubs

If you are not going to the Saut du Doubs by boat, take the not very clearly signposted left fork out of Morteau, at the Hôtel de France, for Saut du Doubs and Maiche. The road climbs steeply, giving a splendid view across the river, which has just become the Franco-Swiss border.

From the second car park there is a 500-m walk down to the cafés and souvenir stalls and a further 500m to the belvedere overlooking the fall itself. Boats come down river from Morteau and from Villers-le-Lac as well as from the Swiss shore. The border is marked by a garland of floating plastic buoys.

## Villers-le-Lac

Boat trips along Lac de Chaillexon and to the Saut du Doubs start from here. The river has spread across the valley, before being confined again at Chaillexon.

The exterior of the 17th-century Chapelle de St-Joseph-des-Bassots might not suggest that a stop is called for. However, the ceiling, formed of lozenges and hanging spindles, in blues, reds and gold, is unique. The reredos and choir-stalls also bear witness to the taste of the patron, Claude Binétruy, who built this sanctuary.

*The Saut du Doubs plunges over a 27-m high ledge before being dammed.*

# CIRQUES OF THE JURA

B aume, Revigny, Ladoye – dead-end valleys known as *les bouts-du-monde* – are among the most spectacular cirques of the region. The Jura is also well worth visiting for the 12th century abbey of Baume-les-Messieurs, the Royal Saltworks at Arc-et-Senans, for its rather exclusive but delicious wines, and for Comté cheese.

## Arbois

The wine capital of the Jura, Arbois is said to have produced one of the favourite wines of Henri IV. So, we are told, did Chalon, Jurançon and many other vineyards. Louis Pasteur, born at Dole in 1822, spent most of his youth and all his holidays in Arbois. The family home is now a museum explaining his research into rabies and serums, his contributions to the silk industry and, above all, his seminal work in the field of fermentation and wine production.

*At the bottom of the Cirque de Baume lies Baume-les-Messieurs, a village perhaps best known for its ancient abbey.*

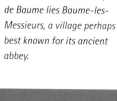

## Cirque de Baume

The best vantage point from which to see the many small valleys that make up the Cirque de Baume is the Belvédère des Roches de Baume. A gorge over 1,500m long, 300m wide and up to 200m deep suddenly opens at your feet. At the bottom of the gorge is the abbey and village of Baume-les-Messieurs.

## Cirque de Ladoye

Seen from the top of its sheer 200-m cliffs, or from the bottom, this 600-m wide *bout-du-monde* is equally striking. A mountain road winds down the side of the cirque and the northern source of the River Seille rises, in a fountain called locally a *doye*, at the bottom of the cliffs.

## Creux de Revigny

The River Vallière bursts forth from the foot of the escarpment. It is difficult to appreciate the sight without climbing part of the way up the overgrown scree slope. In the cliff face itself are a series of interconnecting grottos and caves, carved by underground rivers which have long since disappeared. These served as refuge for the inhabitants of the village, terrorised for many years during the Thirty Years War by the Swedes.

## WINES

The Côtes du Jura produce only 1 per cent of the wines of France, but their distinctive bouquet has a growing following. Local wine growers do not make a wine to suit supermarket customers: 'Let the customer come and try our wines and he will soon appreciate them. If not, let him go back to the supermarket!'

At Château-Chalon is produced a deep-yellow wine with a distinctive nose and flavour. Is matures for a minimum of six years in part-filled barrels, under a yeast skin that excludes air. But 38 per cent of the wine evaporates – *la part des anges*, the angel's share – a much higher proportion than in cognac. Château-Chalon is the only wine sold in a 62-cl bottle rather than the EC 75-cl standard.

Several grape varieties are grown hereabouts. Château-Chalon is made from Savagnin grapes, little grown elsewhere. Pinot Noir was introduced from Burgundy, having a more reliable record of production than the grapes that give such distinctive character to the local vintages. These grapes are the Trousseau, which is used for Montigny, and Poulsard, from which Pupillin is made.

## SALT SPRINGS

*Salarium* meant wages – with which to buy salt – such was the importance to the Romans and others of salt. Production of salt by evaporation of brine has been a valuable trade in this part of France as well as in the area around Marsal in Lorraine, for thousands of years. Salins-les-Bains, built along a river valley, is still guarded by two forts, Belin and St-André. It is the only place in the region where you can still see and understand the work of extraction and evaporation.

As wood was replaced for firing boilers by more expensive coal and as the warmth of the Mediterranean sunshine began to be used to do the job of evaporation almost free, Salins went into decline. The museum, in the 18th-century workings, gives a clear idea of the whole process. At Arc-et-Senans (above) the brine was pumped from Salins, along tree-trunk pipes, much being lost on the way. The project, which began in 1779, seldom produced even half of its Utopian target. It closed in 1895 but has been restored and since 1983 has been listed by UNESCO.

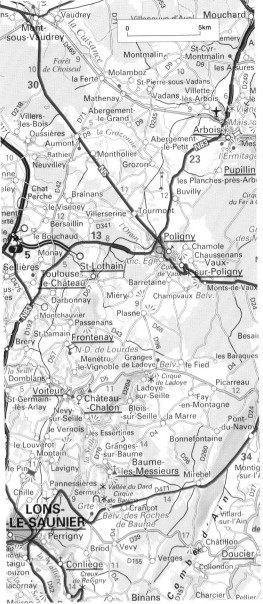

## Lons-le-Saunier

Lons-le-Saunier is a pleasant centre from which to explore the 'Reculées', as the many spectacular gorges and chasms in the region are called. Salt springs exploited by both Gauls and Romans ceased production in the Middle Ages. Waters with some of the highest concentrations of chlorine and iodine in France are used today to treat lymph and rheumatic troubles.

Only the Tour de l'Horloge, the clock tower, remains of the town's medieval walls. The archaeological museum, housed in the former Vache Qui Rit cheese factory, contains some interesting displays, including a life-size replica of France's oldest-known dinosaur, a 210-million-year-old plateosaurus.

Without a doubt, the town's most famous son is Rouget de Lisle. An engineer officer garrisoned at Strasbourg in 1792, he composed the *Marseillaise*. The theatre clock, in the Place de la Liberté, chimes a

couple of bars of the national anthem each hour.

## Poligny

As with wines, there is an *Appellation Contrôlée* for Comté cheese. Poligny is the capital of this industry, with its museum dedicated to the cheese, the Maison du Comté. Only cows fed on fresh grass can supply the milk.

Since no silage is used, there is little production in winter. As with Munster, some cheese is made straight away from the morning milking and another batch in the evening. Other Comté is made from a mixture of the two. The cream having risen and been skimmed off, this Comté has a lower fat content.

For a view over the whole town, climb up to the 'Trou de la Lune' near the Château de Grimont, once home to the counts of Burgundy. Among the roofs of the town seen from here are those of the Hôtel-Dieu which has a fine collection of Poligny pottery, apothecary jars for the pharmacy (visits by arrangement with the tourist office only), and of the Clarisses convent.

## Pupillin and Fer à Cheval

Just south of Arbois, the Poulsard grapes planted around the village produce a light red wine, unusual and very fruity. After a *dégustation*, the nearby Fer à Cheval is another of the cirques well worth seeing.

*The Tour de l'Horloge in Lons-le-Saunier's Place de la Liberté once formed part of the town's medieval walls.*

**Comité Départemental du Tourisme du Jura**
8, Rue Louis-Rousseau
39000 Lons-le-Saunier
Tel: 03 84 87 08 88
www.jura-tourism.com

**Touring:**
AA Road Map France
series 13: Bourgogne
Franche-Comté

# DOULX LIEUX

'*Doulx lieux*', gentle places. Thus did Cardinal Granvelle, a native of Ornans himself, counsellor to Philip II of Spain, describe his Jura to a friend at court. The Parc Naturel Régional du Haut-Jura, between the Swiss frontier and the road from St Claude to the Cascades du Hérrison, is a wilder, though equally inspiring landscape: convoluted limestone crags carved by tumbling rivers into sheer gorges, fertile alpine meadows and crystal-clear streams full of trout.

## Col de la Faucille

*The layers of rock of the Chapeau du Gendarme, near St Claude, have bent upwards without breaking.*

Climbing up from the valley of the Valserine on a clear day, you may be lucky enough to see Mont Blanc nearly 100km away. It is a memorable sight, although more memorable still is the view from the top of Petit Mont Rond (1,534m). The view down over Lac Léman, with Geneva to your right, is stupendous.

## Forêt du Massacre

This is another reminder of the region's turbulent past, the name recalling the massacre, by Savoyard troops besieging Geneva, of a force sent to the aid of the city by François I in 1535. The forest is criss-crossed with tracks and the views, especially from Crêt Pela (1,495m), are splendid.

## Gorges du Flumen

Outside St Claude the D436 runs through the Gorges du Flumen, where the river drops spectacularly, one fall after another. From the Saut du Chien there is a view back to one of the best of these. Near by is the Chapeau du Gendarme: a huge slab of sedimentary rock that was thrust up in the Tertiary era and has been gently bent without cracking or shattering.

## Les Rousses

Situated at an altitude of 1,100m, the village of Les Rousses is a prime winter sports centre. For summer visitors it has its lake and, just to the north, the Crêt des Sauges, and the Forêt du Risoux, which stretches into Switzerland. For some reason the timber cut here has special qualities of resonance and is much sought after by makers of musical instruments, such as those of Mirecourt.

### HÉRRISON FALLS

These are among the finest falls in the region, the river dropping nearly 300m in about 3km. Within sight of the top car park at the end of the road from Bonlieu is the Saut de la Forge, a wide 12-m drop into a small shallow basin, where optimistic fishermen gather. The river tumbles on, over numerous small limestone lintels and steps, to Grand Saut, 500m downstream. Here the drop, confined in a V-shaped cleft, is a spectacular 60m. The path can become very slippery and muddy, so wear shoes with rugged soles.

Further downstream is the Cascade de L'Éventail. Both the Grand Saut and the Éventail, where the river cascades 65m over a series of rounded steps, looking not unlike a bridal veil, are best seen from below. To this end, take the D326 out of Val-Dessous and park amid the myriad coaches, cafés and souvenir shops, from where it is a five-minute walk to the bottom of the Éventail

*A series of waterfalls set in beautiful woodland, the Cascades du Hérrison are accessible on foot.*

## Morez

The River Bienne drops by more than 300m between Les Rousses and Morez. The town stretches for nearly 3km along the valley, its single street dominated by high escarpment walls and impressive railway viaducts.

The Bienne was a useful power source and around 1796 Morez became to spectacles what St Claude is to pipe making and it was here that the pince-nez was invented. There is a secondary industry, that of clock making, and a third, winter sports, as well as cheese making.

## St Claude

This town is the natural centre from which to explore the region and possesses two tourist attractions itself: the Cathédrale St-Pierre and a pipe-making industry dating back 150 years. Near the cathedral is a museum combining this and another established St Claude industry, the cutting and polishing of diamonds and gemstones.

St Claude clings to the precipitous banks of the ravine carved out by the Bienne and the Tacon, and the best overall view is from the Grotte Ste-Anne.

The site where the cathedral now stands was chosen as a retreat by two monks, the brothers Romain and Lupicin, in the mid-5th century. Monastic wealth soon attracted the worldly nobility, and monastic discipline relaxed scandalously over the years.

The glory of the 14th- and 15th-century cathedral are the choir-stalls, finished in 1465 after 15 years' work, by the Geneva sculptor Jehan de Vitry. Carvers of the period seem to have had a similar puckish sense of humour and caricature: see, for example, the choir-stalls of the Collégiale St-Thiébaut at Thann, in Alsace. Unfortunately some 200 carvings, all those on the south side, were destroyed in a smouldering fire on the night of 26 September 1983. Careful restoration has taken place.

### PIPE MAKING

The making of pipes at St Claude grew from the religious objects – rosaries and crucifixes – produced by local wood carvers for sale to pilgrims. A French ambassador to Portugal introduced both tobacco and the pipe to France in 1560. Early pipes with silver bowls were beyond the means of most would-be smokers. Pipes of porcelain and meerschaum from Germany were also expensive but, above all, fragile.

Experiments with boxwood, pear, maple and walnut had little success. The wood burned as fast as the tobacco and the taste was horrible. Trials with horn were even more unpleasant. In 1854 the idea of using briar root was introduced from Corsica, where the root grew in abundance. By 1914 there were 1,300 workers making five million pipes a

year, most for export. Mass production since 1945 has removed St Claude from its place as the maker of 90 per cent of the world's briar pipes.

A large collection of pipes can be seen at the Maison du Confrérie des Maîtres Pipiers (open 1 June –15 November), near the cathedral.

**Comité Départemental du Tourisme du Jura**
8, Rue Louis-Rousseau
39000 Lons-le-Saunier
Tel: 03 84 87 08 88
www.jura-tourism.com

**Touring:**
AA Road Map France series 13: Bourgogne Franche-Comté

*The main part of the Cathédrale St-Pierre in St Claude was built in the Gothic style in the 14th and 15th centuries, but in the 18th century the classical façade was added.*

# THE ATLANTIC COAST

The Mediterranean may be warmer than the Atlantic, but in many other respects the Atlantic Coast and its hinterland have as much to offer as the more popular, more crowded, Côte d'Azur.

You can certainly eat well here, seafood and goat's cheeses being just two of the regional specialities. As for wine, very few people would deny that the best wine in the world comes from Bordeaux. This is also France's famous cognac region, and although it is not covered here, you will almost certainly drive through it.

If you are interested in history and ancient monuments you will love this region. Here were fought many bitter battles during the Hundred Years War. There is an abundance of churches, châteaux and museums to explore, particularly around Poitiers. But you do not have to be a history buff to enjoy the atmosphere of the many medieval villages. If you like night-life and shopping in smart shops, there are the stylish resorts of Arcachon and La Rochelle. Here, and in many other seaside towns, you can pamper yourself by having thalassotherapy – smooth and invigorating sea-water treatment, very popular with the smart set these days. For sport, take your pick from walking, cycling, windsurfing, sailing, diving, canoeing, horse-riding, golf, swimming or simply paddling in the ocean.

For many city dwellers one of the most appealing aspects of the Atlantic Coast is quite simply that there is so much of it. It is very easy to find peace and quiet here, and even in the height of summer there are deserted beaches. But you need not be from the city to appreciate the pure air for which the whole region is known. Elsewhere the world's rain forests are being denuded, but the soil of the Landes area – a former swamp below Arcachon – has been fixed in place by the planting of thousands of pines, whose heady scent fills the air and clears the lungs.

The Atlantic Coast is also a haven for the environmentalist and nature lover. Offshore islands are on the migratory routes of many birds. On the islands themselves you can see the old salt plains as well as oyster beds and mussel farms. Inland, the mysterious reclaimed landscape of the Marais Poitevin, the 'Green Venice', exerts a powerful charm of its own. Its waterways are best explored by boat.

In some ways time seems to have stood still in this region, where the fields are still cultivated with the same crops and vines as they have been for centuries. But you can be abruptly brought back into the 21st century by the Parc du Futuroscope, near Poitiers. The northern part of the region's coastline is known locally as the Côte de Beauté, and the southern, below Arcachon, as the Côte d'Argent. The whole Atlantic Coast could, equally aptly, be called the 'underrated coast'. But those who know it have always appreciated its charms.

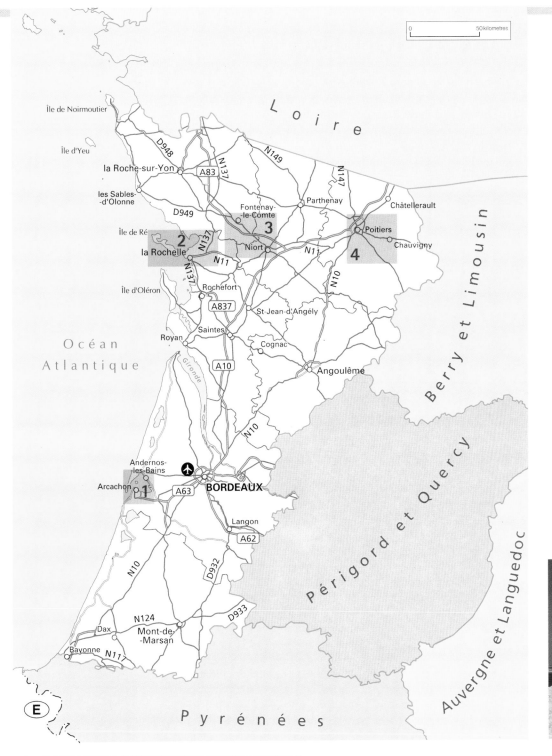

*The Écomusée de Marquèse shows Landes life, including the shepherds' use of stilts (below).*

*The Dune du Pilat is the highest sand dune in Europe (below).*

*A fireman is wed in Civray (bottom).*

*A 3-D cinema and the 'Gyrotour' are among the many thrills offered by the Parc du Futuroscope (below).*

# THE ARCACHON BASIN

The sheltered basin of Arcachon, fringed with pine forests that anchor the sand dunes, is where the rolling Médoc meets the sea. Here the traditional industries of oyster and mussel farming still flourish. The basin is dotted with small resorts, varying from the simple to the stylish, but Arcachon is usually described as its pearl. To the south of the town, the local capital, lies the impressive Dune du Pilat, Europe's tallest sand dune.

*The air in Arcachon is scented with a mixture of sea and pine, and sometimes on a breezy day there is a heady smell of eucalyptus. From the beach you can see Cap Ferret across the bay.*

## Andernos-les-Bains

Andernos has a picturesque harbour where you can watch the oyster boats being loaded. The Église St-Éloi was built on the site of a much older Gallo-Roman church and you can still see the 4th-century remains of the old basilica. Pines, oyster farming and tourism made this prehistoric village prosperous. The actress Sarah Bernhardt settled here during World War I.

## Arcachon

This is one of France's most stylish seaside resorts and is very popular with the rich of Bordeaux, many of whom own weekend homes here. Originally a sleepy fishing village, it started to expand in 1857 with the arrival of the railway.

The town was formerly divided into four quarters named after the seasons of the year, and still has distinct summer and winter areas. The Ville d'Été is closest to the beach, and used to have a spectacular Moorish casino, but this was destroyed by fire in 1977. The surrounding park and gardens are still there, however, and from the lift there are fine views of the town and bay. The Ville d'Hiver is a more residential area.

Parking can be a problem in the town, and the best way to explore it is on foot.

## Arès

This small oyster-farming and resort town was not given separate borough status from Andernos-les-Bains until 1851. A lady named Sophie Wallerstein was the resort's main benefactress, and her large home in the middle of the park is now a retirement home for teachers.

Near the jetty is an old tower, all that remains of a former mill. It had started as a windmill, but when taxes were increased the sails were removed and the battlements added to make it look like a watch-tower. David Allegre, the inventor of the steam trawler, lived here. And it is perhaps surprising to discover, in such a sleepy town as Arès, that the world's first UFO-tracking station was launched on the beach here on 15 August 1976.

## Cap Ferret

This is the long sand jetty that protects the Arcachon basin from the ocean. From its lighthouse there is a wonderful view back of the whole basin, and of the Atlantic ahead. Until 1928, when the road was built, you could reach Cap Ferret only by boat, and this is probably still the nicest way. Another enjoyable excursion is to ride to the beach on the miniature steam train.

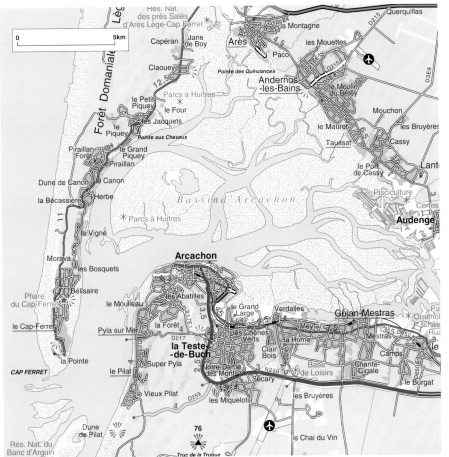

Comité Départemental du Tourisme de la Gironde

21, Cours de l'Intendance 33000 Bordeaux Tel: 05 56 52 61 40 www.tourisme-gironde.cg33.fr

**Touring:** AA Road Map France series 5: Aquitaine

## LANDES LIFE

Until the 19th century the Landes was a huge swamp, edged by dunes. Today the area is planted with thousands of kilometres of trees. At the Écomusée de Marquèze (below), 15km east of Labouheyre on the N10 from Bordeaux to Bayonne, the traditional Landais way of life can be seen.

Shepherds used to wander the land on stilts and many of their dwellings were built on legs. Sheep and bees were the main basis of the economy, and today nearly every small farm still sells honey and every market sheepskin jackets. To reach the Écomusée you take a small steam train from Sabres to

*At over 100m high, the impressive Dune du Pilat (above) is the tallest sand dune in Europe.*

*The lighthouse on Cap Ferret (left) gives an excellent view of the Arcachon basin*

## Dune du Pilat

Sometimes called 'Sahara by the sea', the Dune du Pilat is a must for anyone visiting the area. This natural sand dune, more than 100m high and over 3km long, has continued to change and move since its formation. You can climb to the top up 190 steep wooden steps: the view of the sea, the channel between Arcachon and Cap Ferret, the thick forest of the Landes and the rolling dunes themselves are well worth the climb. And children love the (perfectly safe) slide down the dune.

## Gujan-Mestras

This town is known as the oyster capital of the Arcachon basin. From its seven harbours you can find out everything you ever wanted to know about oysters and oyster farming – though tasting them is probably the best test.

The town has a fine old church, and even an oyster museum at the the Maison de l'Huître. For children, there is the Aqualand leisure centre, an adventure park, the Ile d'Aventure, and the Coccinelle zoo. There is also a botanical garden to explore, the Jardins du Bassin.

## L'Herbe

This tiny oyster-farming village attractively sited between the sand dunes and the sea, with its narrow streets and its pine trees, is one of the most picturesque places in the Arcachon basin.

In the 19th century its most famous residents were the Lesca family, who made a fortune in Algeria and built an Algerian-style villa and chapel here. Today only the chapel remains.

the clearing, with its re-creation of a typical Landais homestead. You can watch stilts being made and bread cooked traditionally over a fire. There is also a recreation area and restaurant. In addition, 20km north of Marquèze, you can visit a restored typical 19th-century Landais farmhouse and an old pine-resin processing plant.

# BORDEAUX AND WINE

## 18th-century Bordeaux

Behind the Quai Louis XVIII, on a curve in the river, is the Esplanade des Quinconces. Reputedly the largest square in Europe, it was established in the early 19th century. The statues of two of Bordeaux's most famous sons, Montesquieu and Montaigne, are at the river side of the square. This is the best place from which to begin a tour of old Bordeaux.

The Grand Théâtre is spectacular, with the style of an ancient temple but built in 1780. It is sumptuously decorated, and has an Italian-style auditorium with seating for 1,000. Its fine

domed staircase inspired the Paris Opera over 100 years later.

Among the city's many museum's is the Musée des Beaux-Arts, a very special collection of paintings, including works by Titian, Van Dyck and Goya, housed in part of what once was the 18th-century Archbishop's Palace.

The Place de la Bourse, Place du Parlement and adjacent buildings are other 18th-century reminders of what was Bordeaux's Golden Age.

---

The city of Bordeaux and its most famous product, wine, owe their origins to the Romans. Like Celtic tribes 300 years earlier, the Romans were attracted to the great crescent of the River Garonne. And today the port is still at the centre of Bordeaux's fame and fortune. The waterfront remains an impressive feature, with imposing houses built in the 17th and 18th centuries by wealthy wine merchants, currently undergoing cleaning and restoration.

Bordeaux is synonymous with wine. What started as a result of the Roman's irritation that their precious cargoes of Italian wine were always late has culminated in the city's pre-eminence in the production of fine wines.

The land drained by the Rivers Dordogne, Garonne and Gironde is host to 112,000 hectares of vineyards that make the Bordeaux region the world's largest producer of fine wines. Each year the area's 3,000 châteaux and 20,000 vineyard owners sell 3–5 hectolitres of wine – a total of almost 500 million bottles.

*The historic importance of wine to Bordeaux is underlined by eyecatching architectural detail.*

*A fine memorial to the Girondins graces Bordeaux's magnificent Esplanade des Quinconces.*

## The Medieval Quarter

Medieval and Gothic Bordeaux, just behind the dazzling range of buildings to be found in the Place du Parlement, is easy to miss. The Porte Cailhau is a fine example of Gothic military architecture, built in 1500. The Grosse Cloche is a 13th-century gate, restored 200 years later. The oldest of the churches dotted around the old town is the Basilique St-Michel, close to the river.

## Modern Bordeaux

Bordeaux today is a young, lively university city, as a stroll down its main shopping street, the Rue St Catherine, will confirm. It is a centre for major trade exhibitions, as well as providing good sporting and cultural facilities. The city has been enhanced in recent years with some striking modern architecture, whilst retaining its sense of history. One example of this is the conversion of a former warehouse into the innovative Museum of Contemporary Art.

## The Vineyards

In some ways the vineyards for which Bordeaux is famous are not of great interest to the sightseer. Most are in flat, dull countryside with few of the pleasant villages or even eating places that elsewhere make touring French wine regions such an enjoyable experience. There are relatively few places where *dégustation*, wine sampling, is readily available. By contrast, St Émilion is a beautiful old wine town within well-preserved city walls on a hill. It features a monolithic church carved out of the hillside, a medieval fortress and fine yellow-stone houses.

A tour of Bordeaux vineyards begins right in Bordeaux itself, with the Graves-producing Château Haut-Brion. 'Graves' refers to the gravelly soil that sometimes produces white and red wines from the same vine. Start a visit to the region with the best known château, although this is not connected with a vineyard at all. La Brède, built in the 15th century, was the birthplace of Baron de Montesquieu. About 15km from Bordeaux, this fine old château is surrounded by a beautiful functioning moat.

*Some 3,000 châteaux produce wine in the Bordeaux area (above).*

*Bordeaux's old quarter (left) recalls the long history of this great city on the River Garonne.*

## Wine Châteaux

The winding lanes leading to Sauternes are explained by the fact that the vineyards there produce some of the most expensive wines and therefore no land will be sacrificed for the sake of straight roads.

The most famous producer of the rich, sweet wines of the Sauternes district is Château d'Yquem. The medieval château is admirable but is not open to the public. However, it is close to Château Filhot, which offers tastings. Just across the Garonne, Ste-Croix-du-Mont presents a beautiful vision of church and château perched on a cliff top.

Four great towers mark a medieval fortress built by Pope Clément V and the home of Roquetaillade. Another such château is Villandraut, the scenic background to the Uzeste music festival held during late August.

The most celebrated of all Bordeaux wine regions is Médoc. The definitive wine of the region, Médoc is produced by a thin strip of vineyards north-west from Bordeaux along the west bank of the Gironde estuary. Most of the 180 Médoc châteaux are open to the public, although it is necessary to book for the most celebrated of all, Mouton-Rothschild. A visit to the highly ornate mansion and the home of some of the world's rarest wines is a delight not to be missed. The wine museum there contains priceless exhibits and wine labels featuring the work of artists such as Salvador Dalí.

*The grapes of Bordeaux (above) produce classic wines such as those of Moulis-en-Médoc (right).*

In Pauillac there are many well-known vineyards including Château-Latour and Château-Lafite, which has guided tours. In St-Estèphe the architecture of Cos d'Estournel is reminiscent of the Orient and recalls the days when estate owners returned from the East Indies with ornaments. The Margaux château, designed by a pupil of the architect responsible for Bordeaux's Grand Théâtre, is similarly well worth a visit. The architectural style is based on Greek temples.

Only in the Bordeaux region does the word 'château' refer to the house, farm buildings and vineyard – the whole wine-producing estate. Many of these buildings are pleasing examples of local architecture.

# LA ROCHELLE AND THE ILE DE RÉ

Linked by a modern road bridge, La Rochelle and the Ile de Ré are together the most attractive resorts on France's northern Atlantic Coast. Historically the Ile de Ré served variously as a protector to the harbour of La Rochelle and as a transit point for convicts awaiting deportation. Once an important maritime centre – the navy is still based nearby – the area is now more popular with well-heeled sailors of leisure, and gets extremely busy during the summer.

**Comité Départemental du Tourisme de Charente-Maritime**
85, Boulevard de la République
17076 La Rochelle Cedex 09
Tel: 05 46 31 71 71
www.charente-maritime.org

**Touring:**
AA Road Map France series 4: Poitou-Charantes

## Ile de Ré

Known locally as the 'white island bathed in light', the Ile de Ré is said by some to owe its name to the *ratis*, the fern with which it was covered in prehistoric times. Others say it was named after the Egyptian sun god Ra. Whatever the truth, this 30km-long island does have its own microclimate. It is, in fact, two islands – Loix and Ars – joined together by a narrow strip. It has had a turbulent history, mainly involving rivalry with Britain. However, today it is best known for the quality of its oysters, sandy beaches, pretty villages, wild birds and whitewashed cottages with green shutters. This is not to forget the taste of the local white wine, which some claim has the tang of seaweed. It is just right to accompany trout, oysters or other local seafood dishes.

## Abbaye des Châteliers

Driving along the main road from Rivedoux, the most striking sights you are likely to come across on the island are the ruins of the Abbaye de Notre-Dame de Ré, more commonly know as the Abbaye des Châteliers. Originally founded in the 12th century, it was burned down and rebuilt again many times until it finally fell into ruin in the early 17th century. There have been several excavations, and the Musée d'Orbigny-Bernon at La Rochelle contains a 13th-century tombstone from the abbey.

## Ars-en-Ré

The economy of the Ile de Ré was founded on salt and wine. Many of the original salt marshes have now been converted to oyster beds but you can still see others stretching for kilometres, in places such as Le Fier d'Ars. Ars-en-Ré, which today is a popular yachting centre, has very narrow streets, and you may notice that some of the corners

*A striking modern road bridge joins the Ile de Ré to La Rochelle.*

The harbour of La Rochelle is guarded by twin towers. For a contrast with the city's many historic buildings, you can enjoy a stroll in the beautiful wooded Parc Charruyer just behind the old city wall.

have been cut off. This was so that people could turn round in the days when the horse and carriage provided the main form of transport.

Those interested in history should visit the 11th-century Église St-Étienne. Its black and white bell tower is a landmark for the island of Ars, and was in centuries past also used by navigators of passing ships. The church contains a 17th-century pulpit, an 18th-century lectern of painted and gilded wood and some interesting statues. Sunbathers may prefer to head for the lovely beach south of the town.

## La Pallice

The commercial port on the western side of La Rochelle could scarcely be called attractive. But it has its points of interest, despite being heavily bombed in the war after the Germans built some huge concrete sheds as submarine bases. Being too difficult to demolish, some still remain in use. The navy has a base here. Close to La Pallice is the bridge linking the Ile de Ré

with the mainland. The 2.9-km bridge was opened in 1988, 14 years after work began.

## Pointe des Baleines

If you travel to the north-west tip of the Ile de Ré, you cannot miss the lighthouse on the Pointe des Baleines. It is one of the most powerful on the Atlantic coast, with its 47-km range. From its top you can see the whole island and get a good view of the Vendée coast. Children – and adults with a sense of fun – will enjoy a visit to the nearby 'Noah's Ark'.

## La Rochelle

Sometimes called the French Geneva, this city claims, with some justification, to be France's most handsome port. Eleanor of Aquitaine granted La Rochelle its charter in 1199, and ushered in a period of prosperity. Its still-bustling harbour is guarded by two towers that were part of its 14th-century fortifications: the Tour St-Nicolas (the patron saint of navigators) and the Tour de la Chaîne, the latter named after the heavy chain that was drawn between the two towers each night to seal off the harbour. The harbour was once the site of a bitter siege. In 1627–8 Cardinal Richelieu blockaded the port because of the town's Protestant resistance to national unity. The population of 28,000 was reduced by famine to 5,000. In more recent times it was the principal port for trade between France and Canada.

One interesting legacy of the association with Canada is the Musée du Nouveau Monde in Rue Fleuriau, which contains fascinating photographs of American Indians and old maps of America. The whole town is steeped in history, but you do not have to be a history enthusiast to enjoy atmosphere, the cobbled streets, beautiful parks, stylish shops and fabulous seafood restaurants.

La Rochelle can also claim to be one of France's most environmentally friendly towns. Its forward-thinking municipality was the first to introduce the idea of pedestrian-only streets back in 1971, together with a fleet of free bicycles for use in the town. More recently electric cars have also been introduced, both for local residents and for those visiting the town on a short-term basis. The only drawback: take care when crossing the road in La Rochelle, as these vechicles make none of the usual traffic noise and can creep up silently on unwary pedestrians!

## CONVICTS

In the 17th century the Citadelle de St-Martin, on the northern coast of the Ile de Ré, served to protect the island from foreign invaders. Later it found another use – as a prison, particularly as a transit point for deportees. The island was at one time known as the 'land of exile'.

The most famous deportees were the communards – 400 souls who were condemned by the Third Republic for insurrection. In 1872 they were sent to St-Martin before being shipped to New Caledonia. Many political or other prisoners who had been sentenced to hard labour or deportation found themselves spending a few months at St-Martin first. The prison was in use until 1947.

A statue in La Rochelle honours Eugène Fromentin, the 19th-century writer, who was born in the city.

# THE MARAIS POITEVIN

Between Niort and the Atlantic lies the strange, misty landscape of the Marais Poitevin, reclaimed from the sea in the 11th century. It comprises two distinct areas, the dry marshes and the wet marshes, together now designated a Regional Nature Park. The wet marshes, known locally as the 'Green Venice', are the more beautiful and are best explored by boat. A further attraction is the surprising sight of churches and old abbeys – the legacy of the monks who originally drained the land.

**Comité Départemental du Tourisme en Deux-Sèvres**
19, Rue Thiers
79000 Niort Cedex
Tel: 05 49 77 19 70
www.tourisme-deux-seures.com

**Touring:**
AA Road Map France series 4: Poitou-Charantes

*The Marais Poitevin is a secluded area divided up by an extensive network of canals. It is said that to this day not all of the 15,000 hectares of wet marshes have been fully explored.*

## Abbaye de St-Pierre

Situated right in the middle of the Marais Poitevin is the town of Maillezais, best known for the ruins of the Abbaye de St-Pierre, just outside the town. The abbey was originally built on an island in the 11th century and added to during the 14th and 16th centuries. In summer it is used for a dramatic *son et lumière*.

## Château de Coudray-Salbart

About 6km north of Niort, on a rocky cliff overlooking the valley of the Sèvre Niortaise, are the ruins of the château, built by the lords of Parthenay in the 13th century. It is built in the form of an irregular quadrilateral with six towers. One of these, the Tour Double, has walls over 6m thick.

## Coulon

In the heart of the Marais Poitevin's wet marshes is the village of Coulon, with its low houses typical of the region. Each house has its own small canal, and many farmers still rely on flat-bottomed punts for transport. Coulon is the best

*The remains of the 11th-century abbey of St-Pierre, near Maillezais. Boat trips can be taken from the quay at the abbey.*

place to hire a punt to explore the whole area.

The area is now classified as a regional nature park. You can spot eels, pike, herons, snipe, duck, orioles, kingfishers and many other forms of wildlife. World-wide interest in ecology is making this once relatively isolated area much more popular with tourists. Nevertheless it remains largely unspoiled, and has a slightly mysterious quality, owing to the fact that it is neither entirely land nor sea.

*At Coulon, as elsewhere in the Marais Poitevin, punts provide a relaxing means of transport. The light filters gently through the poplar, ash and willow trees that line the tranquil canals.*

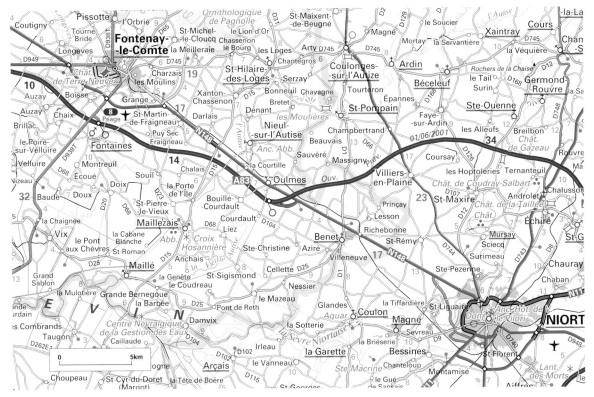

## MARAIS POITEVIN FOOD

The Marais Poitevin has a whole host of regional specialities when it comes to food and drink. Many include salt and cognac, which is produced nearby. Eels cooked in red wine sauce and snails in wine are very popular. Saddle of young goat with green garlic, mutton leg and local ham rubbed with salt and cognac are also local favourites. Meals are often served with *mojettes*, kidney beans, cooked in local butter, which is made from pasteurised cream. Goat's cheeses served with raspberry sauce make a rich ending to the meal. The whole region is proud of its goat's cheeses, which come in many different shapes.

## Fontenay-le-Comte

Once the capital of lower Poitou, this town was given its motto by François I. It is engraved on the Renaissance Quatre-Tias fountain: 'Fountain and source of great minds'. During the Renaissance many influential writers and poets, including François Rabelais, lived here Today the old town still has many 16th- and 17th-century manor houses, as well as a château and a local history museum. Even the tourist office is sited in an old toll-house, and pretty walks abound.

## Nieul-sur-l'Autise

This village is worth visiting for its Romanesque church, established in the 11th century. It has the only complete Romanesque cloister remaining in the entire Poitou region, and there are some good capitals on the main doorway.

## Niort

A busy town situated on the Sèvre Niortaise, Niort once boasted a Plantagenet castle rumoured to be built by Henry II and Richard the Lionheart. All that remains is the keep (Le Donjon), but it has a museum of Poitevin costumes where you can see jewellery, costumes and old tools.

Niort was once a thriving port and traded extensively with Canada. It also used to cultivate angelica and the local drink, *angélique de Niort*, dates from this time. Other local dishes include *matelotte des anguilles* (eels fried then baked in a wine sauce) and *mojettes à la maraîchaine* (kidney beans). Today the town's biggest industry is insurance, and many of France's major insurance companies have their headquarters here.

The town has a number of interesting museums, including the Musée des Beaux-Arts, with several Dutch old masters in the gallery, and old houses. However, like so many of the towns in the Marais Poitevin, its chief attraction is its water, in this case the Sèvre Niortaise. There are also some very pretty walks near the town.

The river makes an attractive setting for the Regional Arts and Crafts Centre on Quai Cronstadt, which displays the best of the area's creative work, while just across the river, in the Moulin du Roc National Theatre are two concert halls, three exhibition galleries and one of the oldest libraries in France, which is also a national ethnological centre.

## St Pompain

This is the site of one of the many Romanesque churches in the area. Monks were among the first settlers in the marshlands. The very first canal was called the Canal des Cinq Abbayes. These five abbeys were built on the first 'islands' left by the departing sea.

## OYSTERS AND MUSSELS

A luxury in most parts of the world, oysters are everyday fare on the Atlantic Coast. But they need a lot of care and attention and can take four years to mature. In the autumn lime-washed clutches are placed in oyster parks. After 10 months they are transferred to oyster beds, then to *claires*, running water beds where they fatten. Oyster farmers must continually clean out the algae and weeds that inhibit the growth of the oysters.

Their green exterior colour comes from a seaweed, the *navicule bleue*.

Mussels are grown on *bouchots*, wooden posts planted in the open sea to which the broods stick and grow. The traditional way to cook mussels is to place them upright on a wooden board, cover them with pine needles and then set these alight.

# POITIERS AND CHURCH ARCHITECTURE

The rolling plains around Poitiers, with their crops of wheat and maize, have been marched across by many invaders over the centuries. Moors, Arabs, Visigoths and the English have sought control of the area and have left a rich legacy for today's tourist, particularly of religious architecture. Poitiers itself used to be on the pilgrims' route to Santiago de Compostela and lay at the heart of Eleanor of Aquitaine's domain.

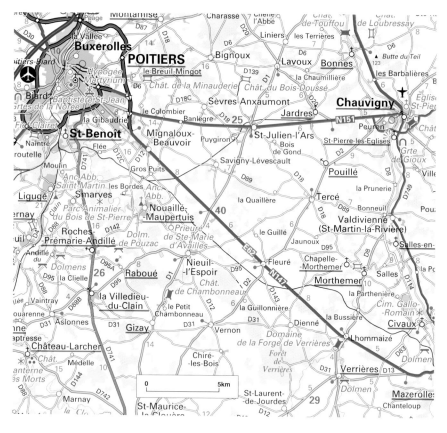

## Chauvigny

This town boasts the ruins of five medieval castles set alongside the 11th-century Église St-Pierre, grouped together on a hill overlooking the town. The sculpted capitals of the church are justifiably famous, depicting scenes that are the stuff of nightmares – for example, a Siamese twin being gnawed by monsters!

Try to visit Chauvigny on a Saturday, when its lively and colourful market is in full swing. On the river at the far south end of the town, St-Pierre-les-Églises has some 9th-century frescos.

## Civaux

Civaux, a tiny hamlet on the west bank of the Vienne, has a 12th-century church in the middle of a Merovingian

**Comité Départemental du Tourisme de la Vienne**
1 bis Rue Victor Hugo
86000 Poitiers
Tel: 05 49 37 48 48
www.vienne.org

**Touring:**
AA Road Map France series 3: Pays de Loire, and 4: Poitou-Charantes

## Chapelle-Morthemer

To get an idea of the immense power wielded by the barons of Poitou in the Middle Ages you have only to visit the château and church of Morthemer. Built on a massive scale, they tower somewhat menacingly over the little village and valley of the Dive. The buildings date back to the 14th century, though architecture buffs will notice that the church has a strange mixture of Gothic and Romanesque styles. There are frescos of Christ and the Virgin, from when the church was first built. Another of the church's claims to fame is the 16th-century tomb of Renée Sangler.

The most striking aspect of the château is its rectangular, turreted keep. Among the many who no doubt came to a sorry end in this gloomy prison was one John Chandos, a lieutenant of England's Black Prince who was wounded in the battler of Lussac.

cemetery. Here was once a city of the dead with 20,000 tombs. Today there are still 2,000 4th- and 5th-century sarcophagi containing the remains of those who fought valiantly to hold this land.

### CHURCH MURALS

Some 20km to the east of Chauvigny is the small town of St Savin. Its abbey church, probably built in the 11th century on the site of a church founded earlier by Charlemagne, contains what is believed to be the finest example of Romanesque murals in France, if not in Europe. The wall paintings, which have been designated a UNESCO Heritage Site, include scenes from Genesis and Exodus, including Noah's Ark and workmen building the Tower of Babel. In the summer there are daily guided tours. While in St Savin you should also visit the international centre for mural art and the medieval bridge over the River Gartempe, from where you get a beautiful view of the abbey church and its Gothic spire.

*St-Pierre-les-Églises at Chauvigny boasts fine relief carvings*

## FUTUROSCOPE

In Jaunay-Clan, 7km north of Poitiers, is Futuroscope (below), Europe's first park devoted to technology: France's answer to the USA's Epcot Center. Its numerous attractions include: a Kinemax cinema with a 600sq-m screen; a 3-D cinema; the 'Magic Carpet' cinema, with a screen under your feet; a 'dynamic' cinema where spectators' seats react to the picture – for example, they shake when an earthquake is shown; a Gyrotour from which those with strong nerves can see the park from a rotating tower at a height of 45m; and an 'enchanted lake' with fountains. Behind the scenes, not open to the public, Futuroscope has a serious side and includes a research centre, university and telecommunications centre.

*There is a heavy concentration of ancient and beautiful churches around Poitiers. In the heart of the city is the 12th century Notre-Dame-la-Grande.*

## Nouaillé-Maupertuis

Every June there is a medieval festival in the town to commemorate the battle between England's victorious Black Prince and John the Good (Jean II), during the Hundred Years War. Even if you miss the festival, the town is still worth a visit. There is a Romanesque church with a 12th-century belfry, and a Benedictine abbey surrounded by walls, a moat with fortifications and a medieval garden.

## Poitiers

Set on a hill overlooking the Rivers Clain and Boivre, Poitiers used to be the capital of the Poitou region. From a distance it does not look inspiring. However, once you are inside the old city – and plenty of it remains – Poitiers reveals its true charms.

Historians rate it as one of France's most important cities, particularly for Romanesque art. In the Middle Ages it was a very important commercial and religious centre, at one time hosting 67 churches.

One of the most famous sites in Poitiers is the Église Notre-Dame-la-Grande, a 12th-century church originally built in the reign of Eleanor of Aquitaine. The sculptures on the outside, particularly the western front, are a masterpiece of

Romanesque art. Today the church is surrounded by an open-air market where you can buy some of the goat's cheeses for which the area is famed. A short walk away is the Cathédrale St-Pierre, Poitiers' largest church. This has some spectacular 12th-century stained glass windows, and its wooden choir-stalls are believed to be the oldest in France.

Other Romanesque churches worth visiting include St-Hilaire, Ste-Radegonde and St-Porchaire. The oldest building in Poitiers is the 4th-century Baptistère St-Jean. Try to see also: the French, Flemish and Italian paintings in the Musée Ste-Croix (the museum also has a section devoted to the history of Poitou – a useful prelude to a tour of the historical sites); the palace of the counts of Poitou; and the half-timbered houses of Rue de la Chaîne. Also worth visiting is the 7th-century subterranean chapel, the Hypogée des Dunes, and the Pierre Levée dolmen, where Rabelais once scratched his name. The more modern – that is 19th-century – building of the Palais de Justice encloses a medieval tower and parts of a ducal palace where Joan of Arc was cross-examined.

*The 4th-century Baptistère St-Jean is France's oldest Christian church.*

# BERRY AND LIMOUSIN

Aforgotten region ignored by tourists in favour of the more spectacular, Berry and Limousin have few great monuments and little dramatic scenery. Nor is the area renowned for its food or wine. Yet the few that know better call it paradise. It has bred some of the greatest cultural achievements in France – Limoges enamel and porcelain and the Aubusson tapestries, to name but three – and inspired deep devotion in writers and artists, natives and visitors alike.

'I prefer to have a nettle in my Berry than a magnificent oak tree in any other place,' declared Georges Sand, the region's most famous daughter. The sentiment might sound extravagant, but it has long been shared by countless others.

Berry and Limousin lie at the heart of France. They also have a good claim to being its historic centre. As far back as the 6th century BC, Bourges, then known as Avaric, was a thriving Celtic city. At the collapse of the Roman Empire this was the first area settled by the Franks, who gave France its name. During the lengthy struggles leading up to and forming part of the Hundred Years War, it was within the island of land that was never ruled by England. In 1429 the Duc de Berry became Charles VII of France, the monarch who finally found the resources and the strength to drive the English out of France.

Since then, the region's historic importance has faded. Limoges is the only city of any real size, and the only major industrial centre. Visitors today find themselves in a gentle agricultural backwater dotted by small market towns and tiny villages, modest châteaux and minute Romanesque churches. In the north the great plain of Berry-Champagne is an area of open skies and prairie-like fields of wheat, framed with scarlet when the poppies are in flower. Further south the landscape gently gives way to rolling pasture patchworked by hedges and oak woodland. Creamy Charentais cows and russet Berry goats graze quietly while eagles and hawks swoop high above the fields. Wild boar and deer still roam the forest reserves.

Four main rivers – the Cher, the Indre, the Creuse and the Vienne – meander languidly across the limestone plateau, feeding the crops and drawing the tourists. Many of these come also for the water sports on the two main lakes, Chambon and Vassivière. But by contrast with the more famous neighbouring areas, here there are no great armies of tourists, no batteries of souvenir stalls, no vast complexes of holiday homes. Yet the area has plenty to offer sightseers and those who prefer to take it easy.

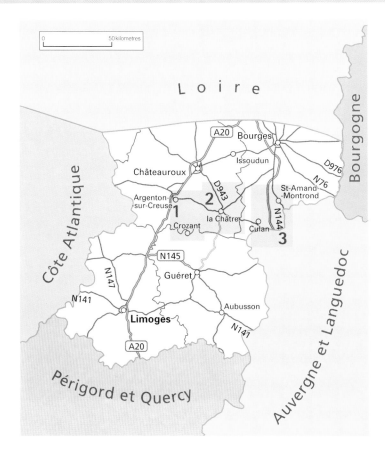

*Berry is famed for the cheese produced by its russet goats (left).*
*Georges Sand and Chopin stayed in the Château de Culan (left below).*
*Sunflower crop (left, bottom)*

*In a region so fond of meat as Berry and Limousin, the butcher, like this robust-looking character from the old quarter of Chénérailles, near Montluçon, plays an important role in everyday life.*

*Wine-growers in Berry (top) produce a number of good red, white and rosé wines (above).*

# ALONG THE CREUSE VALLEY

U nlike the gentle countryside near by, this stretch of the Creuse (literally 'hollow') cuts deep into the granite hills to create a long series of spectacular gorges beloved of many artists, including Rousseau and Monet. There are several historic sights of great interest, but this area is renowned above all for its scenery and as a centre for water sports.

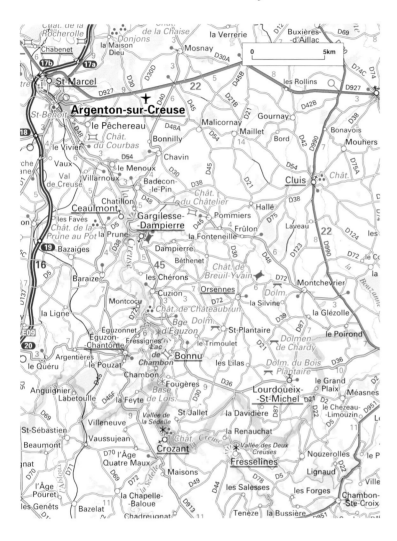

## Château de Crozant

The fortress at Crozant was once one of the largest and most important in France. Built between the 13th and 15th centuries, it has walls over half a kilometre long, ten towers and a garrison of several thousand.

The château played a key role in the defence of Limousin and Aquitaine during the Hundred Years War (1337–1453) and the Wars of Religion (1562–98). However, severe damage, sustained both in battle and during an earthquake, meant that it was already in ruins by the 17th century. Nevertheless it remains one of the most spectacular sights in the region, since it is set high on a promontory overlooking the gorges of the Creuse and the Sedelle.

*The ruins of the château at Crozant. Overgrown footpaths lead between the ivy-clad remnants of towers that still cling precariously to the wooded cliffs. There are magnificent views from the fortress.*

## Fresselines

The little cliff-top village of Fresselines has an august artistic pedigree: Monet, Rousseau and Rodin all worked here. It was also for a long time the home of the 19th-century poet and musician Maurice Rollinat, to whom there are two memorials: a bas-relief by Rodin in the back wall of the church, and a bust by Paul Surtel.

From the bridge over the Petite Creuse on the road to Nouzerolles, there are good views of both Fresselines and the Château de Puyguillon.

## GOAT'S CHEESE

The one great claim of this area to gastronomic fame is its goat's cheese. There are six varieties, both hard and soft, all made from whole milk, with a creamy texture. None is strong. The best known is the *crottin*, which is the shape of a flat-topped cone. Its name comes from the small, clay oil lamp of the same shape that was at one time used in the area. The best cheese is said to come from the milk of the smooth-haired Berry goat.

**Comité Départemental du Tourisme de l'Indre**
1, Rue St Martin
36003 Châteauroux
Cedex
Tel: 02 54 07 36 36
www. berrylindre.com

**Touring:**
AA Road Map France series 4: Poitou-Charantes, and 8: Centre

## Argenton-sur-Creuse

This bustling market town grew up at the foot of a vast fortress built in 761 by Pepin the Short, King of the Franks. Today only a few sections of the château walls and its chapel remain. The chapel was built in the 15th century on the site of the 2nd-century sanctuary of St Ursin, the first Bishop of Berry. In 1899 it was topped by a vast, gilded statue of La Bonne Dame d'Argenton. More than 6m high and weighing six tonnes, this has become the main local landmark. There is a panoramic view of the town from the terrace by the chapel, and from the Vieux Pont there are views of old riverside houses and mills.

*Well preserved 13th- and 15th-century frescos decorate the walls of the crypt of Notre-Dame-de-Gargilesse. The novelist George Sand gave a description of Gargilesse as it was in the last century in her* Promenade autour d'un village.

## Gargilesse-Dampierre

One of the prettiest villages in Berry, Gargilesse–Dampierre is tucked away in a steep river valley. Probably the best view of the village, as well as of the confluence of the Rivers Gargilesse and Creuse and the iron Pont Noir, is from just across the bridge over the Creuse.

It is a place of narrow streets and stone-built, geranium-clad cottages, liberally sprinkled with artists' studios. At the end of one alley is 'Algira', the small cottage bought for George Sand as a writing retreat by her lover, Alexandre Manceau. Today the cottage is a museum, with mementoes and work by both George Sand and her son, Maurice Sand.

The 18th-century château contains an exhibition gallery. In its grounds is the Romanesque Notre-Dame-de-Gargilesse, which has magnificent frescos and carvings. There are 129 capitals, all different. The themes include the Old Men of the Apocalypse, Old and New Testament stories and decorative designs. All are finely carved and in a remarkably good state of preservation. The frescos in the crypt date from the 13th and 15th centuries. Those in the apse and the two side chapels are still glorious. Centred round a huge portrait of Christ at the Apocalypse are scenes from the life of Christ and the Old Testament, and the patron saints of the various donors.

## Lac de Chambon

This lake was created by the Barrage d'Éguzon, which, when it came into operation in 1926, was one of the first major dams to be built in Europe. Built primarily as a hydroelectric project, the dam is 59m high and 300m wide. There is an excellent view from beside the power station above the dam wall.

The narrow, 16-km long lake has become a major water-sports centre with its activities centred on Éguzon. This was once a fortified medieval village, although only the château's gateway remains as a sign of its illustrious past. Near here are a beach and a nautical club where you can swim or hire boats. The small roads round the lake do not follow the shoreline, but there are frequent access points.

## Le Pin

About 2km north of Gargilesse–Dampierre, near the tiny hamlet of Les Chocats, there is a superb view over the Creuse gorges. Nicknamed Le Boucle, this stretch of the river loops tightly around the promontory of Le Pin in a last flamboyant gesture before leaving the granite hills for the gentle, flatter plain of Berry-Champagne. High on the opposite cliff, the Romanesque church you can see belongs to the village of Ceaulmont.

## CRAFTS

Fine enamels have been produced in Limoges since the 12th century. Early work was all *champlevé* ware, with the enamel being layered into hollows on an engraved copper base. Since the 14th century, however,

Limoges has produced painted enamels. Porcelain production in the region was first made possible by the discovery of local kaolin deposits in 1768, allowing for the first time in France the production of delicate hard-paste porcelains based on a mixture of kaolin and sand. The first porcelain factory in Limoges was founded in 1771. Today Limoges produces more than half France's china.

# GEORGE SAND AND THE VALLÉE NOIRE

B ut for George Sand, few would have heard of the Vallée Noire. The novelist set a series of pastoral romances here, creating an image of rural bliss. The farmers might no longer wear smocks, but this stretch of the Indre still exudes a sense of calm well-being that makes it easy to understand the writer's deep devotion to her lifelong home.

## Château de Nohant

George Sand lived and worked in this rather run-down 18th-century château for most of her life. Here she gathered around her an artistic and literary circle of extraordinary talent, including Chopin, Liszt, Balzac, Flaubert, Dumas and Delacroix.

Now a museum, the château feels as if time has stood still since Sand's death. Faded place cards stand on the dining table, her pens wait to be to be picked up again and the curtain is ready to rise in the tiny theatre where she tried out her plays in front of a local audience before taking them to Paris. Georges Sand died at Nohant in 1876 and is buried in the family plot in the grounds of the château.

There are two piano festivals at Nohant each year, in June and July, the latter dedicated to the music of Frédéric Chopin, who lived with Sand from 1838–47.

*The keep, with its tiled pepper-pot towers, is all that has survived of the Château de Sarzay. In her novel* Le Meunier d'Angibault *George Sand refers to this château as Blanchemont.*

## Château de Sarzay

Built in the mid-14th century by Matthieu de Barbançois, the Château de Sarzay was in its prime a vast, moated edifice covering five hectares, with 38 towers and two drawbridges. All that remains today is the keep, a rectangular building with four circular corner towers, the fortified chapel and fragments of the outer wall. Even so, the château is remarkably impressive, its sombre elegance visible for several kilometres on every approach.

The current owners live in the farmhouse next door, the approach to which is through an attractive working farmyard. Inside, a thick layer of dust over the simple furnishings, together with the signs warning of ongoing restoration, give it an intensely atmospheric air, part building site, part fairy-tale castle. There are magnificent views over the surrounding countryside from the turrets.

## La Châtre

Although it has a population of only just over 5,000, this little market town is the main centre on this stretch of the Indre. It is a charming place, built round a central market square, with a fine collection of half-timbered, 15th-century buildings as well as a number of 17th- and 18th-century stone houses.

The keep, which is all that remains of the 15th-century Château de Chauvigny, now houses the eccentric Musée George Sand et de la Vallée Noire, with a collection of 3,000 stuffed birds and a floor devoted to George Sand, with photos, original manuscripts, letters and first editions. The second floor is given over to the work of local artists.

In August the town echoes to the sound of hammers, as the annual stone carving competition takes place.

### LA BONNE DAME DE NOHANT

George Sand (1804–76) was born Aurore Dupin. Her father had royal blood, her mother was the daughter of a bird seller. Married briefly and unhappily to Baron Dudevant, she went on to live with various other lovers, both in Paris and at her family home of Nohant. She took her pen-name from Jules Sandeau, the lover with whom she collaborated on writing her first novel.

Today George Sand is commonly remembered both as Chopin's mistress and as a great eccentric (she occasionally wore trousers and a top hat and smoked cigars). During her life,

*La Châtre is an important market town in the heart of the Vallée Noire.*

**Comité Départemental
du Tourisme de l'Indre**
1, Rue St Martin
36003 Châteauroux
Cedex
Tel: 02 54 07 36 36
www. berrylindre.com

**Touring:**
AA Road Map France
series 8: Centre, and
9: Auvergne, Limousin

however, her reputation as a writer was immense, and she enjoyed simultaneous critical and popular acclaim.

Sand was extremely prolific, writing 28 plays, and over 100 other works including 80 novels. Some 20,000 of her letters have also been published. May of her peers, from Dostoevsky to George Eliot, openly acknowledged her influence on their work. She was a committed socialist and remained politically active for most of her life. Although George Sand did not regard herself as a feminist, she was an early and influential exponent of women's rights.

In Berry George Sand still enjoys the state of a saint; she is 'La Bonne Dame de Nohant'.

## Neuvy-St-Sépulchre

Neuvy-St-Sépulchre lies about 20km to the west of La Châtre and there is a story attached to its name. When Eude de Déols came home from pilgrimage in the Holy Land in 1042, he was so taken with Jerusalem that he decided to build a copy of the Holy Sepulchre. The result is this extraordinary little basilica. The 22-m two-storey rotunda has a central ring of 11 heavy columns with fine sculptured capitals, and seven apsidal chapels around the outer wall. Above, a somewhat lighter ambulatory surrounds a central dome. An exhibition of sacred art is held here every summer. A central altar is placed directly under the dome. The iron strapwork door at the entrance dates from the 12th century.

The basilica was built on to an existing rectangular church with several small side chapels. This was to be demolished until word cam from Jerusalem that the Holy Sepulchre had been extended, when it was decided to leave it in place. It was vaulted over in the 13th century and has been restored many times since. The resulting church is fascinating, if somewhat awkward, its two halves being forced by design to function separately. A few old buildings surrounding it are all that now remain of the canons' cloisters that were once attached to the church.

## St Chartier

Chiefly famous as the setting of George Sand's novel *Les Maîtres Sonneurs*, this is a small attractive village with a pretty but undistinguished church that was heavily restored in the 19th century, and a 14th century château, not open to the public. Each summer, however, it hosts a major international folk festival that keeps alive local musical and dance traditions. There are concerts and demonstrations by makers of bagpipes, lutes and hurdy-gurdies, all of which were traditionally made in the area.

## Ste Sévère-sur-Indre

Perched on a cliff top overlooking the Indre, this pretty village has had an eventful history. Founded in AD 630 around an abbey long since vanished, it was later ruled by bandits, was sacked twice, and during the Revolution became a commune. In the central square are a 15th-century fortified gateway a 16th-century stone cross and an open-sided 17th-century market hall, as well as other old buildings.

*In Berry and Limousin most people still live close to the soil (top).*

*The ancient beamed market hall in Ste Sévère-sur-Indre (above)*

# THE ROUTE JACQUES-COUR

The Berrichons have given the name of Jacques Coeur, the most famous son of the great medieval city of Bourges, to a route that carves its way through the heart of France. Few of the châteaux and churches along the way have any historical connection with Jacques Coeur, but together they paint a fascinating picture of French history, from the fearsome fortresses of the 11th century to the studied frivolity of the 18th.

**Comité Départemental du Tourisme du Cher**
5, Rue de Séricourt
18000 Bourges
Tel: 02 48 48 00 10
www.berrylecher.com

**Touring:**
AA Road Map France
series 8: Centre

*The cloisters of the abbey at Noilac. At its height Noirlac's 150 monks and 150 lay brothers spent eight hours a day in church, starting at 2am.*

## JACQUES COEUR

Despite humble origins in Bourges, Jacques Coeur made a fortune and became Master of the Mint to Charles VII, and thus one of the most powerful men in France. In 1451 jealous rivals falsely accused him of murdering the king's mistress, and the king seized his fortune and exiled him. But in 1457, a year after Jacques' death, Charles finally acknowledged his innocence.

## Abbaye de Noirlac

Founded in 1150 by Abbot Robert de Clairvaux, a cousin of St Bernard, the abbey at Noirlac, set in a peaceful river valley, is the only French Cistercian monastery to have survived almost intact.

The vast, austere abbey church has no capitals, sculpture or paintings, and its windows are of grisaille glass, yet its simple arches have immense grace and its honey-coloured stone lends warmth and charm. Only three sides of the more elaborate 13th- and 14th-century cloister, with its ogival arches and traced windows, have survived.

## Bruère-Allichamps

Since 1865 this little village on the banks of the Cher has been officially recognised as the geographical centre of France. It has a monument to prove it.

Yet France has three hearts, say the diplomatic Berrichons, for two other nearby villages, Saulzais-le-Potier and Vesdun, hotly contest the honour – and they also have monuments to prove it.

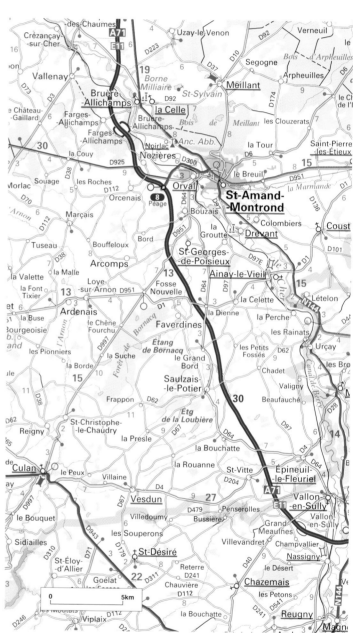

## Château d'Ainay-le-Vieil

This small, octagonal, moated fortress is by some nicknamed 'little Carcassonne'. Originally built in the 13th century, its nine towers and rampart walls have all survived intact. It was owned briefly by Jacques Coeur, then sold in 1467 to the Bigny family, who still own it today. In the late-

*Restored in recent years, the Château de Culan (above) has a number of attractions, including exhibitions of medieval weapons of war and tapestries from several countries.*

*The extravagant external ornament of Meillant (above right) is matched by the attention to detail inside the château. In addition, the chapel in the courtyard has a beautiful 16th-century Rhenish altarpiece.*

15th century they built an Italianate Renaissance château into the wall. This has a small, highly decorated octagonal tower at the entrance and magnificent painted coffered ceilings in the main public rooms.

In the grounds a beautiful rose garden includes a number of old species, some of them dating back to the 15th century, as well as some scented and newer varieties.

A tiny but charming village is tucked under the château's walls.

## Château de Culan

The setting of the Château de Culan is one of the most dramatic in this area: perched heavily on a cliff top over the gorge of the River Arnon, dominating both the town and its approaches. The château was begun in the 11th century, but only one side of the original massive, rectangular fortress still exists. This remnant is forbidding enough, with the circular towers at its corners in perfect condition, complete with roof and machicolations. The inner face and lower levels of the château were rebuilt in the 17th century, to create an elegant and comfortable stately home.

The tour follows the centuries, with displays of 13th- and 14th-century armour, 17th- and 18th-century salons with fine Flemish and Aubusson tapestries, and a look at the bedroom used by Georges Sand and Chopin on their many visits. There are magnificent views over the valley from the terrace, and of the château itself from the bridge on the Montluçon road.

## Château de Meillant

The Romans first settled Meillant as a garrison town. The village today is an attractive if slightly dilapidated place, with buildings that date back to the 17th century.

The present château, an architectural gem, has its origins in the early 14th century moated fortress built by Étienne de Sancerre. In the late 15th century the Amboise family destroyed much of the rampart wall, incorporating some of the medieval towers into the south face of their new château. The curved east façade is a riot of decoration, a perfect example of 'flowering' or High Gothic architecture that nevertheless foretells the more classical lines of the Renaissance. Particularly spectacular is the central Tour du Lion (so called because of the small lead lion on its roof), which was designed by Giocondon, a close colleague of Michelangelo. The chapel and well date from the 16th century.

Inside, the sumptuously decorated rooms have a festive air. Especially notable are the dining-room, with hand-painted, embossed wallpaper, carved, painted frieze, painted ceiling and stained-glass windows, and the medieval Great Hall with is wooden ceiling and vast, formidable bosses of knights in armour.

## BOURGES

The capital of Berry, Bourges is a medieval masterpiece, a warren of cobbled streets lined with beautiful buildings, from humble stone cottages to timber-framed shops and grand palaces. The huge Cathédrale St-Étienne, built between 1135 and 1324, is one of the finest in France, with a series of magnificent stained-glass medallion windows (1215–25) in the apse. The Palais Jacques Coeur,

commissioned in 1443 but not completed until after his disgrace, is grander than many royal palaces of the period. Other attractions include the 16th-century Hôtel Cujas, containing the archaeological and folklore collections of the Musée du Berry.

# Auvergne and Languedoc

Though well below the high Alps and the Pyrenees in altitude, and lower than the peaks of Haute-Provence, the Auvergne and Languedoc region is thought of by many intending visitors as mountainous. This is because Auvergne in particular is synonymous with the Massif Central. Although they quickly change their minds, they are never disappointed, for what the region lacks in height and snowy peaks it more than makes up for in the sheer diversity of its scenery. Close to Clermont-Ferrand is the Parc Régional des Volcans d'Auvergne with its range of ancient volcanic cones.

Further south, the scenery of the Cévennes is so special that the area is designated a Parc National, one of only seven in France, and is the only non-alpine such park on the mainland. Close by are the Causses, a huge area of raised limestone pavements that create a virtual rocky desert, the heart of which has been honeycombed by rainwater to produce some of the finest show caves in the world.

Between and around those high land blocks, the valley and plan scenery is equally good. Auvergne, which lies to the north of Languedoc, starts with Bourbonnais, a gently rolling pastoral area surrounding the towns of Vichy and Montluçon. Vichy was, and is, a spa town. By contrast, Montluçon is a large industrial city.

Here we concentrate on that part of Auvergne below Clermont-Ferrand, exploring the unique scenery touched on above. Clermont-Ferrand is a sprawling industrial city, but it does have its points of interest, in particular the Basilique de Notre-Dame-du-Port, believed by many to be the finest example of Auvergne Romanesque architecture.

We also explore southern Auvergne, an emptier landscape where the visitor can the more easily appreciate the feel of the countryside. At inns in or between the villages and small towns the visitor can sample the enticing local foods. Auvergne is said to be the cheeseboard of France, such is the variety and quality of its cheeses. Then there is *potée auvergnate*, a stew of salt pork and vegetables; and Auvergne claims to have invented *coq au vin*.

To the south we enter Languedoc, an empty, secret land of lush valleys and low, wooded hills. This is beautiful country, so very different from Provence to the east, even if the menus of the two areas occasionally look very similar. To taste the difference, try *cassoulet*, a casserole of pork and haricot beans spiced with garlic and herbs, or *cousinat*, a stew of chestnuts (a local speciality), cream and fruit. Montpellier, the area's largest city, well planned and attractive, lies close to the Mediterranean.

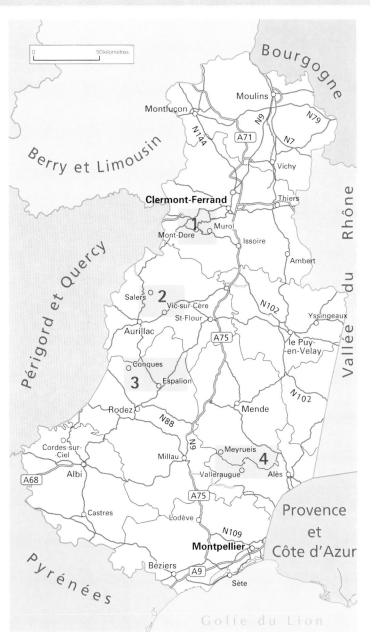

Of the more than 100 volcanoes of the Monts Dômes, the Puy de Dôme (above) is the oldest. The Salers (below left) is a hardy breed of cow – nowadays very popular throughout France.

The region's many markets offer fresh local produce and provide a good meeting place.

Much of Auvergne and Languedoc is an agricultural region, whose inhabitants are fond of the outdoor life.

# THE MONTS DORE

To the west of Clermont-Ferrand lies the Parc Régional des Volcans d'Auvergne, one of the most spectacular landscapes in France. The old volcanoes are laid out in a chain, with the Monts du Cantal to the south and the region's oldest and best known peak, the Puy de Dôme, lying to the north. Between these two are the Monts Dore, a superb piece of country, with impressive peaks hovering above equally fine villages.

**Comité Départemental du Tourisme du Puy-de-Dôme**
Place de la Bourse
63000 Clermont-Ferrand
Tel: 04 73 42 22 50
www.planetepuydudome.com

**Touring:**
AA Road Map France series 9: Auvergne, Limousin

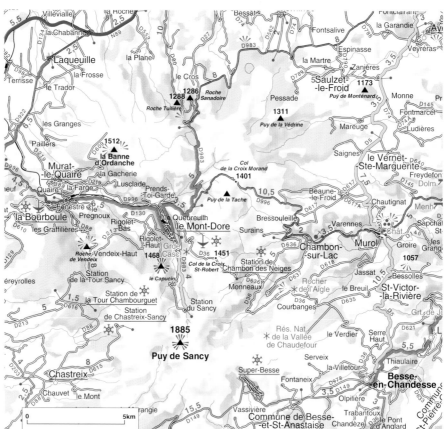

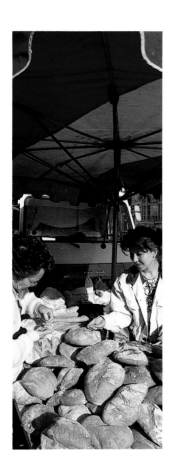

*In an area of scattered rural communities the market town is an essential feature.*

## Besse-en-Chandesse

The old and picturesque town of Besse-en-Chandesse was fortified in medieval times, though of the defences only the 16th-century Porte de Ville and the Tour de la Prison remain. The town is also famous for its production of St-Nectaire cheese. Modernity is represented by the nearby centre for the study of plants and animals, an outpost of the university at Clermont-Ferrand, and the new winter-sports complex of Super-Besse. The best of the old town is seen in the Rue de la Boucherie, where the delightful houses are built of black lava. The Maison de la Reine Margot is said to be named after Marguerite de Valois, wife of Henry IV. The Église St-André is, in part, 12th-century and is famous for its 16th-century choir-stalls and the ancient statue of Notre-Dame de Vassivière.

## La Bourboule

Though it has been a recognised thermal centre since the 15th century, La Bourboule was really only developed as a spa town in the early 19th century, so that little of it is more than 150 years old. Nevertheless it is a delightful spot, with pleasant bridges over the youthful River Dordogne, and the airy Parc Fenêstre. The spa water has the highest arsenic content of any in Europe, though it is still recommended as a medicine rather than banned as a poison.

From the Parc Fenêstre, with its fine river and lakeside strolls, a cableway serves the Plateau de Charlannes, where there is winter skiing and summer walking. It is possible to walk to the top of the Rocher des Fés, the 50-m granite mass that dominates La Bourboule. There is a fine view of the town from there.

*La Bourboule, seen from the River Dordogne. The Rocher des Fés gives a contrasting panoramic view that many prefer.*

*A six-hour walk from La Bourboule will take the serious walker to the top of the Puy de Sancy, at 1,885m the highest peak in the Monts Dore range, from where there are spectacular vistas.*

## Col de Guéry

Those travelling north from Le Mont-Dore pass the Lac de Guéry, a high (1,244m) lake formed when a volcanic lava flow blocked the river valley. Further on is the Col de Guéry, a little higher at 1,264m. From here there is a tremendous view of the valley, looking towards Rochefort-Montagne.

## Le Mont-Dore

Although beautifully located, Le Mont-Dore is purely a spa town, with a single and very particular reason for its existence: a ready supply of natural hot water.

The town has a long history: there was a Roman settlement around the spring and perhaps even a Gallo–Celtic one before that. Those who are interested in the thermal station itself can take a guided tour.

## Monts Dore and Puy de Sancy

The Monts Dore are the glaciated remains of a late Tertiary volcanic range, the volcanoes therefore being around three million years old, though the glaciers retreated only 10,000 years ago. The highest of the Monts Dore peaks, and also the highest peak of the Massif Central, is Puy de Sancy (1,885m). The peak is the source of the River Dordogne, and its summit is easily reached by cableway. Leave Le Mont-Dore southward on the D983 to reach a large car park and restaurant. From the top of the cableway there is a short walk to the summit proper, from where, on a clear day, the Dauphiné Alps can be seen, as well as virtually all the major local mountain groups.

## Murol

East of Le Mont-Dore is Murol, a delightful village set among trees, with a castle that seems out of all proportion to the village's size and position. The castle is both picturesque and interesting: it dates from the 13th century, with the final touches being added by the d'Estaings, one of Auvergne's noblest families. Among the family's 20th-century descendants is ex-President Valéry Giscard d'Estaing.

## Super-Besse and Lac Pavin

Close to Besse-en-Chandesse is the new winter-sports resort of Super-Besse, at an altitude of 1,350m. It has good facilities for both downhill and cross-country skiing, and is also a convenient centre for summer walkers. A cableway links the resort with the summit of the Puy de Sancy, and a road links it with Lac Pavin. The lake, with its surrounding roads and trees, is claimed to be the most beautiful in Auvergne – a title for which the competition is stiff – and is on the route of the GR4 and GR30 long-distance footpaths. It is a popular spot with anglers, for it is well stocked with trout and *omble chevalier*, a species of char sometimes referred to as mountain trout.

Lac Pavin is almost exactly circular and very deep – nearly 100m. Its name derives from the Latin *pavens*, frightening, because at one time it was said that if a stone were thrown into the lake violent local storms would threaten.

## BLACK VIRGINS

It is believed that the first 'Black Virgin' was brought back from the Holy Land by Louise IX on his return from the Seventh Crusade. The original statue was lost in a fire at the time of the Revolution – the one now seen in the cathedral at Le Puy-en-Velay is a 19th-century copy – but its influence can be seen in churches all over Auvergne.

Black Virgins were carved from walnut or cedar, which both age to almost jet-black. Originally the Byzantine icon style was used for the Virgin, but later statues used the faces of local girls for a more pleasing effect.

The Black Virgin of Besse-en-Chandesse is one of the most famous statues. Each year on the first Sunday in July the statue is carried in procession 3km uphill to the Chapelle de Vassivière, and on the Sunday after St Matthew's Day it is carried back down to Besse's church.

# MONTS DU CANTAL

At the southern end of the Parc Régional des Volcans d'Auvergne are the Monts du Cantal. It is now believed that the peaks of this range are the remnants of one massive volcano perhaps as much as 3,000m high and over 70km across the base. Wind, rain, and Ice Age glaciers have eroded the huge peak down to the *puys* we see today.

*The Monts du Cantal (top), of which the highest point is 1,855m, are thought to be the product of the erosion of a single, much higher volcano.*

*Salers (above), with its ornate, mainly 15th- and 16th-century houses, has a magical quality.*

## Monts du Cantal

At 1,885m the Plomb du Cantal is not as high as the Monts Dore's Puy de Sancy, but is still an impressive peak. It is also a good viewpoint, but by common consent the best panorama is provided by the summit of Puy Mary.

This top (at 1,787m) is reached in about 30 minutes from the Pas de Peyrol, at 1,582m the highest pass in the Massif Central. From Puy Mary the volcanic ruins of the Cantal peaks are seen to perfection, as are the results of later glaciation. Laid out below are numerous valleys, enclosing the rivers that drain the high peaks.

## St Cernin

This pretty village has a fine old church well known for the quality of its wooden panelling. To the west of St Cernin, a drive along the D43 and then the D9 reaches the excellent Gorges de la Maronne. Beyond lies the Château de Bronzac, a picturesque ruin set on a ridge above the same river.

## Salers

Make your way to the Grande-Place, the heart and centre of Salers, and look towards the church. This is a magical town: angled roofs set at all orientations, seemingly without order; turrets, chimneys and gables; an elegant bell enclosed in its wrought cage; old lamps and signs. It would be easy to see this small town, with around 600 inhabitants, as having been built to a design in a children's fairy-tale. Except, that is, for the dark, sombre nature of all the houses, which are built of the local lava.

Salers is set high, at 950m, which adds to the fairy-tale quality, and has almost no buildings from before the 15th century or after the 16th, which explains the architectural similarity among the apparent chaos. The earliest houses were built when the village was a refuge from bands of English soldiers and other ne'er-do-wells during the Hundred Years War. The later houses date from the time when it was a successful local market town. The Hôtel de Ville, in Grande-Place, was built in the 15th century, as was the nearby Maison de Bargues, though this house – which is open to the public – is furnished in 17th-century style. Another fine building is the Maison des Templiers, just off Grande-Place, which

## PARC NATIONAL DES VOLCANS D'AUVERGNE

About 60 million years ago, during the Tertiary era, the Massif Central was formed in the squeeze that created the Alps and Jura to the east, and the Pyrenees to the west. Faulting in the rocks of the Massif allowed magma from the earth's core to vent to the surface, creating volcanoes. This area's volcanic activity was neither continuous nor short and violent when it was in progress. In fact three distinct periods of activity are recognised. During the earliest, from 13 million to 3 million years ago, the volcanoes of the Monts du Cantal were active; from 6 million to 250,000 years ago those of the Monts Dore were erupting; while the youngest group, the volcanoes of the Monts Dômes, were probably still active when the earliest man arrived in the Auvergne.

The Volcano Park is, at 348,000 hectares, the largest park in France set up to protect natural scenery. Within it, all the best features of volcanoes are present – typical volcanic craters, crater lakes, hot springs and pillars of volcanic rock. The latter are produced by the erosion of softer rock from around the hard-rock intrusions. The most famous examples are at Le Puy-en-Velay, which in fact lies outside the Park's boundaries.

The hot springs were known to the Romans, and indeed many of Auvergne's spa towns sit on Roman foundations. The spa water emerges at about 40°C, heated by sub-surface contact with rocks still hot from volcanic activity.

The most famous of the volcanic areas is the Monts Dômes, where there are over 100 old volcanic vents spread

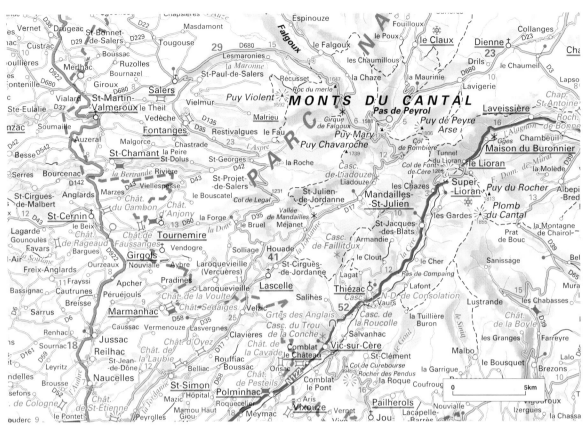

out in a 30-km ridge. The best known of these peaks is the Puy de Dôme. This has been an important pilgrimage site for thousands of years: it was a Gaulish holy site before the Romans built a temple to Mercury, and in the 12th century a chapel was erected on the summit. Part of the explanation for this mystical hold on the locals could be the surprisingly warm temperatures recorded at the peak.

*The town of Salers gave its name to a highly prized local breed of cattle*

houses a folklore museum. Go past the museum to reach the Esplanade de Barrouze and a wonderful view of the valleys below Puy Violent (1,592m).

Finally, the bust in Grande-Place is of Tyssandier d'Escous, the man responsible for obtaining countrywide recognition for the local breed of cattle, the Salers, which in France is now second only in popularity to the Charollais of Burgundy.

## Vallée de la Cère

Many believe that the Cère valley is the finest in the Cantal, and with its lush greenness and the fine gorges of the Pas de Cère and Pas de Company it is certainly a strong candidate. At Thiézac, a village between the gorges, the valley opens a little, so that the village is delightfully situated. The chapel above the village, Notre-Dame de Consolation, was visited by Anne of Austria, who prayed to a miraculous Virgin there for nine days.

At the valley head is Le Lioran, with the ski centre of Super-Lioran. A tunnel driven through the mountain here allows access to Murat even when snow blocks the high pass. The tunnel was hand-cut in 1839 and, at 1,412m, was the longest in France at the time.

## Vic-sur-Cère

This spa village is set in the lush lower region of the Cère valley. As a spa it was popular with the Romans, but achieved real fame as a result of a visit by Anne of Austria in 1837. Anne, wife of Louise XIII, was childless despite 22 years of marriage, and was doing the rounds of spas and miraculous statues of the Virgin in the hope of providing the king with a legitimate heir. In 1838 she gave birth to the prince who would become Louis XIV, the Sun King, though there are several other places on her itinerary of the year before that could presumably claim equal credit for the 'miracle'. A fine 15th-century house in the village is named after the Princes of Monaco, Louis XIII having given an area around the town to them.

South of the village is the Col de Curebourse, the Pass of the Cutpurses, a favourite haunt of highwaymen. Further on is the Rocher des Pendus where the highway robbers met their end by hanging after capture and sentence. The view from the rock is superb.

**Comité Départemental du Tourisme du Cantal**
11 Rue Paul Doumer, BP 8
15018 Aurillac Cedex
Tel: 04 71 46 22 00
www.cdt-cantal.fr

**Touring:**
AA Road Map France series 9: Auvergne, Limousin

# CONQUES AND THE VALLÉE DU LOT

The flat plain of Midi-Pyrénées lies between Auvergne and the Pyrenees themselves. Across it drains the River Lot, which rises in the Massif Central and links with the Garonne before heading off to Bordeaux. In its early stages the Lot flows through a beautiful gorge in charming countryside.

## Conques

*The ancient village of Conques was a major religious centre in the Middle Ages and is still on one of the principal pilgrimage routes through France to Santiago de Compostela in northern Spain.*

The highlight of the area is Conques, a truly delightful village of golden-brown houses beneath grey shingle roofs, which spills its way down the valleyside of the River Dourdou. At least as winning as the setting is the fact that Conques makes few concessions to tourists, who must make their own arrangements, not only about parking but also about accommodation, as there are few hotels (and even fewer souvenir shops) in the village. The visitor must wonder whether the same regard was paid to pilgrims in the 12th and 13th centuries, when Conques was one of France's leading pilgrimage centres. Then, the line of visitors sought the reliquary of St Foy in Conques before moving on to seek the indulgence of St James of Compostela.

The Église Ste–Foy is Conques' great treasure. It is built in 11th–12th-century Romanesque stylewith a tympanum that drawss experts from all over Europe. The work is above the west door and is a 12th century representation of the Last Judgement. St Foy is depicted on the left side (as viewed).

Within the church, the treasury holds the finest work, the church itself being either dignified or austere, depending on your taste. The complete treasury represents one of the finest collections of early-medieval religious art in France, but the main attraction is the 10th-century statue of St Foy, carved in wood, covered in gold and set with precious stones. The saint is seated, with a small vessel in each hand.

At the top end of the village is the recently opened European Centre for Medieval Art and Civilization, which has exhibitions in summer. Finally, for the best view of the village, take the D901 Rodez road and go left over the Dourdou after 500m to reach the Site du Bancarel.

## Entraygues-sur-Truyère

Although named after the Truyère, the village actually sits at the confluence of that river and the Lot. The Truyère is usually a limpid river at Entraygues, the clamour of its excellent gorge – best reached from the village – being far behind. As it enters Entraygues it is crossed by a beautiful bridge, built at the end of the 13th century and comprising heavy buttresses separated by pointed Norman arches. In the village there is a fine collection of old houses, especially in the pedestrian-only Rue Basse, which represents the old quarter. Beyond, an old castle stands at the point where the Truyère meets the Lot.

East of the village the summit of the Puy de Montabès, reached by a straightforward

## RURAL BUILDINGS

In Languedoc, to the south of the region, there is clay in the valleys and the houses are of brick, the roofs of clay tiles. This is a wine-growing area, the ground floors of the houses being wine 'cellars', the farmer and his family living on the first floor. The houses have small doors and windows so that the interior – and, most critically, the wine – is kept cool.

Further north the domestic architecture changes. In the Causses the walls and roofs are of limestone, as would be expected. What is not expected is that the roof trusses are also of limestone, for this countryside has few trees, and those stunted, making timber trusses a luxury. Since stone was in good supply the farmers had separate buildings for their animals, though the family still lived on the first floor, the lower floor being a tool shed. By contrast, in the Cévennes animals occupied the ground floor of the slate and schist (*lauze*) houses. Perhaps the difficulty of working the stone meant fewer buildings, perhaps it was the fact that 'spare' slate was used to face the windward side of the houses, as an extra protection against the wind and rain.

North again the building material was volcanic rock, the houses being built smaller so as to offer a low profile to the wind and so that less stone was needed. Typical of this area is the *buron*, a cowman's shed that could be thatched or stone-roofed, and the *bergière*, a similar building for sheep.

*Just outside Entraygues-sur-Truyère the river is spanned by a superb late-13th-century bridge.*

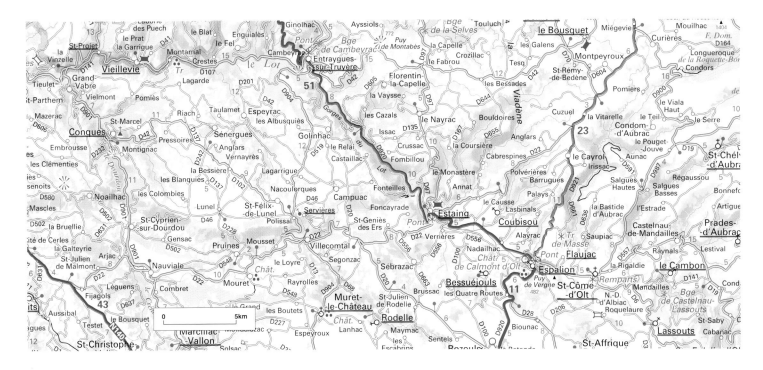

10-minute walk from a car park, offers a superb panorama. With the help of a panoramic table and a little clear weather, you can pick out the Monts du Cantal and the plateau of Aubrac.

## Espalion

Set on the Lot, and with a bridge as old as that at Entraygues, Espalion is another delightful village. From the viewpoint near the car park on the southern side of the Lot, the old palace, the houses rising straight out of the river and the bridge make a beautiful picture. The palace is a 16th-century mansion in fortified Renaissance style. In the village centre old houses group around a good church dedicated to St Hilarion, a confessor of Charlemagne who retired to Espalion after a life of hectic service, only to be beheaded by Saracen invaders. Built in pink sandstone, the 11th-century church is a fine example of the Romanesque.

The Musée Joseph Vaylet, housed in an old church, has a collection of local arts and crafts as well as a section devoted to diving, as the inventors of the diving suit came from the village. It was also the home of composer Francis Poulenc. The Château de Calmont d'Olt, perched high aove the village, is also worth a visit.

## Estaing

At the entrance to the Gorges du Lot stands Estaing, a small village nestling below an old château and with a fine old bridge over the river. The name of the village recalls its association with the early history of the d'Estaing family. The statue of another member of the family, François d'Estaing, a bishop of Rodez, stands close to the Lot bridge. The d'Estaings lived at the château, but the family lost the building at the time of the Revolution when it was discovered that Charles-Hector d'Estaing, though a Republican sympathiser, had exchanged letters with Marie-Antoinette in the hope of securing the successful escape of the king and his family. Charles-Hector was arrested and, not surprisingly, executed. The château, built in the 15th and 16th centuries, is a fortress-like building, the interior of which may be visited on application to the local tourist office in the village.

## Gorges du Lot

Between the villages of Estaing and Entraygues the Lot, which until here has flowed in a wide valley, is cramped into a very picturesque gorge. The high, steep sides are topped by a ragged, rocky crest, the whole offering a very wild, if wooded, view. The Barrage de Golinhac, the 36-m high dam that is passed along the way, feeds water to a hydroelectric station.

**Comité Départemental du Tourisme de l'Aveyron**
17 Rue Aristide Briand
12008 Rodez Cedex
Tel: 05 65 75 55 75
www.tourisme-aveyron. com

**Touring:**
AA Road Map France series 6: Midi-Pyrénées, and 10: Languedoc Roussillon

*A villager from Estaing*

# THE CÉVENNES

Of the seven French Parcs Nationaux, five are high mountain parks and one a marine reserve. The seventh is the Cévennes, covering a series of modest – by Alpine standards – peaks, deep gorges cut through green hills and the limestone plateaux known as the Causses. The area is distinctive and beautiful, its villages quiet and secret, its wildlife a naturalist's paradise.

## Abîme du Bramabiau

Travelling from Meyrueis to the Col de la Séreyrède, the visitor passes the Abîme du Bramabiau. This is a chasm, the second part of the name meaning bellowing ox and referring to the noise the foaming stream makes as it emerges.

This stream, the Bonheur, has cut down into the limestone plateau and then, instead of creating a deep gorge, has cut an underground channel about 700m long before returning to the surface. To date, over 10km of passages have been explored in the chasm.

## Col de la Séreyrède and L'Espérou

The Col de la Séreyrède can be reached from the summit of Mont Aigoual by road or by a fine 5-km walk along GR7. The Col is a surprisingly good viewpoint, despite being 250m lower than the summit, and can be used as a starting point for a trip to the waterfall on the River Hérault.

Nearby L'Espérou – also on GR7 – is set against the flank of the Col, which shelters it from northerly winds. Since it also faces south towards the Mediterranean, the little village has an enviable climate, warm in the summer with masses of flowers, shrubs and trees, yet high enough to be a small winter-sports centre.

## Gorges du Trévezel and Gorges de la Dourbie

The northern flank of the Aigoual massif is drained into the Dourbie valley by the Trévezel stream, which passes through the wild and narrow Gorges du Trévezel. The narrowest part of the gorge, no more than 35m wide, is known in local dialect as the Pas de l'Ase.

In its lower reaches the Dourbie flows through a pleasant valley, but its youthful vigour is entrapped by a delightful gorge, not as tight as the Pas de l'Ase, but with the attraction of a string of fine villages.

## Meyrueis

Set at the junction of not two but three rivers, Meyrueis is a pleasant little town that is a good centre for local explorations. One of the town's hotels, an old Benedictine monastery, boasts General de Gaulle as a former guest. Its old round tower, part of the original town fortifications, is topped by a clock tower, which is itself finished by a caged bell.

### PARC NATIONAL DE CÉVENNES

Of the six Parcs Nationaux that are land-based (the seventh is part island and part marine), the Cévennes is the only one that does not lie in high mountain terrain, this section of the Massif central being, in the main, a medium-height (around 1000m) plateau.

The park was created in 1970 and covers a triangular section of limestone plateau around which are grouped several mountain chains. The Lozère range, grouped around the Mont Lozère itself, the park's highest peak at 1,699m, are volcanic plugs, characterised by poor soil and a harsh climate, with peat bogs and a strange flora. The Bougès are lower and granitic, with a thin soil, except in the valleys, which are deeply wooded. The final group, Aigoual/Lingas – including Mont Aigoual, perhaps the park's finest peak – are limestone peaks rising to 1,500m with a typical limestone flora, inset by granite masses that add a variation to the scenery. Set between these ranges are

*In parts of the Gorges de la Dourbie rocks tower some 300m above the river.*

**Comité Départemental du Tourisme de Lozère**
14, Boulevard Henri-Bourillon
48001 Mende Cedex
Tel: 04 65 05 60 00
www.france48.com

**Comité Départemental du Tourisme du Gard**
3, Place des Arènes, BP 122
30010 Nîmes Cedex
Tel: 04 66 36 96 30
www.cdt-gard.fr

**Touring:**
AA Road Map France series 10: Languedoc Roussillon

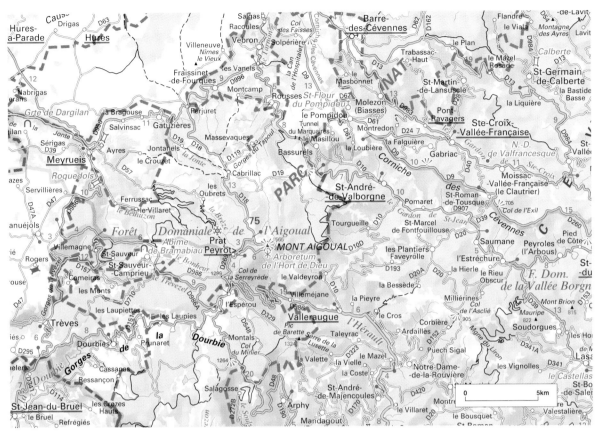

good valleys, the best of which are the Gardons valleys, cut in schist and the most agricultural area of the park. The agriculture supports few now, though life has always been hard in the Cévennes, where summers are very hot and winters are very cold. Today under 1,000 people inhabit the high central section of the park. A few of them are engaged in bee-keeping (left).

The park's wild flowers include beautiful tracts of wild daffodils in spring and over 40 varieties of orchid. Its birds include the Egyptian vulture (if you are really lucky), golden eagles and eagle owls, hen and Montagu's harriers, little bustards, stone curlew and choughs. And for the animal lover there are wild boar, genet cats and several species of deer.

## Mont Aigoual

The Massif de l'Aigoual, of which Mont Aigoual is, at 1,567m, the highest point, is of critical importance to the water flow of the country on all sides. It stands between the Atlantic and the Mediterranean and collects clouds from each, the rain from which averages over 2m annually. This is not a great deal in comparison with some of the wetter areas of Europe, but for the peak's position, close to the arid south of France, it is a very great amount and has earned it its name, from the local dialect word for water, *aiqualis*, It must also be said that it does not rain often on Mont Aigoual, but when it does it comes down in torrents.

The summit is easily reached – by road, with no walking involved – and there the visitor finds a meteorological station built in 1887 for the Water and Forests Department. This organisation planted trees on the peak, turning a bare mountain into one that became covered in beech and pine in only 100 years. From the summit the view towards the Mediterranean is superb, as is that towards the closer Causses country. On clear days Mont Blanc is visible to the north-east, beyond Mont Ventoux in Provence, while to the west the Pyrenees can be seen.

## St André-de-Valborgne

With its narrow streets hemmed in by old houses of great character, this charming village owes its prosperity to the local silk industry. Those wanting to know more about this fascinating subject should visit the Écomusée de la Soie at St Hippolyte-du-Fort, which lies about 20km to the south-east of St André. The eggs of the moth, whose caterpillars are the silk 'worms', were incubated in pouches hung between local women's breasts.

## Valleraugue

This pleasant market town is also a centre for apple growing as almost any visitor will realise on seeing the orchards on both sides of the D986 into Valleraugue. The town offers gentle strolls with no particular highlight, and those looking for a more energetic outing and a genuine goal should visit the 12th-century church. From there a long walk – known, optimistically, as the Path of 4,000 Steps – leads to the top of Mont Aigoual.

*In the predominantly rural Cévennes there is plenty of local produce on sale in the market towns dotted throughout the area.*

# LIMESTONE SCENERY

In addition to the volcanoes of Auvergne the region possesses one other unusual feature, the Causses. This area, bordered by the Cévennes to the east, the eastern edge of Aquitaine to the west, the valley of the River Lot to the north and the Hérault plain of Bas Languedoc to the south, is a limestone plateau of around 1000m in height and presenting a chiselled landscape to the visitor. Its climate is harsh, with hot, dry summers followed by cold winters during which the area is scoured by high winds. The limestone is carboniferous, permeable to water, so that vegetation has little soil and even less water.

The Causses is divided into four blocks by steep valleys that carry rivers out of the region. These rivers spring from neighbouring hill ranges and traverse the area along beds of the impervious marl strata that lies below the limestone. The Causse de Sauveterre lies between the Lot and the Gorges du Tarn; it is the least arid and is mostly arable. The Causse Méjean is next. Lying between the Gorges du Tarn and the Jonte, it is the highest Causse, a harsh area. The Causse Noir lies between the Jonte and the Dourbie. It is the smallest Causse, named after an ancient, dark, pine forest that once grew on it. Finally, south of the Dourbie, is the Causse de Larzac, the largest of all, mainly a high, dry plateau covering over 1,000 square kilometres.

*The harsh Causse Méjean is the highest-lying of the Causses.*

These dry tunnels – and occasionally the wet ones – are the caves explored by speleologists. Ultimately the underground river reaches a layer of impervious rock – under the Causses it is a bed of marl – runs along it and reaches the surface again at a point where the limestone cap has been eroded, or at a geological fault. The point of re-emergence is known as a resurgence.

Sometimes the surface rainwater erodes the rock into a shallow depression known in the region as a *cloup*. As the depression erodes down it

## Caves

The limestone of the Causses is a basic calcium-carbonate rock. Rain, a mild acid, attacks the rock when it falls on it. In some cases rainwater percolates down vertical fault lines, eventually reaching horizontal or inclined rock beds along which it can flow. The flowing water carves out tunnels and chambers in the rock, and occasionally eats is way through to a lower level so that a tunnel or series of tunnels are left literally high and dry.

## Martel, Speleologist Extraordinary

Though Stone Age man inhabited caves perhaps as long as 50,000 years ago, by medieval times the holes and caves of the Causses had become places of dread for the locals. At best they were the homes of demons, at worst gateways to Hell. No one contemplated entering them for fun.

It was not until the 18th century that the first tentative explorations were made, and not until the late 19th century that any systematic exploration took place.

At the forefront of cave exploration was Édouard-Alfred Martel. Born in 1859, he was interested in geology and geography from a very early age, and explored the caves of the Causses, often in the company of Louis Armand, a locksmith from Rozer.

Most of the great caves of the area were first explored by Martel: Demoiselles

*The Grotte des Demoiselles lies south-east of Ganges.*

from 1884, Dargilan and Bramabiau from 1888 and Armand from 1897. Martel also explored caves in Spain, Austria and Britain, and virtually founded the science of speleology with his writings on underground geography. Back in the Causses he also helped the locals by studying regional water flow, so aiding the creation of a more hygienic water supply.

## Rochers Ruiniformes

Interspersed within the calcium-based limestone matrix of the Causses are nodules of a magnesium-based rock known as dolomite. This rock is more famous as the basis of the sharp towers it has produced in the region of northern Italy that bears its name, but since it was named after Dolomieu, a French geologist, it is not out of place here. Dolomite is a harder rock than limestone, more resistant to water and wind. Where it outcrops it therefore tends to be left behind as the softer, calcium-based limestone dissolves or erodes. Where this happens the lumps of dolomite that remain form *rochers ruiniformes*. The name means "town-ruin rocks', because, from a distance, they look like the remains of an old town. The best example is Montpellier-le-Vieux in the Causse Noir.

The site can be explored on foot: drive to the car park from the Auberge de Maubert on the D110 and start from there. The path around the site from there is about 1.5km long and very worthwhile. At the first path junction go left, to reach the viewpoint of Rampart. Beyond is the Porte de Mycènes, one of the site's best features, a 12-m natural arch, named by Martel after the Lion Gate at Mycaenae. Further on again, beyond a rock evocatively named the Nez de Cyrano, is a cave, the Grotte de Baume Obscure (*baume* being a local word for cave), in which Martel found the remains of cave bears. On again is a superb viewpoint and a 53-m deep *aven*.

The rocher ruiniformes *of Montpellier-le-Vieux (left and right) cover 100 hectares. Edouard-Alfred Martel drew the first plan of the site in 1885.*

becomes a *sotch*, more of a pit than a hollow. Further erosion creates an *aven* or *igue*. *Avens* are steep-sided chimneys and are at their most spectacular where they link with underground chambers.

In such chambers water from the *aven*, or just from percolation, creates stalagmites as calcium carbonate is redeposited, having been taken into solution as the water dissolved the rock. It is these formations that make a visit to the caves of the area so worthwhile.

The Grotte des Demoiselles has a chamber 120m long and over 50m high. The Grotte de Dargilan, with its 100-m wide and 40-m high waterfall, and its Salle Rose, is also spectacular.

## Aven Armand

This superb cave started with the percolation of water through the Méjean limestone pavement, the water forming vertical chimney-like holes that all joined together in a huge, water-eroded chamber. Ultimately the detached blocks formed at the base of the percolation chimneys collapsed into the chamber, blocking the outflow from it. Much later the blockage also collapsed so that water could again flow freely. Then, on top of the blocks on the chamber floor, and from the chamber roof, respectively, stalagmites and stalactites began to form.

Local shepherds knew of the *aven* and Martel, hearing of it from them, brought a ton of equipment and his trusted partner Louis Armand for an exploration. It was Armand who first descended into the cave, bringing out news of the wonders below. Today's visitors enter by way of a 200-m tunnel bored directly into the main chamber. When they emerge into it they are confronted by an extraordinary forest of stalagmites.

## Gorges

These are formed either where the rock roofs above underground rivers have collapsed, or, more usually, where surface rivers have cut right through the limestone plateau to reach the impervious marl bed beneath. Occasionally the cutting has created ordinary valleys, wide and lushly vegetated, but more frequently the gorges are tight and high-sided, the scenery dominated by angular rocks.

The gorges of the Jonte and the Dourbie are worth visiting, but best by far is the Gorges du Tarn. This beautiful gorge is 5km long and can be followed by car (the easiest way), by

*Whether seen from road, cliff top or river, the Gorges du Tarn (above, right and below) are among the most dramatic sights in France.*

boat (the most exciting) or on foot. The last way is hard work but undeniably worth the effort.

The Tarn has no tributary streams in the Gorges, other than one or two that are a few tens of metres long, but is fed by water from over 40 resurgences – much of the water inflowing as waterfalls. This gives some impression of the degree to which the Causses are penetrated by rainwater. Never more than 500m wide and occasionally narrowing to just 30m, the sides of the Gorges are always steep, sometimes vertical and occasionally overhanging.

Consequently the drive along the Gorges is thrilling. If you are driving, start at Molines, passing the 16th-century Charbonnières castle near Montbrun, before reaching the enchanting village of Ste Énimie. Beyond are two *cirques*, the Cirque de St Chély and the Cirque de Pougnadoires, before the Point Sublime is reached. From the Point, close to which is a memorial to Martel, there is the very best view of the Gorges. The section in prospect includes Les Détroits and the Pas du Souci, but both of these features are best viewed from the boat that can be boarded at La Malène. Les Détroits are 400-m sheer cliffs, while in the Pas du Souci the Tarn flows over and under huge blocks created by the collapse of part of the wall of the Gorges.

# Roquefort

Many thousands of years before the village of Roquefort existed, the edge of the Cambalou plateau collapsed into the Soulzon valley, creating a jumble of huge rocks on the impervious marl of the valley's floor. In the caves created by the stabilised blocks a specific form of penicillin, *Penicillum glaucum roquefortii*, formed. Neolithic man inhabited the caves, but it is doubtful whether he noted the effect of the bacteria on cheese – though it was known by the time of the Romans. Nowadays the cheese is big business.

The basic ingredient of the cheese is sheep's milk, the efforts of half a million sheep in the Causses now being supplemented by imports. The milk (obtained by milking machines, just as from cows) is not pasteurised or in any other way altered before 'standard' cheeses are made from it. After the round cheeses have been formed – by about 10 cheesemakers, a number that is surprisingly large in modern industrial terms, but small for such a cottage industry – they are taken to the caves formed by the ancient rockfall and stored on oak tables for three months. In the cool (about 10°C), humid air the penicillin grows in the cheese, producing the famous blue marbled appearance.

# Cirques

Occasionally the rivers that cut down through the limestone form a meander and then, by cutting away a cliff in the bend, cut a straighter path, leaving the old bend behind. In a river plain, and on more impermeable soil, the old bend usually remains filled and is termed an oxbow lake. In the Causses the bend empties of water and becomes a dry gorge called a *cirque*. The best example is the Cirque de Navacelles, close to the Gorges de la Vis on the Causse du Larzac. The tiny village of Navacelles has a splendid bridge over the River Vis and is a good starting point for a trip to the local viewpoints. To the south is La Baume-Auriol, while to the

*The region's best-known* cirque *is that of Navacelles (left).*
*Mourèze (above) is near a fine* cirque.

north is the honestly named Belvédère Nord, and from either the bleached, plant-free sides of the cirques are well seen. For those wanting a clearer look, GR7, one of France's system of long-distance footpaths, visits the Cirque.

Another fine *cirque* is to be found close to Mourèze at the southern end of the Causse du Larzac. Rocks at the Cirque de Mourèze have weathered into fantastic shapes.

# THE RHÔNE VALLEY

France's main north–south highway, the Rhône Valley is used by travellers by road, rail, river and canal, and consequently there is a sense of frenetic rush throughout its length. A great deal of industry is concentrated in the river valley itself and with it all the ugliness that industry attracts. But concentrating too much on these aspects is unfair to the Rhône Valley, for they are arguably the price of modern living, and besides there is much more about the region that is positive.

In the valley itself the countryside is largely spoiled and uninteresting in its flatness. Yet not very far from either side of the river, hills rise, steep and high, in places, opening up huge vistas of the valley, which from a distance gains a beauty not always evident at close quarters. These hills also allow visitors wishing to escape the rush and industry of the valley floor to enter a world of peace and beauty.

To the north-east of Lyon, that tranquillity comes in the strange world of Les Dombes, a flat region dotted with hundreds of lakes and home to many species of bird. West from there, on the right bank of the Saône and between the vineyards of Burgundy and the Côtes du Rhône, lies the Beaujolais region, where attractive little villages quietly prepare their young red wines for the mad November rush. Much farther south, to the south-west of Montélimar, there are the Gorges de l'Ardèche, without a doubt some of the most dramatic scenery in the whole region.

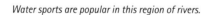

*Water sports are popular in this region of rivers.*

*A game of boules (right)*

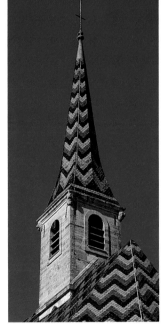

*The Chartreuse de Valbonne (left) lies in attractive wooded country south of the Gorges de l'Ardèche, spectacular cliffs towering over the river.*

*At Juliénas a colourful mural can be seen in old wine cellars. It depicts the frolics associated with Bacchus, the Greek and Roman god of wine.*

# ALONG THE RHONE

The Rhône traces a major communications corridor between northern and southern France, sharing its valley with two trunk roads, the RN7 and RN86, an autoroute, the A7, and two railway lines. Despite these, and a subsequent growth in industry that demands three nuclear power stations between Lyon and Pont-St Esprit, there is much along the Rhône valley to draw the traveller's attention.

Comité Départemental du Tourisme du Rhône
35 Rue St Jean
69005 Lyon
Tel: 04 72 56 70 40
www.rhonetourisme.com

Comité Départemental du Tourisme de la Drôme
8 Rue Baudin
26000 Valence
Tel: 04 75 82 19 26
www.drometourisme.com

**Touring:**
AA Road Map France series 14: Rhône Alpes

## Corniche du Rhône

A high-level route between Tournon-sur-Rhône and Valence, passing on its way the lofty ruins of the Château de Crussol, the Corniche du Rhône runs to the west of the river via St Romain-de-Lerps.

From various points along its route there are marvellous views of the valley, but the best is at St Romain itself. All-round panoramas from the viewing table at the tiny Chapelle du Pic are immense, encompassing no fewer that 13 *départements*.

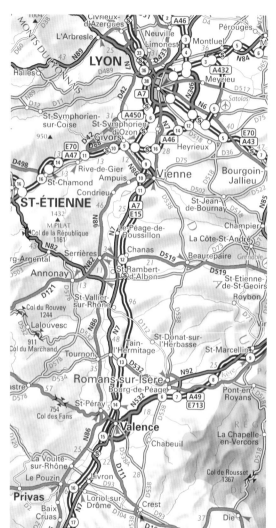

*The centre of Lyon retains a wealth of Renaissance building. Its narrow streets, most of them pedestrianised, are lined with many fine mansions of the period.*

## Lyon

Situated at the confluence of the Rhône and Saône, France's third-largest city is worth a visit of several days. Built on silk, banking and insurance, Lyon is a prosperous city with hundreds of restaurants and 24 museums (from fine arts to puppets).

The heart of the city is the Place Bellecour, one of the largest squares in Europe, from where it is just a short distance across the Saône to Vieux Lyon, the area around the Cathédrale St-Jean.

Overlooking the old quarter of Lyon is the Fourvière district, where the city was founded by the Romans. Visitors can take a funicular railway to the top of the hill to see the gaudy Basilique Notre-Dame, the Roman amphitheatre and the Musée de la Civilisation Gallo-Romaine. Views from the basilica's terrace are extensive, stretching from the Parc de la Tête d'Or in the north to the riverside petrochemical works in the south, and show a red-roofed city virtually devoid of high-rise buildings. The exception is the soaring Crédit Lyonnais tower.

## THE SILK TRADE

Lyon owes much of its wealth today to the silk industry established in 1536. Progress was slow at first and in the latter half of the century was interrupted by the Wars of Religion. With peace restored, the famous horticulturist Olivier de Serres suggested to Henri IV that to help revive the economy, silkworms and their staple diet, mulberry trees, should be introduced to the Rhône valley. Several farms were established and by the mid-17th century locally produced raw material was supplying 10,000 looms in Lyon.

The Revolution caused further setbacks and Napoleon came to the industry's rescue. New looms

were introduced, enabling one *canut*, as the weavers were called, to do the work of five, and new premises were built in the Croix-Rousse district to accommodate them. But workers' pay and conditions were far from good and the mid-19th century saw bloody revolts. With the advent of mechanisation in the early 20th century, the Croix-Rousse workshops fell into decline and today most of

*Tournon-sur-Rhône is a compact little town facing Tain-l'Hermitage across a broad stretch of the river.*

**N 7 MONTELIMAR NOUGAT LE BOUQUET**

Z.I. Nord du Meyrol BP 71
26202 MONTÉLIMAR CEDEX

the city's silk production has dispersed to high-tech factories elsewhere in the region.

Lyon's Musée Historique de Tissus, to the south of the Place Bellecour, has a particularly fine collection of silk, and at the Maison des Canuts in the Croix-Rousse a small number of artisans produce silk by traditional methods.

One of the last silkworm farms still operating can be visited at Les Mazes, near Vallon-Pont-d'Arc in the Ardèche.

## Montélimar

A quiet but colourful town just east of the Rhône, Montélimar is best known for nougat. This is made with almonds, which were first introduced from Asia by the horticulturist Olivier de Serres in the early 17th century. Other ingredients, such as honey and eggs, were available locally and for the next 300 years nougat thrived as a cottage industry. Only since the early 20th century has production been factory-based.

The town centre, around the 15th-century church of Ste-Croix, is pedestrianised and has several old mansions, while at the eastern edge is the feudal castle of Mont-Adhémar, which gave the town its name.

## Tournon-sur-Rhône

The Rhône is wide at Tournon, slowly flowing between the town and the vine-covered slopes of Tain-l'Hermitage opposite. It was between these twin towns that the first suspension bridge across the river was built in 1824 by the engineer Marc Seguin, who was also responsible for the first steamboat service on the river and for the first French railway, between Lyon and St-Étienne. A steam railway still runs from Tournon, following the scenic Gorges du Doux to Lamastre.

Tournon, with its attractive riverside terrace shaded by huge plane trees, has several other interesting sights. Overlooking the river is its 15th-century château, which houses a museum showing the use of the Rhône for trade. In the Grande Rue are several imposing town houses and the 14th-century church of St-Julien with its unusual timber ceiling.

## Valence

Squeezing the RN7 and A7 to the banks of the Rhône, Valence rises on the slopes to the east and for travellers from the north offers the first taste of the Midi. Enclosed within broad boulevards, the town centre hides tree-shaded squares where numerous restaurants vie for business. Among several Renaissance houses is the Maison des Têtes in the Grande Rue, which has 45 heads carved on its façade, in the entrance passage and in the interior courtyard. On terraces overlooking the Rhône are the Cathédrale St-Apollinaire, rebuilt in the 17th century, and the lovely Parc Jouvet.

## Vienne

A town of churches and Roman remains, Vienne is not a place to hurry past. The Cathédrale St-Maurice is one of the most important Romanesque and Gothic churches in the Rhône Valley, but much older is the former church of St-Pierre, now an archaeological museum, parts of which date from the 5th and 6th centuries. The Romanesque St-André-le-bas has a charming little cloister.

For a town of its size, Vienne has a remarkable number of Roman remains. The largest is the amphitheatre below Mont Pipet, which is still used. Other remains include the Temple d'Auguste et de Livie, an archaeological garden, the settlement of St-Romain-en-Gal on the opposite bank of the Rhône, and a strange structure called the Pyramide, formerly an arena.

**VIVARAIS RAILWAY**

Running between Tournon-sur-Rhône and Lamastre, the Chemin de Fer du Vivarais is the only passenger service operating in the Ardèche *département*. Built in 1891, the line winds through the Gorges du Doux, the steam locomotives and wooden carriages taking two hours to complete the 33-km journey.

The train first passes orchards and vineyards before reaching the wilder mountain scenery of heather and fir. Just before reaching Lamastre the line crosses the 45th parallel, which is where the Midi, or southern France, begins.

Train run daily in July and August and on a restricted basis from the beginning of April to the end of June and from the beginning of September to late October.

# THE ARDÈCHE GORGES

The Ardèche region, with its many outstanding natural sights both above and below ground, makes an attractive contrast to the rush and industry of the nearby Rhône Valley. A sparsely populated limestone plateau covered in forest, it has been shaped by the action of water, and the visitor is presented with one of the most beautiful gorges in France as well as a number of spectacular caves.

## Aven de Marzal

Reached by a staircase through its roof, this chasm is not as big as that of Orgnac, but it is just as beautiful. Strategically placed lights pick out the shapes and colours and cause minute crystals in the rock to sparkle. On the surface there is a museum of caving.

## Aven d'Orgnac

This is the largest of the caves in the Ardèche open to the public, but despite its size it is only a fraction of a system that has still to be fully explored. Strictly speaking a pothole because it has a vertical entrance, it was known for many years but only entered for the first time in 1935 when the speleologist Robert de Joly made a descent. Consisting of several chambers, one of them 250m long, it has magnificent stalactites and stalagmites in all sorts of weird and wonderful shapes and colours,

some reaching 25m in length. The growth rate is about a centimetre per century.

## Gorges de l'Ardèche

For around 30km between Vallon-Pont-d'Arc and St Martin-d'Ardèche, the Ardèche flows through some of the most spectacular scenery in southern France, part of it a nature reserve. Precipitous limestone cliffs, some 300m high, tower over the river, which from autumn to early spring rages with white water. A road follows the northern rim but the best way to see the Gorges is from the river itself and every spring, especially during May and June, when conditions are at their best, thousands make the journey by canoe, most completing it within a day.

For those who prefer a more leisurely pace there are a couple of riverside camp sites. One of the most fascinating sights on the way is the Pont d'Arc, a huge natural arch over the river.

### THE *MAS*

The *mas* is the typical farmhouse of the region. Quite low despite its two storeys, it has stone walls beneath a gently sloping roof of curved terracotta tiles. The windows are small to keep it cool in summer but large enough to allow in light.

The focal point of the house is the kitchen, which traditionally comprises a hearth, sink and oven plus simple furnishings. The bedrooms and sometimes a sitting-room, all with terracotta-tiled floors, are upstairs.

The outbuildings, grouped round a courtyard, consist of a cellar, storeroom, bread oven and sometimes a cocoonery from the days of silk production.

*Spanning the Ardèche some 4km below Vallon-Pont-d'Arc, the Pont d'Arc is in summer a popular place to relax and sunbathe.*

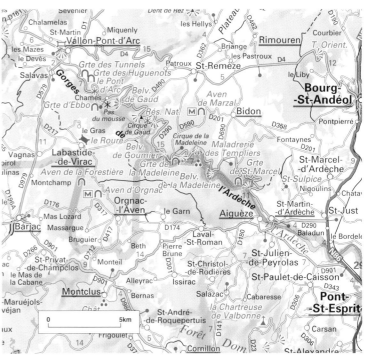

*The Belvédère de la Madeleine is one of the finest viewpoints on the high cliffs of the dramatic Gorges de l'Ardèche.*

## Haute Corniche

Opened as recently as the late 1960s, the D290 road along the Gorges de l'Ardèche follows as closely as it can the curves of the river, often along the clifftops.

There are frequent stopping places, but the most spectacular section of the journey is the Haute Corniche, from where at almost every bend in the road there are outstanding views of the river below. Particularly dramatic are the views that can be enjoyed from the Belvédère de la Madeleine and the Belvédère de la Cathédrale.

## Grotte de la Madeleine

This cave, which overlooks the Gorges de l'Ardèche and was discovered in 1887, has been open to the public only since 1969, shortly after the scenic road was built. In its chambers are beautiful and richly decorated rock formations, some flowing almost like water or shaped like hanging curtains,

others having the appearance of flowers and coral. In addition, the remains of Ice Age animals such as reindeer, stags and bears have been found in the cave.

## Grottes de St Marcel

These caves are not far from St Martin-d'Ardèche at the southern end of the Gorges. Discovered in 1835, they have only recently been opened to the public. Previously access was restricted to scientists, who have explored a network of more than 20km.

Some of the chambers are enormous and have outstanding natural vaulting and concretions – that is, small, round masses of rock particles which are embedded in the limestone.

## Vallon-Pont-d'Arc

This town is the main tourist centre for the Gorges de l'Ardèche, with many hotels, campsites, restaurants, bars, souvenir shops and canoe rental centres. For most visitors Vallon-Pont-d'Arc is the starting point for the journey through the Gorges, either by canoe or by car.

Wandering around the town, though, away from the hubbub, the visitor will find attractive old squares and alleyways reminiscent of some of the medieval villages in the area. The town hall, a Louis XIII-style mansion, has on show a fine collection of Aubusson tapestries.

**Comité Départemental du Tourisme de l'Ardèche**
4, Cours du Palais, BP 221
07000 Privas
Tel: 04 75 64 04 66
www. ardech-guide.com

**Touring:**
AA Road Map France series 10: Languedoc Roussillon, and 15: Provence & Côte d'Azur

# THE ALPS

Bordering Switzerland and Italy, the French Alps offer a diversity and grandeur unmatched in Europe. They include not only the single highest mountain, Mont Blanc, but also hundreds of other peaks that attract climbers and tourists alike. In the north of the region is Chamonix, the world centre for Alpinism, where dozens of needle-like peaks thrust skywards, demanding attention and holding a fascination for all who gaze up at them. Beyond, the creamy-white summit of Mont Blanc lures thousands of climbers each year.

To the south, huge valleys linked by high passes delineate different Alpine regions. The Parc National de la Vanoise, a magnificent area for wildlife, is far less commercialised than the northern Alps, as is the Parc National des Écrins, south-east of Grenoble. This latter area is one of the largest mountain bulks in the Alps, and although it is popular with Alpinists, it remains free from the heavy tourist-related developments of many other areas.

Towards the Italian frontier is the Queyras, famous for its wild flowers, high villages and stunning scenery, while to the south again is the Vercors. Gorges of unfathomable depth, tremendous limestone cliffs leading on to huge plateaux and dense woodland characterise this landscape of outstanding quality.

To the south-west of Chamonix, Lac d'Annecy and Lac du Bourget and their surroundings demonstrate yet another stark contrast. The larger towns are important cultural and historical centres, while the lakes themselves are the perfect complement to the nearby peaks.

Wherever there are mountains there will be climbing and walking, and the Alps have a superb selection of both, from the gentlest stroll to the most demanding north face. In addition there are many other activities, such as paragliding, canoeing, mountain biking, skiing and sailing, making the Alps one of the world's great outdoor playgrounds.

Below the majestic peaks are dozens of small and friendly villages, ranging from the austere, granite-clad settlement of the high eastern Alps to the mellow, bleached limestone houses of the Vercors. Each area has its own distinctive quality, and in many cases its own food and wines. The traditional dishes of Haute-Savoie are the fondue and the *raclette*, both of which can take several forms. You may have sampled these delights elsewhere, but they are even better in the right environment, ideally after an energetic day on the mountain, when your appetite is likely to match the generous portions. Locally produced wines are also a good bet.

Some places have had to be left out, for lack of space. Grenoble is one of these. A modern city often referred to as the capital of the French Alps, Grenoble is strategically placed, economically important and a good cultural centre.

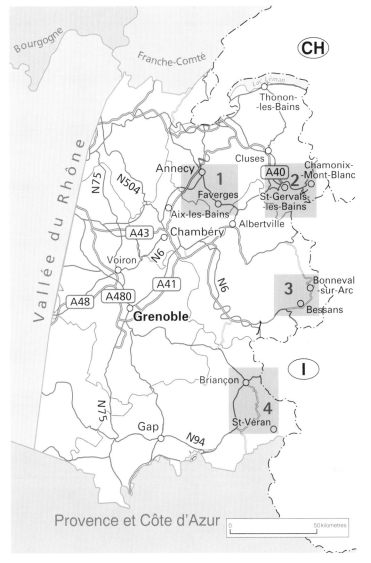

The old quarter of Annecy (left) is largely built around the River Thiou.

Rural Savoy is proud of its crisply starched traditional costume (below).

The town choir of Beaufort (right), a strong community, rehearses for a festival. The Beaufortin is a gentle Alpine area with no massive peaks of glaciers.

Behind the village of St Michel-le-Portes (above) Mont Aiguille (2,086m) can be seen to the left and the Grand Veymont (2,341m) to the right.

# LAC D'ANNECY

Annecy, the lake bearing its name and the surrounding peaks and forests all possess a character very different from that of the higher region to the east. The land is gentler, the accent is on sailing as much as climbing and the climate is less harsh. Annecy itself is a marvellous centre, charming and with an air of well-being. The region provides cultural and outdoor interests to suit all tastes.

## Annecy

*Annecy is an ancient town, its name deriving from the Roman Villa Aniciaca. A large part of the town's old quarter grew up around the River Thious. Important past residents of Annecy include St François de Sales and the 18th-century writer and philosopher Jean-Jacques Rousseau.*

This fine town commands a magnificent position at the northern end of the lake. On the lake front are the Jardin d'Europe, the boat-lined Canal du Vasse, with its photogenic Pont des Amours, and the wide, open spaces of the Parc du Paquier. From here can be clearly seen the saw-tooth ridge of the Tête du Parmelan and the jagged pinnacles of La Tournette. With the royal, tree lined Avenue d'Albigny behind it, the park is a deservedly popular place. Opposite the inland end of the canal is the Centre Bonlieu, which houses an information centre, library and theatre.

The old quarter is worth a special visit. On its lakeside edge are the Église St-Maurice and the Église St-François. The former has a mural dating from 1458 and representing the mortal remains of Noble Philibert de Monthouz that was rediscovered during the restoration of the church in 1953. Much of the old town is built around the River Thiou, which is bridged several times in this short length. The sinuous streets are lined with houses painted grey, ochre, fern and salmon, and window boxes brighten the bleached paintwork. Some streets have squat, pillared archways and small, cave-like arcades with dozens of inviting shops and bars. An exceptionally fine and busy food market can also be found here, where superb cheeses are brought in and sold by farmers from the nearby hills. The Palais de l'Isle, which divides the river like the bows of a boat, is one of the most famous attractions in the old town. Formerly the Governor's house, a court, prison and mint, it now contains a small but interesting museum of local history.

## Cimetière des Glières

Between Annecy and Thônes, and overlooked by the Tête Ronde, the Tête de Turpin and the Plateau des Glières, there are a cemetery and a museum dedicated to the Resistance. The message on the cemetery's monument reads simply 'Live free or die'. The place is a forceful reminder of the dark days of World War II.

## Crêt de Châtillon

A gruelling drive up through the forests and then out into the Alps, the high pasture land that gave these mountains their name, leads to the area just below the summit of the Crêt de Châtillon. Ten minutes' walk up to the cross on the summit itself is rewarded with a stunning 360-degree panorama. The orientation panel will help you to pick out Mont Blanc and the Aiguilles de Chamonix, the Dents de Lanfon, La Tournette and the Dents des Portes, among many other peaks.

This is a popular paragliding, walking and Nordic-skiing centre.

**Agence Touristique Départementale Haute-Savoie/Mont-Blanc**
56, Rue Sommeiller
74000 Annecy Cedex
Tel: 04 50 51 32 31
www.hautesavoie-tourism.com

**Touring:**
AA Road Map France series 14: Rhône Alpes

## COMBE D'IRE

At the southern end of Lac d'Annecy lies the long valley of the Combe d'Ire. Even at the beginning of the 20th century this was one of the least known valleys in the French Alps. Although it is possible to drive some way up the valley, through dense

woodland and alongside a swift stream, there is no vehicular access into its upper part, which is a strictly controlled nature reserve. Chamois, ibexes, marmots and many other forms of Alpine wildlife inhabit this area, which has well-marked footpaths.

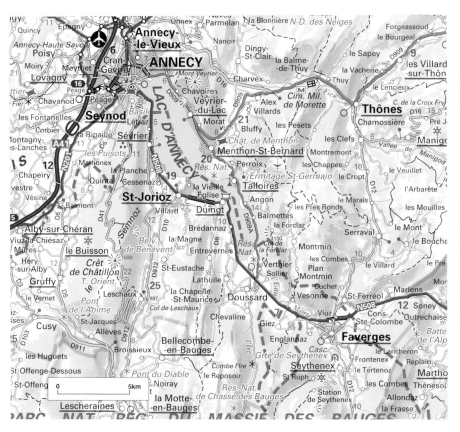

## Duingt

Despite its main-road location, Duingt is a delightful lakeside village. The ancient wooden houses, with their exterior stairways and trellises overflowing with honeysuckle and wistaria, are fine examples of Savoyard domestic architecture.

On the lakeside is the Château de Duingt, also known as the Châteauvieux, property of the de Sales family and best viewed from the small square named after St François de Sales.

## Ermitage de St-Germain

This impressive spot is where St François de Sales came to see out his days in 1621. The tiny church has many paintings and sculptures, and the Belvédère de la Vierge presents a wide and truly superb panorama over Lac d'Annecy, to Duingt and to the Crêt de Châtillon.

## Lac d'Annecy

The lake is now well protected, and is reputed to be the purest in Europe. There are plenty of opportunities for water sports and fishing, and many beaches have lifeguards.

With a water temperature as high as 23°C in midsummer, swimming is possible from June to the end of September.

## Talloires

This is a well looked after and popular village that exudes affluence and a high quality of life. There are plenty of outdoor activities on offer, including paragliding, sailing, diving and water-skiing.

In 1031 a Benedictine priory was established at Talloires, serving as the residence of the head monk and a centre of daily monastic activities until the Revolution. Now it is a centre for international conferences and academic studies.

## Thônes

The approach to Thônes is industrial and unattractive, but the town centre is open and pleasant, sheltered by the surrounding tree-clad hillsides, The regular cheese market is a gastronomic delight and the church, with its typically baroque interior, and the nearby museum of local history and arts and crafts, should be on every visitor's itinerary.

## Viuz

Just north of the industrial centre of Faverges is Viuz, which has a small archaeological museum next to its 12th-century church. It also gives views of the creamy-white summit of Mont Blanc, which peeps over the nearer Mont Charvin.

*Pleasure boats make regular trips around Lac d'Annecy from the mouth of the River Thiou in Annecy.*

### CHÂTEAU DE ST-BERNARD

The château occupies a truly commanding position. The site probably dates back to pre-Celtic times, though the château is the result of work carried out between the 12th century and World War II.

The Menthon family has occupied the château for a virtually unbroken period of over 700 years and has played prominent roles both locally and nationally. St Bernard de Menthon, the patron saint of mountaineers and mountain dwellers, is reputed to have been born there in 923. There are regular trips around the château, which has a beautiful chapel and a fine library.

*Lac d'Annecy, widely regarded as the jewel of the Savoy Alps, is used for water sports of all kinds, of which sailing is the most popular.*

# CHAMONIX AND MONT BLANC

Chamonix and its nearby mountains, the most famous of which is Mont Blanc, dominate a wide area that is without equal for climbing and skiing. Indeed Chamonix has long been known as a centre where the standards of Alpine sports are pushed ever higher. Many of the area's facilities are used by the adventurous and sedate alike, climber and tourist sharing a love for this special place.

## PARAGLIDING

On any fine day in the Chamonix valley you are likely to see dozens of brightly coloured paragliders drifting down to the valley floor, from take-off sites served by the many chairlifts. Pilots seek out the uplift provided by thermals,

which can keep them aloft for several hours, enabling them to fly considerable distances across country. Landing into the wind, pilots apply both brakes at once to slow the canopy, and with luck touch down gently. Dual flights and lessons are available locally, but be warned – the sport can soon become highly addictive.

Agence Touristique Départementale Haute-Savoie/Mont-Blanc
56, Rue Sommeiller
74000 Annecy Cedex
Tel: 04 50 51 32 31
www.hautesavoie-tourisme.com

**Touring:**
AA Road Map France
series 14: Rhône Alpes

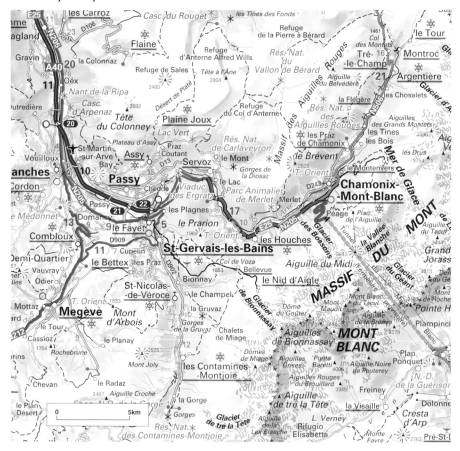

## Aiguille du Midi

One of the most spectacular cable car rides in the world takes you up in two stages via the Plan de l'Aiguille to the summit of the Midi, the most southerly of the famous Aiguilles de Chamonix. The views from here are stunning. The Chamonix valley lies over 2,500m below and behind the town Le Brévent and the Aiguilles Rouges look gentle by comparison with the savage views closer by. Apart from the granite spires of the Aiguilles, you can see the Grandes Jorasses, Mont Blanc du Tacul and distant peaks too numerous to mention. The cable car goes all the way to Helbronner, on the Italian border, after crossing the Vallée Blanche. There is much opposition to this part of the route, as it intrudes into the very heart of the Aiguilles, and its future is in some doubt.

## Argentière

A major settlement of the Chamonix valley, Argentière has retained an old quarter of some character, despite the obvious pressure of more recent development in the town. It is the base for ascents by the Grands-Montets cableway, which serves a very important skiing area.

## Le Brévent

A cableway on the west side of the Chamonix valley gives access first to Planpraz, then to the high summit of Le Brévent.

There are some fine walks and excellent views from the first stage, and a walk back down to the valley is a popular option. From the summit, the views to Mont Blanc and the Aiguille du Midi are superb.

*At 1,252m, Argentière is the highest of the winter-sports centres in the Chamonix valley. Close by are the Glacier d'Argentière and the Réserve Naturelle des Aiguilles Rouges, which has a good variety of wildlife.*

*The imposing Aiguilles de Chamonix looks down on the town. Chamonix also lies close to Mont Blanc.*

## MOUNTAIN GUIDES

The Compangnie des Guides de Chamonix is the oldest and best known of all the Alpine guiding agencies. With 150 members available to guide clients on walks and climbs of all standards, it is well equipped to deal with the demand for activities

around Chamonix, the world's leading Alpine centre.

Popular excursions include the ascent of Mont Blanc by the Dôme du Goûter or Grands Mulets routes, glacier walking and rock climbing of all standards, from the low-level peaks of the Petit Charmoz to the formidable North Face of the Grandes Jorasses. The bronze statue in Chamonix (above) depicts the naturalist Saussure and the famous guide Balmat together contemplating the wonders of Mont Blanc.

## Chamonix

The bustling tourist centre of Chamonix is often described as the world's top Alpine resort, where climbers and visitors of every nationality rub shoulders beneath some of Europe's most formidable peaks. The town is well equipped with all manner of accommodation, a wide range of sporting facilities and entertainment to suit virtually all tastes.

There are many fine examples of Victorian architecture and Alpine chalets, though the mix of these and some of the newer developments is not always pleasing. Chamonix exists above all because of its location at the foot of the highest summit in the Alps, and inevitably mountain views dominate the town. The Musée Alpin relates the history of the Chamonix valley and of mountaineering in the Alps, and holds a mineralogical collection.

## Index

A cableway begins at Praz, a little way to the north of Chamonix, and is in two stages, finishing at the Index station. (The mountain known as the Index is just above here.)

The terminus is a marvellous place to watch paragliders take off and it offers spectacular views of the main peaks, in particular the Grand Dru and the Petit Dru, the Grandes Jorasses and the Aiguilles de Chamonix. The descent from the Index to La Flégère is an easy and popular walk.

## Mer de Glace

A small train from Chamonix ascends the steep, forested hillsides and arrives at Montnevers, right on the edge of the Mer de Glace, probably the most famous glacier in the Alps.

Although this is a very busy place in the high season, the views are exceptional, and particularly prominent are the Grand Dru and the Petit Dru, Le Moine, La Verte and the famous North Faces of the Grandes Jorasses.

## St Gervais-les-Bains

An extremely popular and busy town, famous for its thermal waters, St Gervais-les-Bains is well connected by train and cable car to other parts of the region and is often used as a lower-level alternative base to Chamonix. A popular excursion is to take the small train to the Nid d'Aigle, the Eagle's Nest. At an altitude of 2,386m, this is an excellent viewpoint.

*The Mer de Glace is a huge swathe of ice, cracked, distorted and seamed with crevasses, which flows down unceasingly from the high peaks.*

# ALPINE MOUNTAINEERING

t is difficult to know who first started to climb mountains for pleasure. Perhaps it was one of the early Swiss naturalists, or a shepherd inspired by the promise of some marvellous view.

Probably the first major ascent was that of Mont Aiguille in 1492, made on the orders of Charles VIII of France, and employing ladders in a way that would be more at home on a building site than a mountain. Antoine de Ville and his companions returned with tales of strange and terrible beasts that inhabited the summit plateau, a common fear in those days, and one that was to play its part in inhibiting mountaineering for several centuries.

Mountain folklore was still full of evil in the 17th and 18th centuries. Murderous witches and warlocks were supposed to hurl their terrified victims down hideous precipices, and dragons were allegedly to be found throughout the Alps. Bearing in mind the strength of these fears, and considering the difficulty of normal travel in those times, let alone the hazards of avalanche, glacier crossing and sheer verticality, it is no wonder that the mountains were left well alone.

## Great Adventures

Ever more adventurous feats were attempted during the 18th century, as chamois hunters and crystal collectors made regular forays into the higher Alpine regions. In 1785 Dr Michel-Gabriel Paccard and Jacques Balmat, a crystal hunter from Chamonix, reached the summit of Mont Blanc, the highest peak in the Alps, so beginning an era of great adventure.

The pair returned to Chamonix after three days on the mountain, Paccard snow-blind and both men exhausted. There followed an extraordinary

*Mont Blanc (above) at 4,807m, is the highest peak in Europe.*

*The Aiguilles de Chamonix (right) look down on the town that lies at the heart of Alpine mountaineering.*

series of controversies and infighting, fired by the jealousy and inadequacies of another would-be conqueror of the heights, who suggested that Balmat was the hero, having dragged Paccard to the Summit. In fact, the reverse had been the case. Though Mont Blanc's first ascent will always be tainted by this bickering, it was nonetheless a magnificent feat by two exceptional men. In 1809 the first woman, Marie Paradis, a Chamonix maid servant, reached the summit.

*Bernard Voegeli was the first to climb the Pic du Toedi, in 1837.*

## Personal achievement

As the 19th century progressed people started to climb regularly for reasons other than scientific curiosity or to fulfil a personal ambition. There was an element of joy, of wanting to climb for climbing's sake, to experience the savage grandeur of the mountains at first hand.

The major peaks were gradually conquered in the so-called Golden Age of mountaineering, when climbers could find almost at will an untrodden peak to climb, and when mountaineers of many nationalities joined forces at the Alpine centres.

But later, with all the major summits climbed, a new generation of climbers had to find alternative ways to demonstrate their talents and satisfy their desire for discovery and exploration. They did this by seeking new and more difficult routes up mountains that had already been ascended many times. The quest for ever greater difficulty was on, and this has been the predominant theme of Alpinism over the last sixty years.

*A climber tackles a difficult rock face near Chamonix.*

## Modern Mountaineering

The French have played a great part in the development of mountaineering. Great Alpinists such as Patrick Vallençant, Jean-Marc Boivin, Christophe Profit, Thierry Reneault and Nicolas Jaeger, some of who are now tragically dead, have placed France at the forefront of modern Alpinism, often bringing commercialism into the sport along with very high standards.

In recent years changes in equipment and attitudes have given rise to some remarkable feats. Faces that would once have been considered difficult climbs have been descended on skis, and most of the high peaks have now been descended by paraglider. But there will always be 'the last great problem', and we can be certain that the techniques of Alpine-style climbing will be transferred to the other great ranges of the world, where challenges still beckon.

*Safety in the mountains demands the best modern equipment.*

# THE VANOISE

his remote and spectacular area is crossed by one route only, the Col de l'Iseran, which divides the Maurienne and Arc valleys from the Tarentaise mountains to the north. The scenery is characterised by a bleak grandeur that is reflected in the squat stone houses, built to withstand the harsh climate. For high-level mountain walking the region ranks with the best, and is less touched by man's influence than many other Alpine areas.

## Bessans

This village is situated on a small, high plain surrounded by steep-sided peaks, and it seems that whichever direction you look in there is a glacier, high snowfield or milky waterfall tumbling down from unseen heights. Lying in the heart of the Maurienne mountain region, Bessans retains much of its traditional character, despite being an increasingly popular winter-sports centre, and has some fine old buildings.

Above the village stands the church and the Chapelle St-Antoine. The church has some statues from the 17th century, but it is the chapel that is particularly impressive. It houses some tine examples of the ornate works that are found throughout the Arc valley, as well as murals, wood carvings and frescos dating from the 15th century.

*The village of L'Ecot perches on the mountainside above Bonneval-sur-Arc, and is right on the edge of the Parc National de la Vanoise.*

## Bonneval-sur-Arc

Situated at the very foot of the Col de l'Iseran, Bonneval is one of the classic villages of the French Alps. There are no telephone lines, television aerials or electricity cables to be seen, and only local vehicles are allowed into the village. The houses huddle together as if sheltering one another from the harsh climate, and the rough, rust-coloured stone roofs are almost works of art. Wooden balconies and ancient doors complete this rustic scene, and when it is quiet you could be in another century.

In the village centre is the Grande Maison, a huge old chalet that now houses the butcher's and baker's shops and an information centre. On the outskirts of the village is a cheesemaker who sells local cheeses such as Emmental and Beaufort.

### PARC NATIONAL DE LA VANOISE

Covering 7 per cent of its land surface, France's Parcs Nationaux are a relatively recent contribution to conservation. The Parc National de la Vanoise is the oldest, founded in 1963. Sandwiched between the high valleys of the Maurienne and the Tarentaise mountains, the Vanoise has a high point of 3,855m and a low point of 1,280m. A wide variety of rock types has led to a great diversity of flora and fauna, the alpine and sub-alpine zones being especially interesting. These hold chamois, ibexes, golden eagles and a splendid selection of Alpine plants.

**Agence Départementale du Tourisme de la Savoie**

24, Boulevard de la Colonne
73000 Chambéry
Tel: 04 79 85 12 45
www.savoie-tourisme.com

**Touring:**

AA Road Map France series 14: Rhône Alpes

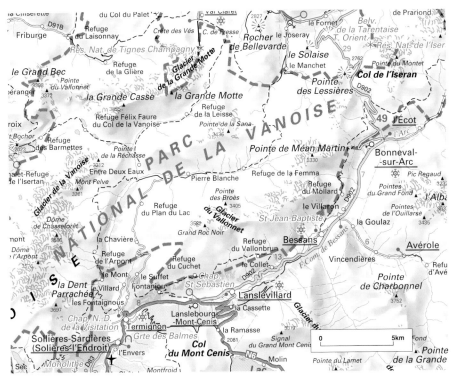

## Col de l'Iseran

The highest major European pass, the Col de l'Iseran is a desolate and austere place. From Bonneval the road twists tortuously up very steep hillsides (with good views of the village), rising almost 1,000m from the valley to the Col itself. There are several excellent viewpoints, for example the Belvédère de la Maurienne, located immediately past the Pont de la Neige tunnel. This provides a particularly good view of the Albaron, the snowy pyramid of the Pointe de Charbonnel, the Pointe de Ronce and the dramatic ridge of the Massif du Mulinet.

*The stern beauty of the Col de l'Iseran, with its fine viewpoints, attracts many walkers. Bonneval-sur-Arc, situated at the foot of the Col, is the closest village to the Col's summer skiing area, and is a good base for both summer and winter activities.*

There is always plenty of snow near the Col, and there is a summer ski area, the Glacier du Grand Pissaillas, which is well signposted. Snow can fall at any time of the year here, and the road is almost certain to be blocked from November to June. At the Col itself there is a shop, built to withstand the extremes of climate, and a small church built in 1939, just three years after the route was opened.

The finest viewpoint of all is the Pointe des Lessières, the peak to the immediate west of the summit. However, this is a route for experienced and properly equipped walkers only.

## Vallée d'Avérole

This is a remarkable high valley of the Haute Maurienne that contains tiny, unspoilt villages such as La Goula, Vincendières and Avérole.

It is overlooked and dominated by the Pointe de Charbonnel, with its attendant glaciers and ice cliffs that teeter on the edge of the vast rock walls below.

This is a wild and savage landscape, where large, dirty snow patches, often the residue of winter avalanches, lie next to the road until well into the summer.

## CHALETS OF THE MAURIENNE

The high valleys of the Maurienne contain villages that have survived and developed despite the harsh environment. The hardy and adaptable inhabitants have had to construct homes able to withstand the extremes of climate. The traditional permanent chalets at lower levels are normally constructed of stone, with some wood, and have barns to the rear for hay, tools and implements. At higher levels the chalets are constructed solely of stone, their front sections designed to house both animals and people, while at the rear hay is stored for winter. The roofs are often striking, with their huge granite tiles.

*Vincendières, nestling beneath the massive mountainsides that form the Vallée d'Avérole, is a typical stone-built village of the Haute Maurienne.*

# THE QUEYRAS

The Parc Naturel Régional du Queyras is a mountain paradise, closed off from Italy by a wall of 3,000-m peaks and presenting a fine combination of flowery meadows and high pastures, villages that cling doggedly to steep hillsides and a reasonable climate. Further north the awesome Col d'Izoard leads to Briançon, a strategic stronghold since Roman times and now a busy Alpine centre.

**Comité Départemental du Tourisme des Hautes-Alpes**
8 bis, Rue Capitaine-de-Bresson – BP 46
05002 Gap Cedex 2
Tel: 04 92 53 62 00
www.haute-alpes.net

**Touring:**
AA Road Map France series 14: Rhône Alpes

*From the perimeter of the fort of Château-Queyras, perched on an outcrop of rock, there are fine views to the east. The village nestles just below, in times past grateful for the fort's protection.*

## PARC DU QUEYRAS

France's Parcs Naturels Régionaux differ from its Parcs Nationaux in that alongside the promotion of nature conservation and the protection of sites of, for example, archaeological, historical and geological interest (below), they also encourage outdoor sports. These include walking, ski touring, paragliding and canoeing, and the establishment of a long-distance footpath, the Tour du Queyras, is a good example of this initiative. As a result, economic considerations do not predominate over landscape and wildlife conservation.

The Parc Naturel Régional du Queyras, which is famous for its wildlife, was created in 1977, and provides an excellent illustration of how careful development can coexist with a policy of conservation of the environment.

## Briançon

The highest city in Europe, and the most important in this part of the Alps, thriving Briançon developed as a result of its strategically valuable position. There have been military fortifications here since Celtic and Roman times and the Fort des Salettes still stands impressively above the Ville Haute. This part of the city is particularly worth a visit. After parking at Champ de Mars or Porte d'Embrun, you can gain access on foot through stout, studded wooden doors. The newer, low town has excellent year-round sporting facilities.

Shops and bars are plentiful in Briançon and through it is a busy place, the mellow colours of the rock, the steepness and the pleasing architectural styles lend it a

relaxing air. In the north-west corner is the Collégiale Notre-Dame, built between 1703 and 1726. Inside is a 16th-century tapestry of St George and the Dragon and many other superb paintings and tapestries. There are many other things to see, including the Place d'Armes with its sundials, the town hall and the Pont d'Asfeld.

## Château-Queyras

The huge fort of Château-Queyras, which remained in military use until 1967, completely dominates this upper part of the valley. There have been important fortifications on this natural rock barrier since the 14th century, but most of the present structure was built in the 18th and 19th centuries.

*In the Parc Régional du Queyras, a mountainous and wooded area on the border with Italy, efficient environmental management goes hand in hand with prudent development of leisure activities.*

## CASSE DÉSERTE

From Château-Queyras, the road north to Briançon runs over the Col d'Izoard, a high-level pass often blocked by snow from October to June. However, it becomes accessible in summer, when one of its most awesome sights is the Casse Déserte, a huge mountainside of grey scree slopes, out of which sprout dozens of dramatic rocky pinnacles, some in groups, some in isolation. This lunar landscape has been created by natural forces, as wind, rain and extremes of temperature have eroded the softer rock, wearing it down into scree and leaving extrusions of harder rock in the form of these contorted and grotesquely shaped pinnacles.

The true extent of this massive desert of bare scree is difficult to grasp. There are no trees to give it scale, and not even the hardiest plant clings to the ever-moving slopes. The area's beauty lies in its uncompromising barrenness and no one can fail to be overawed by it.

## Col d'Izoard

One of the highest Alpine passes, at 2,360m, this Col is well known as the summit of one of the toughest routes taken by the Tour de France. The approach from either direction is long and arduous, as forest gradually gives way to open mountainside, scree and snow, the road taking an unrelenting series of hairpins. The names of famous riders are painted on the road, and at the summit there is a cycling information centre.

Behind here a short walk leads up to a viewpoint and an orientation panel that points out the magnificent views south to the summits of the Queyras and north to those of the Briançonnais.

Lower down on the south side of the Col is a plaque commemorating Tour de France stars Fausto Coppi and Louison Bobet.

## Montbardon

As you drive through the Combe du Queyras towards Château-Queyras it seems impossible that there should be habitation on the vertical valley sides. Yet there is, and one of the loveliest small villages in the area, Montbardon, lies at the end of a narrow and tortuous road. It is set amid high pastures dotted with fir and pine and carpeted with wild flowers.

## St Véran

The highest village in Europe, at over 2,000m, St Véran is also one of the most visited. All visitors' vehicles have to be left below the village, necessitating a short, uphill walk. Many of the buildings date from the 17th and 18th centuries, with wood featuring strongly in the construction, along with some typical Haute-Savoie stone-tiled roofs. The massively overhanging eaves, wide balconies and contorted, ancient beams, together with the narrow streets, lend a genuinely old-fashioned air to the place. Two old village houses may be visited. One is simply called La Vieille Maison Traditionelle, where the animals lived with the family until 1976. The other, the lovely Musée du Soum, is the oldest house in the village, built in 1641.

## Sommet Bucher

The road to this supreme viewpoint is signposted down in the low town of Château-Queyras, below the fort. The 11-km drive through the forests is rough in places, but presents no real difficulties, and leads eventually to the summit plateau, an open area of high pastures. A short walk from the car parks takes you to the viewpoint, with its beautifully crafted orientation panel.

*St Véran's church, which has a wall-mounted sundial, watches over the upper part of this enchanting village.*

# PÉRIGORD AND QUERCY

There is a magical, almost magnetic, quality about Périgord and Quercy, the areas around the Rivers Dordogne and Lot. The dramatic limestone cliffs, the rivers running down from the Massif Central to their eventual destination in the sea, the waterfalls and the distant views that drew early man to settle here, all exert a similar pull on everyone who visits the region.

This is an area that is rich in many ways: scenery, agriculture, food, caves and other prehistoric sites, châteaux, medieval villages and attractive towns. Lack of space forces us to make a selection of places of interest. But doubtless you will discover many of your own, for if you like to just drive where your fancy takes you, this is the ideal region. Wherever you choose to stop you can be sure there will be something to catch your eye, whether it is a pretty waterside village, a majestic castle perched on a hill, a cave or simply a lively local market or restaurant.

When you first see villages such as St Cirq-Lapopie, set high on a hill, with all its turrets and towers overlooking the winding Lot – which, when full, runs almost blood-red with sandstone – you begin to believe in fairy stories.

Périgord has been conveniently colour-coded by the local tourist office. Historically, there was Périgord Blanc, named after the white rocks that dominate the central region, and Périgord Noir, from the dark leaves of the oaks that covered the southeast of the area. Here, too, you can enjoy those darkest of delights – truffles. To these areas have now been added Périgord Vert (around Nontron) and Périgord Pourpre (near Bergerac and the purple grapes of the wine region).

The Vézère valley, the area between Lascaux and Souillac, including Sarlat-la-Canéda, is the striking heart of Périgord Noir. It is rich beyond belief in cave paintings and historical sites. However, further south, the Quercy region around the Lot is less crowded and also has cave paintings, fine river views and wonderful wine, so deep red it is almost black.

Both the Dordogne and Lot valleys are studded with castles, built mostly for defence and in many cases bearing the battle scars of the Hundred Years War and the Wars of Religion.

Bastide towns, medieval garrisons, today sleepy in the sun and with attractive markets piled high with walnuts, fruits, duck and goose products and wholesome vegetables of every description, are another enjoyable and typical feature of the landscape. It is chilling to learn how bitterly they were fought over.

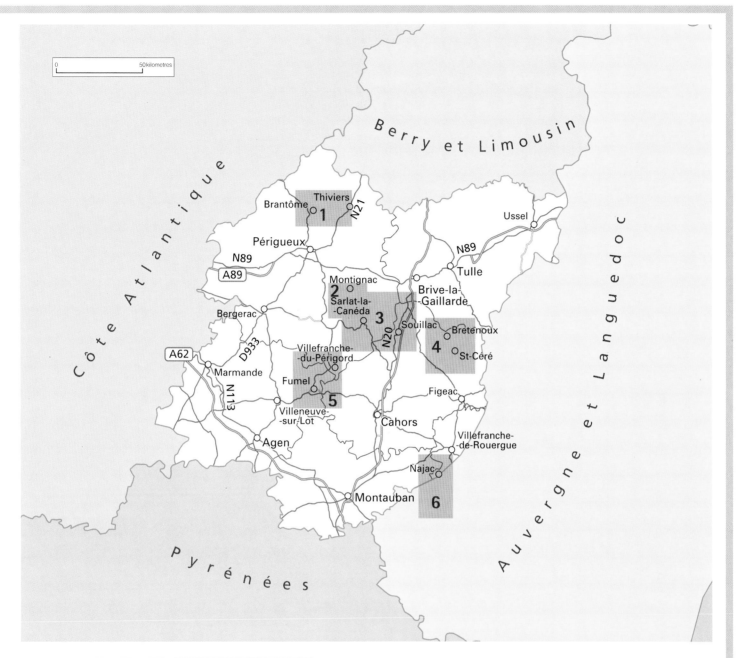

Beynac (right) stands on one of the most attractive stretches of the characterful River Dordogne.

Périgord geese (below) provide renowned pâté de foie gras.

# AROUND BRANTÔME

Brantôme is one of the best gateways to Périgord. Its mellow buildings, its abbey and its island location on the River Dronne are a pleasant foretaste of what is to come in a tour of the region. However, its attractions are so well publicised that you may find it crowded in high summer. The area contains a number of interesting châteaux and a few prehistoric cave paintings, but its greatest asset is undoubtedly the charm of its riverside towns.

**Comité Départemental du Tourisme de la Dordogne**
25, Rue Wilson – BP 2063
24002 Périgueux Cedex
Tel: 05 53 35 50 24
www.perigord.tm.fr/tourisme

**Touring:**
AA Road Map France
series 4: Poitou-Charentes

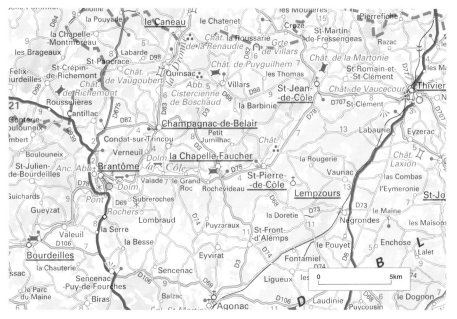

## WALNUTS

Périgord and Quercy are France's second largest producer of walnuts. The main areas of cultivation are north of the Dordogne, south of the Corrèze and many parts of the Lot. During October and November many towns hold walnut markets.

Walnut oil is the chief ingredient of the local salad dressing and is also widely used for cooking. In the Lot Marbot and Grandjean walnuts are often sold broken for making bread, cakes or oil. Many restaurants serve walnut bread with cheese. Walnut mousse is also popular. The chestnut is the other much prized local nut. Even the smallest village shop sells canned *marrons glacés* as souvenirs.

*Monumental rock carvings were executed in the caves behind the abbey at Brantôme in the second half of the 15th century. They depict the Crucifixion and the Last Judgement.*

## Bourdeilles

This was the birthplace of the 16th-century chronicler Pierre de Bourdeilles, who used the pen-name Brantôme. Occupying an imposing position on the rocks above the Dronne are a 13th-century castle and a Renaissance château, with the village clustered below by the river. Among the castle's claims to fame is a bed that was supposedly slept in by Emperor Charles V.

From the castle there is a beautiful view of the restored 17th-century water-mill, built in the shape of a ship and surrounded by the green waters of the river. Canoes may be hired for the trip to Brantôme.

## Brantôme

A beautiful medieval and Renaissance town, Brantôme is known as the Venice of Périgord, as it is a little island held between the arms of the Dronne. It is a wonderful place to stroll, with its old balconied houses with their flowers and trellises and its five bridges. The town is dominated by the abbey, parts of which date back to the 8th century. The abbey has a bell tower built on an imposing rock in the 11th century, while the riverside gardens, originally created by the monks, are one of Brantôme's most attractive features. The monks used the caves behind the abbey to store wines and executed some carvings in them, one of which depicts the Last Judgement. This cave is now used as a theatre, and provides a dramatic backdrop to performances of plays and concerts during the summer.

## FISHING

For the fisherman, a holiday in the Dordogne and Lot region provides plenty of opportunities for sport. It is best to ask for information at the local tourist office first, as you will probably need a temporary licence to fish. Many of these offices have free maps showing where you can fish.

Trout, roach, perch, bream and carp are the local fish. But there are closed seasons for certain fish and the tourist office can advise on the regulations. The best fishing is said to be wherever the river widens. Further information on the Lot can be obtained by writing to the

Fédération Départmentale de Pêche, 182 Quai Cavaignac, 46000 Cahors, or telephoning 05 65 35 50 22. For the Dordogne, contact them at 16 Rue des Près, 24000 Périgueux, or phone 05 53 06 84 20.

Brantôme has not achieved its immense popularity simply on the strength of its archaeological and historical sites; an equal attraction are its many fine restaurants, featuring the best of the region's cuisine.

## Champagnac-de-Belair

If you visit this small town on the last Sunday in August you will see the sheep fair. It has the 16th-century Château de la Borie (now a bed-and-breakfast) and a fine old church. But the town's greatest appeal lies in its location overlooking the Dronne.

## La Chapelle-Faucher

The village boasts a wonderful château set above the River Côle. Although part of the château was destroyed by fire, it is still inhabited. Near by is the little village of Jumilhac, whose springs supply the area with water, where the ruins of the priory of Puymartin and the Château de Bolaurent can be seen.

## St Jean-de-Côle

Situated on the Côle, a tributary of the Dronne, the village has often been used as a location for historical films. Its narrow streets contain half-timbered medieval houses typical of the region and there is a

humpback bridge over the river. The church, which has its origins in the 11th century, has several unusual features, including a curiously shaped bell tower with windows. The remains of the 13th-century Château de Marthonie dominate the village square. Open to visitors in July and August, they house a permanent exhibition of old publicity posters and the handmade paper for which the region was at one time famous.

## Villars

This traditional village, with its old covered market and distinctive fountain set in a circular basin, has three interesting sites. The Château de Puyguilhem was built in the early 16th century by Mondot de la Marthonie, the first president of the Paris and Bordeaux parliaments. It is very much in the style of the châteaux of the Loire on which he modelled it.

Near by are the Grottes de Villars, caves featuring prehistoric wall paintings and stalactites and stalagmites. The most famous painting depicts a blue horse. Unusually, the paintings also show human figures. Also situated near Villars is the 12th-century Abbaye de Boschaud, abandoned at the Revolution. It has undergone restoration but is still partly in ruins. It was one of just four Cistercian abbeys in Périgord.

*Brantôme, with its attractive mixture of medieval and Renaissance architecture, provides an excellent introduction to Périgord.*

*St Jean-de-Côle has provided the location for many films which have a medieval setting.*

# THE VÉZÈRE VALLEY

Although the Vézère valley is best known for its many important archaeological sites, what drew primitive man to the area – its rivers, its lush vegetation and its dramatic cliffs – make it attractive to the modern tourist. It is impossible to visit a region that saw the dawning of early man without finding your curiosity awakened.

*Les Eyzies-de-Tayac lies at the heart of a region renowned for its wealth of connections with prehistory. Near here, in 1868, the remains of Cro-Magnon Man were found.*

## Les Eyzies-de-Tayac

This town, sited dramatically below the limestone cliff where the Vézère meets the Beune, is at the heart of a region where early man is known to have lived, and is therefore known as France's centre of prehistory. The many caves in the cliff reveal some of the secrets of early man, and throughout the area there is a concentration of such caves and prehistoric sites. Situated to the east of Les Eyzies, in a 13th-century fortress on a rock halfway up the cliff overlooking the town, is the Musée National de Préhistorie, which displays, among other items, major archaeological finds.

## Grotte de Carpe-Diem

The cave, off the D47 a few kilometres north-west of Les Eyzies, winds through the rock for 180m and has some fine examples of stalactites and stalagmites. Its mysterious chambers have been named after what these formations suggest – for example, the Salle de la Vierge.

## Grotte du Grand Roc

Close to Laugerie Haute and Laugerie Basse, where primitive man lived for 20,000 years and hundreds of prehistoric items have been found, is the natural cave known as the Grotte du Grand Roc. From the stairs leading up to the cave and the platform at its mouth there are excellent views of the Vézère valley and the valley of Tayac and Les Eyzies. Inside there is an impressive display of stalagmites and unusual crystalline formations, which seem to defy gravity.

## Montignac

This is the only place where you can buy tickets for the cave system of Lascaux II. You can also buy a ticket to include the

### EARLY MAN

The Vézère valley is of prime archaeological importance because it was here that Cro-Magnon Man was discovered. This early form of *Homo sapiens* appeared in Europe about 30–40,000 years ago, after Neanderthal Man, who lived 150,000 to 40,000 years ago. The latter had a short, stocky body, a wide pelvis and an enormous nose, all probably the result of adaptation to the demands of the Ice Age.

Cro-Magnon Man was taller, with a smaller face and a higher brow. He is also distinguished from his Neanderthal predecessors by using tools differently, by the evidence of art and decoration discovered in his dwellings and by his wearing of 'jewellery' such as beads and pendants.

*In the caves of Lascaux II are facsimiles of the paintings in the original caves. Particularly striking is the Salle des Taureaux, the Bulls' Hall, from which a detail is shown here.*

nearby Le Thot visitor centre, which provides background information and a park where many of the anials portrayed in the caves can be seen, both as living examples and animated models.

Montignac, on the banks of the Vézère, was once a fortress town belonging to the counts of Périgord and the original tower

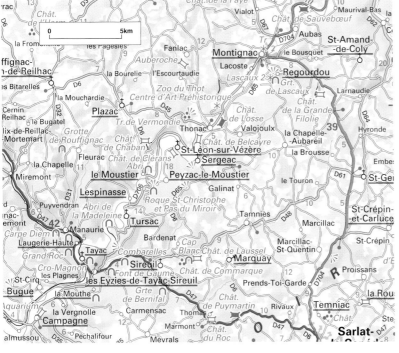

**Comité Départemental du Tourisme de la Dordogne**
25, Rue Wilson – BP 2063
24002 Périgueux Cedex
Tel: 05 53 35 50 24
www.perigord.tm.fr/
tourisme

**Touring:**
AA Road Map France
series 4: Poitou-
Charentes, and
6: Midi-Pyrénées

remains. Thanks to the discovery of Lascaux, it is no longer a sleepy village, but an extremely busy tourist centre. Near by is Régourdou, where in 1954 were found the 70,000-year-old skeleton of Régourdu Man and a burial ground containing the bodies of bears. Montignac is also famous for its association with the writer Eugene le Roy, who died here in 1907.

## Peyzac-le-Moustier

Where the stream of Le Moustier joins the Vézère, there was in prehistoric times an *abri*, a shelter. Apparently, our ancestors preferred to live in shelters formed by overhanging rocks on the cliff face. The cliffs of the Vézère valley are riddled with such shelters, providing archaeologists with rich pickings. At Peyzac in 1908, German explorers discovered a Neanderthal man.

At the Abri du Cap Blanc, a similar shelter east of Les Eyzies, a skeleton of a woman was found. She ended up in an American museum, but you can see a replica of her and some sculpture over 10,000 years old.

## Préhistoparc

You can get a good idea of how our early ancestors lived without setting foot in a cave, by visiting this park at Tursac. It has been laid out with models that reconstruct the life of early man by showing, for example, the cutting up of reindeer, cave painting, fishing and hunting. Early animals are also well represented.

The setting of the park, in woodland between cliffs, where we know prehistoric man actually dwelt, adds a certain magic to what might otherwise be just another theme park.

Also at Tursac is the archaeologically important site of La Madeleine, a narrow, rocky limestone promontory that has been inhabited from prehistoric times, and which has given its name to Magdalenian Culture. By the river in a rock shelter the remains of early man have been discovered.

Further up the cliff are troglodyte dwellings, inhabited from the Middle Ages right up to the beginning of the 20th century.

## La Roque St Christophe

Believed to have been inhabited from prehistoric times to the 16th century, this sheer cliff 80m high and 1000m long is a honeycomb of hundreds of caves and shelters, stacked in five tiers, like a prehistoric block of flats. From the terrace there is a commanding view over the Vézère valley – once the steep steps up to it have been climbed.

This is one of the oldest and most important cliff fortresses in the world, and those who have sought its shelter over the centuries include Neanderthal man, Vikings and Huguenots.

## St Léon-sur-Vézère

This pretty village lying in a loop near the river valley has no caves. But it does boast a fine 12th-century Romanesque church, made of honey-coloured stone, that was formerly a Benedictine priory, and two châteaux which are not, unfortunately, open to the public. Close by is the imposing 16th-century Château de Belcayre.

### MARKETS

Almost every town in France has a market. This is usually held in the main square and takes place on different weekdays according to the town, and sometimes on Saturday as well.

Here is a chance to see – and sample – the local produce: vegetables, fruits, flowers, honey, cheese, bread and of course, the ducks and geese for which the region is renowned.

One of the liveliest markets in the Dordogne is the Tuesday market in Le Bugue, about 30km west of Sarlat-le-Canéda, not far from where the Vézère flows into the Dordogne. Held in the Place de Mairie, the market spills over into neighbouring streets.

# PÉRIGORD NOIR

This area of Périgord is perhaps the most attractive, with its massive cliffs topped by golden châteaux, fascinating history, fine food and the beautiful old regional capital, Sarlat-la-Canéda. Yet the most impressive sights are not the towns, however appealing. It is the landscape of cliffs, rivers and trees that lingers in the memory.

*The Château de Castelnaud looks across a bend in the Dordogne at its former adversary, the Château de Beynac.*

of a rocky cliff. The easy way to reach it is by road, but walking up gives you a better idea of how difficult it was to storm.

A cluster of houses, in the same golden stone, huddle beneath the château: the little village of Beynac-et-Cazenac, where you can visit a small archaeological museum. From the old quays you can take a boat trip along the river, or hire a canoe or kayak. During the Hundred Years War the English occupied Beynac and the French held Castelnaud across the river, the Dordogne forming the boundary.

## Carsac-Aillac

This peaceful village on the green river banks has a beautiful Romanesque church in golden stone, with a huge bell tower and dramatic modern stained-glass windows. It stands beside the ruins of a château, and farther along the river, at Aillac, there is a very similar church, in a similar setting.

## Château de Castelnaud

Beynac's great rival during the Hundred Years War, the château is said to have been destroyed and rebuilt 10 times during its turbulent history. The latest renovation began in the late 1960s and is nearly complete. The château now houses a museum of medieval siege warfare. As with the château at Beynac, one of the best reasons to visit it are the panoramic views over the Dordogne across the terrace.

Close by is Les Milandes, the château where the entertainer Josephine Baker (1906–75) set up a home for orphans from all around the world. A large part of the castle is now a museum dedicated to the artist. There is also a falconry museum, with flying demonstrations in summer.

## Beynac-et-Cazenac

From the terrace of the medieval château here, there is a fabulous view along the winding Dordogne as far as Domme, and of the châteaux of Marqueyssac, Castelnaud and Fayrac. The château is perched on top

## Cingle de Montfort

The great loop in the Dordogne is best viewed from a car park on the D703 built for this purpose. On top of the cliff is the Château de Montfort. Simon de Montfort razed it in 1214, it was rebuilt by the

### TRUFFLES

Probably the most expensive vegetable in the world, truffles are an edible fungus that grows underground close to the roots of certain trees, especially oaks. Truffles like a dry limestone soil, which is why they thrive in Périgord. They are harvested between December and February, when gourmets and chefs from around the world descend on Périgord for the truffle hunt. Traditionally, pigs or specially trained dogs sniff out the truffles when they are in peak condition. Sows were originally used because the smell of a ripe truffle apparently resembles that of a male pig. Neither sows nor dogs have the temerity, it seems, to eat these 'black diamonds'.

There are some 30 types of truffle, but the type from Périgord is the most famous. Truffles feature in many regional dishes, but nowadays only tiny shavings are used, for as with garlic, a little is said to go a long way. A full-grown truffle weighs about 100g. Their aromatic, earthy flavour goes well with eggs, fish and chicken.

Near Sorges, on the N21 north of Périgueux, is the Maison de la Truffe, a truffle museum.

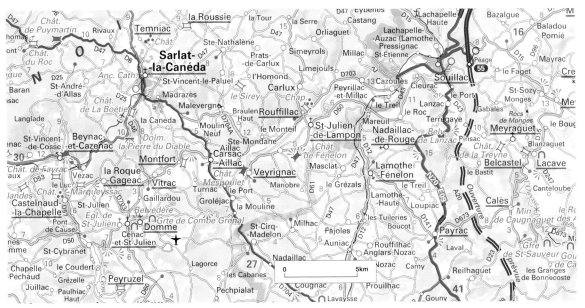

**Comité Départemental du Tourisme de la Dordogne**
25, Rue Wilson – PB 2063
24002 Périgueux Cedex
Tel: 05 53 35 50 24
www.perigord.tm.fr/tourisme

**Touring:**
AA Road Map France
series 6: Midi-Pyrénées

## FOIE GRAS

Geese (below) and ducks are a common sight in Périgord and Quercy, and they feature on practically every menu in one way or anther. *Foie gras* has been popular, particularly in this region, since the 15th century. Often made into pâté, it is produced by force-feeding geese or ducks until their livers swell to an abnormal weight .

Another local speciality is *confit* of duck and goose, in which the wings or legs are preserved in their own fat. The confit was the traditional way of preserving geese before refrigeration was invented.

Turenne family and then it was captured and destroyed twice more; hence the mixture of styles. Unfortunately it is not open to the public, but as it dominates the little hamlet below you can get some good views of it. Near by is the Château de Fénelon, the home of the 17th-century writer and archbishop of that name.

## Domme

This is one of France's most spectacular *bastide* towns, built in 1280 for Philip the Bold. The northern end of the town has such a steep drop down the cliffs that it never needed to be fortified. Domme does not possess the strict rectangular formation of other *bastides*. Instead, its design took advantage of the lie of the land.

The history of Domme is recounted in the Museumof Arts and Popular Traditions. From the traditional covered market in the town centre, you can visit the 400m of caves, where the villagers took refuge during the Hundred Years War. In one of the three gates in Domme's massive walls, the Porte des Tours, are two towers, one of which contains the names of the Knights Templar who were held prisoner there during the 14th century.

## La Roque-Gageac

La Roque-Gageac is frequently described as one of France's most beautiful villages, so in the summer months it is quite busy. Exploration of its narrow streets is best done on foot. There is a 16th-century

manor house with a pepper-pot roof, the Manoir de Tarde. At the other end of the village is the 20th-century Château de la Malartrie, inspired by the style of the 15th-century. Near the riverside car park you can take a trip in a gabarre, a flat-bottomed boat.

## Sarlat-la-Canéda

This medieval town, with its honey-coloured buildings with twisted towers, turrets and gables, alleys and courtyards, is best explored on foot. Parking can be a problem, especially in the summer. Sarlat originated in the 8th century, when a Benedictine abbey was founded there. The monks built their abbey 10km from the river, to protect themselves from river-borne looters. Although the medieval centre has spread somewhat beyond its original boundaries, it is remarkably unspoiled and provides a magical contrast with the suburbs. There is a lot to see in the old quarter, including the Lanterne des Morts, a strange tower with a conical roof, and the Cathédrale St-Sacerdos. But Sarlat's charms does not lie so much in its many individual monuments as in the total feel of the place.

One of the best places to view Sarlat is the park above the Palais de Justice, which were once the private gardens of the bishops of Sarlat. Originally laid our in the 17th century, they are still very beautiful. On Saturdays a market spreads over many streets and all the riches of Périgord Noir, including truffles, chicken, geese and other livestock, can be bought here.

*La Roque-Gageac's Manoir de Tarde, built of the local golden stone and with a pepper-pot tower, stands beneath cliffs that tower over the village and the Dordogne. High up on the cliffs, there are the remains of long-abandoned cave dwellings.*

# UPPER QUERCY

Like much of the region, this is an area of great contrasts. The high limestone plateau that links the Dordogne to the Lot and Célé is nature unrestrained. A trip to the Gouffre de Padirac, for example, makes you realise how hostile the natural world can be. The charm of riverside villages such as Loubressac lies partly in their smallness, which is reassuring when compared with the awesome character of the landscape.

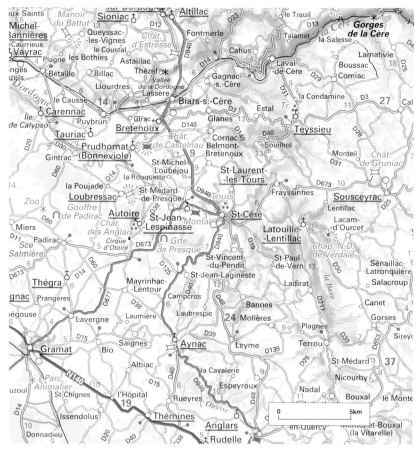

*The lovely village of Autoire is typically Quercynois, with its mellow stone houses with brown-tiled roofs and its turreted grander dwellings.*

## Autoire

This is a well-preserved, picturesque village, officially one of France's prettiest, with its half-timbered houses, turreted mansions and fountain. From the terrace near the beautifully sculptured church you can see the Cirque d'Autoire, an amphitheatre of rocks. Also near by is a ruined castle with a dramatic waterfall tumbling down the cliff face. The gorges of the River Autoire are also a striking sight.

## Carennac

The village benefits from a beautiful setting on the banks of the Dordogne, facing the little island of Calypso. Houses with brown roof tiles, typical of Quercy, and villas with turrets are clustered round an old priory where Fénelon, the 17th-century writer, was

the prior. The 12th-century church of St-Pierre has a handsome carved doorway.

## Château de Castelnau-Bretenoux

At one time 1,500 men and 100 horses were garrisoned in this huge medieval fortress on a spur overlooking the village of Prudhomat, close to the spot where the Cère joins the Dordogne. It was originally built in the 11th century, and was restored at the beginning of the twentieth century by the opera singer Jean Moulierat, who left it to the nation. The château gives superb views over the Dordogne and is an unmistakable landmark. To the north-west you can see the remains of the Château de Turenne, once its bitter rival. Attractions inside the château include Aubusson and Beauvais tapestries and a lapidary museum.

**Comité Départemental du Tourisme du Lot**
46001 Cahors Cedex
Tel: 05 65 35 07 09
www.tourisme-lot.com

**Touring:**
AA Road Map France series 4: Poitou-Charentes, 6: Midi-Pyrénées, and 9: Auvergne Limousin

*St Céré is a thriving market town situated at an important crossroads in the valley of the River Bave. Looking down on the town are the imposing medieval towers of St-Laurent.*

## ROCAMADOUR

The spectacular village of Rocamadour is dramatically sited on a steep rock face in the gorge of the River Alzou. The best view is from the belvedere in the hamlet of L'Hospitalet above it, which still has the ruins of an 11th-century hospital for the care of pilgrims.

Rocamadour is dominated by its 14th-century castle, which is reached from the village by a steep flight of steps marked by the Stations of the Cross. For hundreds of years, pilgrims have flocked here to pay homage to the Vierge Noire, carved out of walnut wood. Penitents used to climb the 216 stone steps in chains to receive absolution in the Chapelle Miraculeuse. The Chapel also houses an ancient bell, said to toll itself before a miracle occurs. Seven churches are grouped together on the site, which was believed to have contained the grave of one of Christ's disciples, St Amadour.

Because of its beauty and history, Rocamadour is the second most visited historic site in France. Inevitably the village gets very congested and is highly commercialised, but it is still a marvellous place to visit.

## Château de Montal

This medieval and Renaissance château on a wooded hillside above the Bave has a sad and romantic history. The widow Jeanne de Balsac d'Entraygues built it in 1534 for her eldest son, who was fighting in Italy at the time. She used master craftsmen and artists, and when it was completed she sat at a high window watching for her son. He never returned, and she had the window boarded up and the words '*Plus d'espoir*' (Hope is no more) carved beneath it. It was restored at the beginning of the 20th century by one M. Fenaille, who gave it to the nation.

## Gouffre de Padirac

This huge crater, 90m in width and depth, was originally caused by the collapse of a cave. Through it flows a subterranean river. Although in the summer it is very busy, it is still an awe-inspiring site. After descending by a lift you can take a boat trip through floodlit limestone caves, of which the enormous Grand Dôme, 100m high, is the most dramatic.

## Gramat

The town is the capital of the Causse de Gramat, the massive limestone plateau that runs from the valley of the Dordogne near Souillac to the Lot and Célé near Cahors. The Causse has an average height of 350m and along its route are some unusual and dramatic landscapes. Gramat itself is a bustling town that serves as a market for many of the villages around, and its many markets sell all the local produce from sheep and nuts to truffles. It is also famous for its training centre for police dogs and handlers, where there are tours and special displays during the summer months. Just outside the town is the Parc de Vision de Gramat, a 40-hectare zoo. Among its attractions are animals in their natural environment and a botanical park featuring typical trees and shrubs of the Causse.

## Loubressac

A charming fortified village built on a rocky spur overlooking the River Bave, Loubressac offers views across the river to the Château de Castelnau-Bretenoux. It is dominated by a 15th-century château of its own, which unfortunately is not open.

## St Céré

A picturesque old town situated 3km west of Montal, St Céré lies clustered in the valley of the Bave, overlooked by the medieval towers and curtain wall of the Tours de St-Laurent. It has many fine old houses, and in the Galerie du Casino there is a large collection of Jean Lurçat's tapestries. Having trained in Aubusson, Lurçat lived in St Céré from 1945 until his death in 1966, when his widow bequeathed a representative selection of his works to the town. The house and studio where he worked are also open.

St Céré is still a prosperous town, with a market that is particularly noted for the plums and strawberries it sells from local farms. Some 16km along the river is Latouille-Lentillac, with the little pilgrim chapel of Notre-Dame de Verdale.

## SOUILLAC

A busy town situated where the main road between Brive-la-Gaillarde and Cahors crosses the Dordogne, Souillac has been an important river trading post and crossroads for hundreds of years. Boats would travel from Souillac to Libourne laden with salt and wood for vine stakes and barrels. It is still an important market town for farms in the region, but now the river is used for swimming, fishing and canoeing.

There is little left of the original medieval town, apart from a beautiful church (above), all that remains of a Benedictine abbey. It is said to compare favourably with the cathedral at Cahors. Souillac also has a fascinating mechanical-model museum.

# LAND OF *BASTIDES*

This landscape is so studded with the fortified towns known as *bastides*, and with castles, that you cannot but wonder about its history, which often turns out to be bloodchilling. But there is a welcome contrast. Pretty riverside towns such as Puy-l'Évêque have great charm, and the best thing about the *bastides* today is their markets, which have long sold all the regional delicacies.

*Originally raised in the 12th century, the Château de Biron (above) is a mixture of architectural styles. It was used as a setting for the French film* Les Visiteurs.

*Monpazier (right), built by Edward I of England, is one of the finest* bastides.

## Château de Biron

Romantically sited on a high rock 8km from Monpazier, the Château de Biron is a massive landmark and from its sentry walks there are wonderful views. It was originally built in the 12th century by the Gontaut family, who held it until the 20th century. It has been added to and altered so many times that it represents nearly every architectural style through the centuries.

The hamlet of Biron is within the outer walls of the château and a remnant of the class system is seen in the chapel, which has an upper storey for the family and one below for the villagers. But you will have to

go to New York's Metropolitan Museum of Art if you want to view what some historians believe were the chapel's best treasures: a carved tomb depicting angels around the body of Christ and a *pietà*.

## Château de Bonaguil

This is one of the last medieval castles to be built. It was begun by Bérenger de Roquefeuil in 1447 and took 40 years to complete. It had 350m of wall, 13 towers and turrets, an inner moat and dozens of concealed passages. Ironically this fortress built to withstand an attack by 10,000 men was never challenged. It came under siege only during the Revolution, and even so the bulk remains. As well as tours of the romantic ruins, musical evenings are held here during the summer.

## Monpazier

Founded in 1284 by Edward I of England, Duke of Aquitaine, Monpazier is a perfect example of a *bastide* town, eight blocks around a central square, and has miraculously survived largely unchanged.

During the Hundred Years War it was captured by the French and English several times in turn, and during the 17th

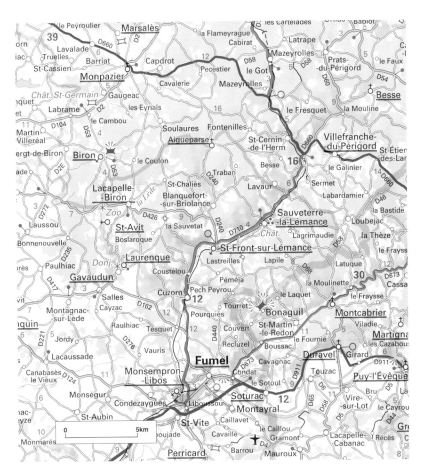

century the town witnessed a bitter peasants' revolt.

The central square, with its medieval covered marketplace, is impressive and on the third Thursday of each month there is a fair. Originally this square was the corn market. The town has many old houses, a *lavoir* where the village women used to wash clothes, an old tithe barn and a 14th-century church. In spring and autumn Monpazier is shaken out of its sleepiness by its renowned mushroom markets.

## Montcabrier

This is a small *bastide* founded by Guy de Cabrier in 1297. Several very old houses overlook the central square. Inside the old church is a 14th-century statue of St Louis, patron saint of the parish, to which local pilgrimages were formerly made.

## Puy-l'Évêque

A good place to stop for lunch, this picturesque town, with its golden-stone houses stretching down to the banks of the Lot, is dominated by the church and the castle keep. The best way to appreciate the

Mushrooms are a speciality of the region, and are sold in many places, including the spacious covered market in Villefranche-du-Périgord.

beauty of Puy-l'Évêque is from across the river. In the town itself there is a stunning view of the Lot valley from the Esplanade de la Truffière, between the original keep and the town hall.

The town's shape is said to have been determined by the English, who occupied it many times and changed its defences. It is now on the official wine route between Cahors and Fumel. The fertile red soil of the area produces what most experts agree are the best wines of Cahors. These rich, red wines are usually matured for three years in oak casks.

## St Martin-le-Redon

A few houses clustered round a church that most people simply drive through on their way to Bonaguil, the village at one time found fame as the source of St-Martial water, which was believed to be capable of curing skin ailments.

## Villefranche-du-Périgord

In times past this Catholic *bastide*, which dominates the valley of the River Lémance, was a great rival to Monpazier, the towns taking it in turns to raid each other. Built over the years to defend the way to Quercy, it was several times captured and destroyed, then rebuilt. Although Villefranche-du-Périgord is not as well preserved as its former rival, its larger covered market surrounded by arcades clearly identifies it as a *bastide*.

*Puy-l'Évêque is a handsome, stone-built town on the banks of the Lot. Its fine castle keep was, in times gone by, the residence of the bishops of Cahors.*

**Comité Départemental du Tourisme de la Dordogne**
25, Rue Wilson
24002 Périgueux Cedex
Tel: 05 53 35 50 24
www.perigord.tm.fr/tourisme

**Comité Départemental du Tourisme du Lot**
46001 Cahors Cedex
Tel: 05 65 35 07 09
www.tourisme-lot.com

**Touring:**
AA Road Map France series 6: Midi-Pyrénées

# THE AVEYRON VALLEY

Dramatic scenery and sparse populations in scattered communities perched on hilltops or sheer cliffs characterise this wild countryside that illustrates so well how France was fought over. The area also possesses several attractive medieval towns where so much remains unchanged after centuries.

*Among the many attractions of Rochers is the Maison du Grand Fauconnier, which has fine carved falcons on its façade and is today used as the town hall. It also houses a collection of contemporary paintings and an embroidery museum. The 14th-century market hall is still intact and has a splendid timber roof and a well said to be over 100m deep. The Maison Portal depicts the town's history. Other attractions include a museum displaying sugar sculptures.*

## Bournazel

The look of this tiny village on a rocky outcrop north of Rochers is typical of the region. It features a 15th-century church with a restored tower and an unfinished château with two 16th-century wings.

## Les Cabannes

The Gothic church has a painting of the Assumption dating from 1653 and an iron cross whose base is decorated with the fleur-de-lys. A broken tower is all that remains of a château. There is a 19th-century bust of Vice Admiral St-Félix in the middle of the beautiful square. He distinguished himself in the American War of Independence. In a battle during the Napoleonic wars he was in command of the only ship that halted the English advance on the French line.

## Cordes

This exceptionally pretty town, sometimes called 'Cordes-sur-Ciel', is built on a hill with a marvellous view of the surrounding countryside, and seems to reach up to the sky. It was a *bastide* town, founded early in the 13th century. But the name 'Rochers'

probably derives from the leather and hemp industries through which the town became prosperous during the 13th and 14th centuries. Energetic visitors leave their cars at the bottom of the hill and walk, the better to imagine the scale of the defensive walls that surrounded the town. Many of the gates remain almost intact and, though tiring, the climb up the steep, narrow streets past old houses with exposed beams is very worthwhile.

## Gorges de l'Aveyron

The River Aveyron forms the south-western boundary of the Massif Central. The main roads connecting Villefranche-de-Rouergue, Albi and Montauban form a triangle of wild, sparsely populated countryside through which the Aveyron runs south to the village of Laguépie and then west to join the Tarn north of Montauban.

The Gorges de l'Aveyron offer stunning steep cliffs, up to 500m above the river, widely contrasting landscapes, grottos, many kilometres of shaded lanes and brooks full of trout. This is an ideal area for those who love to canoe, cycle, ride, walk, climb, pothole or hang-glide.

The area between Laguépie and Villefranche-de-Rouergue has been an important mining area for many centuries. In Roman times metal from local mines was used to make coins and in the 16th century German miners discovered substantial deposits of silver. Although the mines later fell into disuse, it was the wealth they promised that brought the railway to the Gorges de l'Aveyron in the 19th century, during which time they were once again heavily worked. During World War II, it is believed, the Germans carried out exploratory mining for copper here.

*Rochers, with its gateways and steep streets, is a town best explored on foot. Many of the old houses are now occupied by artists and craftsmen, who can be seen at work on canvas or loom, or with metal or stone.*

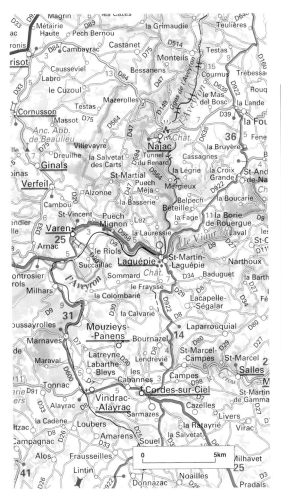

**Comité Départemental du Tourisme du Tarn**
41 Rue Porta – BP 225
81006 Albi Cedex
Tel: 05 63 77 32 10
www.tourisme-tarn.com

**Comité Départemental du Tourisme de l'Aveyron**
17 Rue Aristide Briand – BP 831
12008 Rodez Cedex
Tel: 05 65 75 55 75

**Touring:**
AA Road Map France series 6: Midi-Pyrénées

## QUERCY

The old houses of Quercy are one of the region's greatest attractions. Traditionally built from local stone that seems to glow in the sunlight, they usually had space for animals on the ground floor and living-rooms on the first floor. The top floor was reserved for drying tobacco or preserving foodstuffs. Dovecotes are a common sight, and are mostly balanced on square stone pillars. Pigeons were kept mainly for manure, very important for the land; hence the height of the dovecotes.

## Najac

This is an attractive but rather touristy little town, built, unusually, on twin hills. The houses lie along the ridge of the hills, to one side of which is a sheer drop to the Aveyron, in its beautiful gorge. Najac has always been dominated by the castle, now in ruins, which is located strategically on a cliff and all but surrounded by the river.

This is surely the most romantic setting in France for a medieval fortress. A castle was first built here in 1110 and rebuilt in 1253 by Alphonse de Poitiers, brother of St Louis. Its continuing visual impact on the place is striking: you keep glimpsing it from the hilltops and losing it from view as you dip into ravines.

Despite its predominantly military history, Najac is a colourful, flower-decked tourist centre with adjacent holiday villages. But you will need energy and determination to climb its steep, ancient streets.

## Varen

Situated on the Aveyron about 10km west of Laguépie, and outlined by a string of poplar trees, is the lovely market town of Varen. Long ago it was highly defended,

and you still enter the medieval quarter through the fortified Porte el-Faoure. Here the winding streets have timber-framed houses and interesting flat roofs with round tiles. The tower and gatehouse of the fortified 14th–15th-century château lie beside a 12th-century Romanesque church that has a dungeon in the dean's house.

## Viaur

The River Viaur, which meets the Aveyron at Laguépie, is a water-sports centre, though it has variations in its water level because of its dams. It is fished for trout but the Aveyron has a more varied catch and teems with roach, tench, gudgeon, carp and rainbow trout. About 40km east of Laguépie the river is spanned by the elegant structure of the Viaduc du Viaur, 460m long and 116m high.

## Vindrac-Alayrac

Vindrac-Alayrac, north-west of Rochers, was originally built as a defence for that town, and its church has a watchtower 17m high. The church's interior was restored in the 16th century and its attractions include a gilt wooden statue of the Virgin and St Joseph from that period. Underneath the building is a subterranean refuge. Adjacent to the church is a château that now belongs to the Anselme family but was once the home of the Tapie de Celyrans, relative of the 19th-century artist Toulouse-Lautrec, who are buried in the cemetery.

*Najac is overlooked by a 13th-century fortress and a church of similar date (top). The former occupies a highly defensible position on a cliff encircled by the Aveyron. The Gothic church is plain but distinctive. Most of the houses in the town are of stone (above) or timber-framed and lack cellars because they are built on granite.*

# THE PYRENEES

Stretching the width of south-western France, from the wind-scuffed surf of the Atlantic to the gentle drift of the Mediterranean, the Pyrenees form a magnificent backdrop of mountains some 400km long. In the west they are green and rolling and heavily wooded, with neat Basque villages nestling in their folds. In the east, where the climate of Catalonia influences both landscape and lifestyle, vines, orchards and an aromatic scrub clothe the hillsides.

Between these extremes the region is one of rich scenic and cultural variety, for its history reaches back 20,000 years and more; yet is also at the forefront of modern technology. It is an undulating land watered by big rivers and numerous *gaves* (mountain streams), among them the Nive and Oloron, Adour and Aure, Ariège, Aude and Garonne. There are dramatic waterfalls, stark limestone gorges, snow clad peaks and hundreds of tiny lakes sparkling among glacial cirques.

The Pays Basque, comprising Labourd, Basse-Navarre and Soule, is a land of pelota and sheep; each village has its *fronton*, where *pelota* is played, every hillside its grazing flock. Coastal Labourd has palm trees and sandy bays with great appeal, while inland the pastoral heights of Basse-Navarre are carpeted with bracken and gorse where snaking roads exploit enchanting vistas. Soule, however, is genuine mountain country, sliced by the gorges of Holçarté and Kakouetta on the edge of the High Pyrenees.

Hautes-Pyrénées is truly mountainous, with a number of 3,000-m peaks and the cirques of Gavarnie, Estaubé and Troumouse forming a rim to the Parc National des Pyrénées and the adjacent Réserve Naturelle de Néouvielle. The world-famous pilgrimage town of Lourdes is the gateway to this big country.

Haute-Garonne reaches from the frontier above Bagnères-de-Luchon, beyond magnificent St Bertrand-de-Comminges in the foothills to the plain of Toulouse. Economic capital of the Languedoc and France's fourth town, Toulouse lies too far north to be included here.

The forested heights of Ariège spill down to St Lizier and Foix, whose architectural splendours mark another age. Yet the whole region is riddled with history, from the caves of Lombrives, Niaux and Mas d'Azil, to the cliff-top remains of the Cathar castles of Roquefixade and Montségur.

Far to the east, and with its bright Mediterranean influence, lies the country of Roussillon, whose undisputed overlord is the Canigou rising between the Vallespir and the Conflent. Bleached villages beam at the sun, beneath their undulating, orange-tiled roofs. Orchards and market gardens smother the lowlands, while an extravagant flora, highly fragrant and alive with insects, spreads palettes of colour across the hillsides before these subside among the waters of the Côte Vermeille.

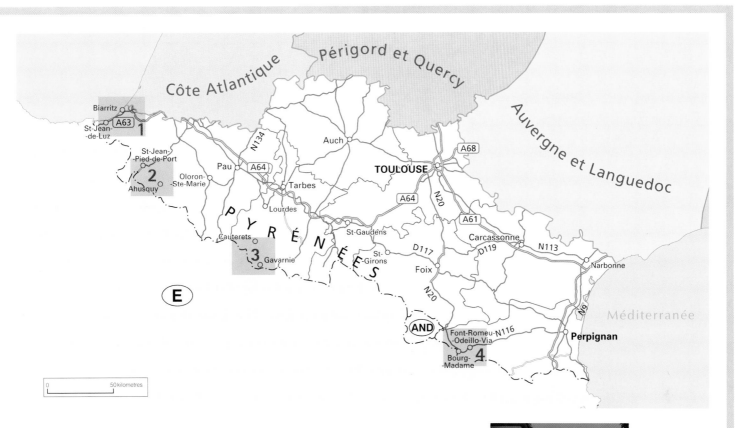

*Away from the coastal resorts such as St Jean-de-Luz (right), life in the Pyrenees is quiet for many people, including this couple (below).*

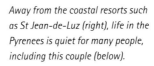

*Sheep farming (above) plays an important part in the economy of the rural Pyrenees.*
*St Jean-Pied-de-Port (right), the former capital of Basse-Navarre, retains its 15th-century Citadelle and defensive walls.*

*The dramatic Col d'Aubisque (above) lies on the 48-km long Route d'Aubisque, which goes from Laruns to Argelès-Gazost. The Col, which is usually blocked by snow between November and June, has in the past been one of the challenges of the Tour de France.*

# THE BASQUE COAST

A gentle, undulating roll of green hills breaks above the sandy bays and coves that line the Bay of Biscay. From Biarritz to St Jean-de-Luz these half-moon beaches receive the Atlantic surge, and the resorts that have grown up behind them offer a wide choice of accommodation and facilities. With a mild climate and glorious scenery, the Basque coast is at its best in the early autumn.

**Comité Départemental du Tourisme des Pyrenées-Atlantiques**
4 Allée des Platanes – BP 811
64108 Bayonne Cedex
Tel: 05 59 46 52 52
www.tourisme64.com

**Touring:**
AA Road Map France
series 5: Aquitaine

## BASQUE MUSEUM

Contained in a 16th-century town house on the right bank of the Nive in Bayonne, the Musée Basque displays artefacts and costumes, reconstructions of dwellings, games and dances, together with historical documents. These combine to summarise the history and traditions of the Basque race in an entertaining yet intelligent way. Here you can learn all about *pelota*, the suppression of witchcraft throughout the region in the 16th and 17th centuries, and the seafaring exploits of its intrepid mariners.

Completely renovated, the museum reopened in 2001.

*The excellent sandy beach at Biarritz (top) helps to make it the main holiday centre on this stretch of the Atlantic coast. At the southern end of the beach is the tiny port from which whalers once put to sea. At the northern end is the lighthouse (above).*

## Biarritz

An air of genteel respectability lingers on in Biarritz, long after the last of Europe's holiday-making monarchs has departed. But it is impossible to visit this 'queen of resorts and resort of kings' and not sense its past grandeur.

The elegance of the Hôtel du Palais dominates the Grande Plage; enlarged and reconstructed, it was originally built for Napoleon III's Empress Eugénie, who brought the town its fame in the mid-19th century. The Grande Plage is a broad sweep of superb sand with bastion-like stacks standing offshore as if to interrupt the endless breakers that make modern Biarritz such a mecca for surfers.

## Bidart

When travelling down the coast from Biarritz, Bidart is the first real introduction to Basque architecture and culture. A handsome village and one of the highest along this stretch of coastline, its open square is dominated by the church and a large, pink-walled *fronton*. Nearby hotels and restaurants, with their balconies, overhanging eaves and rust-coloured shutters, are all the very essence of the architecture of the Basque country.

Inside the 16th-century church triple galleries run round the nave, and from the wood-panelled ceiling there hangs a model sailing barque. An effigy of Joan of Arc stands next to the altar. At the end of a narrow side road leading from the square is the white-walled Chapelle Ste-Madeleine.

## RAVEL

On the quay named after him, the composer Maurice Ravel (1875–1937) was born in a Dutch-style house facing the harbour in Ciboure. Ravel was a highly respected innovator, both of piano technique and of orchestration, whose compositions include piano and orchestral music, ballet, opera, songs, concerti and chamber music.

Although the family moved to Paris when he was only three months old, Ravel often returned to the town of his birth, using it as a 'listening-post' for musical ideas. A number of Ravel's compositions clearly bear a local, or Spanish influence, especially *Bolero*, on which he worked in St Jean-de-Luz in 1928.

## Chambre d'Amour

Anglet's beach, enclosed by rocky projections and backed by vegetated cliffs, is named after a legend that tells of the secret seashore rendezvous of a poor peasant girl in love with the son of a local nobleman. Unable to meet in public, the couple were engulfed in their passion by the onrushing tide, and died in each other's arms. More prosaically, it was here in 1808 that Napoleon I heralded the idea of sea bathing. The water was first tested by members of the Imperial Guard, then Napoleon ventured forth, accompanied by the music of a military band, while the guard stood by in case of accident.

## Ciboure

Linked by a bridge to St Jean-de-Luz, Ciboure escapes the crowds that congregate across the harbour. Smaller, less spread out than its better known neighbour, it hugs the western side of the port from which, in the past, its citizens set sail on voyages of piracy.

*The fishing port of Ciboure, on the left bank of the Nivelle, faces the popular resort of St Jean-de-Luz across the river.*

In the courtyard of the 18th-century town hall there is a bust of Ravel, the town's most illustrious son, and next to it is the *pelota* court. Not far away is a 17th-century fountain adorned with Ciboure's coat of arms. Along Rue Pocalette there are some interesting 17th- and 18th-century houses, and these and the church interior are good examples of the architecture of the Basque country.

## Guéthary

An attractive hilltop village with a number of fine houses, Guéthary is bisected by the Paris–Madrid railway, which passes though a deep cutting. The beach consists of tilted rocks sloping to sand and sea, with a view back to Bidart.

## St Jean-de-Luz

This is a busy resort with the most perfect of bathing beaches: a crescent-shaped bay whose extremities manage to deflect the rolling Atlantic waves and ensure a haven of calm water. The fishing port is likewise protected and is a colourful place at the mouth of the Nivelle.

Adjacent to it is the oldest part of town, that which was rebuilt after the Spanish razed it in 1558. Place Louise XIV faces the harbour and contains the town hall, built in 1635, in which the Sun King stayed before his marriage to the Infanta, Marie Thérèse, in 1660. St-Jean-Baptiste, the church in which the marriage ceremony was performed, is close by. There are also some excellent town houses.

*St Jean-de-Luz is an elegant town with a number of well-preserved mansions in the Basque style, a fine beach and a busy fishing port.*

# THE BASQUE COUNTRY

A green and well-watered countryside adequately describes the *département* of Pyrénées-Atlantiques, a rural landscape abounding in sheep, running with streams and punctuated with delightful villages where art and architecture blend together beneath projecting eaves. But Eskual Herria, the Land of the Basques, is more a country of racial identity than of political boundaries, for the people themselves, unique and mysterious in origin, have dwelt among the western hills and sea coasts of the Pyrenees since long before the birth of France and Spain as we know them today, and with some justification claim to be Europe's oldest race.

Since they have lived in a state of virtual self-isolation for centuries, speaking a language, Euskara, that is unrelated to any other Indo-European tongue, it is perhaps not surprising that the Basques should have developed a number of distinct social, intellectual and architectural features. This uniqueness is most immediately apparent in the difficult, tongue-tying names such as Choldocogagna (one of the western hills), Oxocelhaya (a cave system near Hasparren), the Crête d'Uthurkokotcha in the Forêt d'Iraty, and the minor summit of Léchoukohéguia, to name but a few. Road signs often display two names for a town or village, one being the French spelling, the other giving its Basque identity. These names are almost always polysyllabic and often include x, y or z.

## The Village

While there are several small towns in the Basque country that have undeniable appeal – Cambo-les-Bains and St Jean-Pied-de-Port immediately spring to mind – it is among the neat landlocked villages that the essential Basque quality of bucolic harmony, the peace of the peasant, is best observed. Although each province has its own specific building style, perhaps the most attractive houses are to be found in Labourd in the west. Here the white loam walls contrast with exposed timbers, painted Basque red, beneath large, shallow-pitched, tiled roofs. Individual houses stand out in the pastoral landscape, but gathered together in orderly groups they are some of the loveliest villages in all France. Ainhoa is a classic example, with its wide main street lined with ageing but well-maintained buildings, often with the date of construction and the name of the builder or owner carved in the lintel over the front door. Biriatou, Sare and Ascain fall into a similar category of architectural beauty.

*Typical Basque houses are to be found in many villages, including Ainhoa (far left). The characteristic dress of the Basque region (left).*

## Pelota

No introduction to the Basque country is complete without mention of *pelota*, the game that appears to dominate life throughout the region, and whose top players become local heroes. Age-old in concept, *pelota* has undergone changes and variations, but basically consists of hurling a ball, the *pelota*, against the high *fronton*,

or wall, and playing it back again, either bare-handed or with a curved wicker scoop known as the *chistera* or with a wooden bat, the *pala*. (One of the greatest ever players was Chiquito, who, it is claimed, once won a match using a champagne bottle.) It is a very fast, vigorous sport, with the players dressed in brilliant white and the *chacharia*, the umpire, calling the score.

Most Basque villages have an outdoor *pelota* court, with the *fronton* occupying a prominent position in the main street – usually close to the church.

## A Love of Dance

In many villages the square and *pelota* court are one and the same. The weekly market is held in them, and so too are the dances of which the Basques are particularly fond. Traditional Basque folk dances demand agility and sure-footed

Pelota *is the foremost sport of the Basque country*

concentration, not least for the powerful and spectacular leaps (the famous *saut basque*) required in many of them. The torso and head are held erect, the face set and emotionless. Apart from the *fandango* and *arin-arin*, dances are by custom performed only by males and accompanied by a stringed tambourine, a small drum and a three-holed flute, the *tchirulä*.

The *Zamalzain* is one of the oldest dances, a charade of Good against Evil in which two teams perform. One team is dressed in ornate and colourful costume, with the leader wearing a wicker frame representing a horse, the other in grotesque masks and tattered clothes. As a climax the lead dancer of each team carries out a series of intricate steps around a wine glass, leaping momentarily on to it and then off again. Should the dancer symbolising Good manage to finish the dance without spilling any wine, and Evil knock the glass over – as intended – the dance will have been successfully completed according to tradition, and the future will bode well.

## Galleried Churches

The church plays an important role in the life of the Basque village, although it may not

*The Basque country is mainly green and lush (below) and many white churches, simple in form, punctuate the landscape (inset).*

always be seen as its most notable building. While the exterior varies in architectural style from province to province and is generally rather plain, internally there is a common layout with two, and sometimes three, caved wooden galleries overlooking a wide, wood-floored nave. Men sit in the galleries while women, children and the infirm only are allowed in the nave. In some coastal churches a model sailing ship hangs above the nave as a reminder of the close affinity the Basques have with the sea. Inland, in the province of Soule, many churches have impressive triple belfries, that at Gotein being a fine example.

In a number of churchyards, among them those at Biriatou, Ascain, Sare and Ste-Engrâce, old and unusual discoidal gravestones are seen, some of which have been engraved with the Basque cross, reminiscent of the swastika. Others are decorated with a wheel or solar rose motif.

# THE HEART OF THE BASQUE COUNTRY

Shared between Basse-Navarre and Haute Soule, the heartland of the Basque country is a broad spread of beech woods and steep hillside pasture. It is sparsely populated, with winding, narrow roads and forest tracks that link shepherds' huts and secluded farmsteads. Few villages break the sense of isolation, and only St Jean-Pied-de-Port is large enough to be considered a town.

**Comité Départemental du Tourisme des Pyrenées-Atlantiques**
4 Allée des Platanes – BP 811
64108 Bayonne Cedex
Tel: 05 59 46 52 52
www.tourisme64.com

**Touring:**
AA Road Map France series 5: Aquitaine

## Ahusquy

There is a beautiful, secluded, high pastureland on hillsides between the Forêt des Arbailles to the north and the Forêt d'Iraty to the south. Ahusquy enjoys a magnificent panorama that includes far-off frontier peaks and consists of a lonely hotel, small cottage and a nearby spring, the Fontaine d'Ahusquy. The waters are said to be beneficial to those suffering kidney or bladder disorders. Ahusquy stands at the junction of several narrow roads, variously linking St Jean-Pied-de-Port, Tardets-Sorholus and a number of hidden shepherd's dwellings. The road from St Jean, going through Col d'Egurcé and Col d'Otxolatzé, demands concentration from drivers, but makes a spectacular journey.

## Chapelle St-Sauveur

Unseen from the road but set on a magnificent green crest high on the approach to Col de Burdincurutcheta, the chapel is the site of an annual Corpus Christi pilgrimage. It is barn-like in size and appearance, and surrounded by 13 small crosses with one larger stone pedestal cross set aside from it. On the stone cross is carved a crude but effective Crucifixion. There is a well just below the chapel and a small farm nearby.

## Col de Burdincurutcheta

The main western access to the Forêt d'Iraty is by way of Col de Burdincurutcheta (1,135m), a high, natural gateway in the northern ridge of the Sommet d'Occabé. The road up to the pass from the valley of Laurhibar is long and twisting, but scenically engaging. Views from the pass itself are far-reaching, with Pic d'Orhy (2,017m) peering above the shoulders of nearer mountains.

## Col d'Osquich

On the boundary between Basse-Navarre and Soule, this undemanding low pass (392m) provides the easiest crossing of the hill country east of St Jean-Pied-de-Port and is therefore popular with motorists touring the Basque country. From both sides there are superb views to enjoy – the soft Basque valleys and snow-dusted tops of the frontier range – while from the summit the western Pyrenees spread out in a lavish display of green undulations. An hotel on the pass exploits these views.

### LIMESTONE CLEFTS

South-east of Larrau the frontier hills are sliced by huge limestone clefts sculpted over countless millennia by the industry of innocent-looking streams: the Crevasses d'Holçarté and the gorges of Olhadibie, Kakouetta and Ehujarré. Holçarté and Olhadibie are reached easily from Laugibar below Larrau. Kakouetta and Ehujarré are both accessible from the valley of Ste-Engrâce.

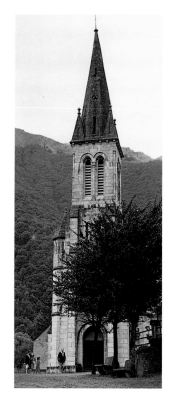

*The Chapelle St-Sauveur, which stands at the entrance to the Col de Burdincurutcheta, is of unusual design, looking rather like a barn from a distance.*

Fortifications dating from the 15th century surround the medieval quarter of St Jean-Pied-de-Port. The ramparts of the Citadelle, built during the following century, make an interesting walk and give fine views over the town.

## GR10 AND THE HRP

The mountains and hill country of the Pyrenees provide some of the most stimulating walking in all Europe, from short outings to multi-day epics full of challenge and reward. Two of the longest are the GR10 (Grand Randonnée) and the Haute Randonnée Pyrénéenne, commonly known as the HRP. Both cross the mountain range from the Atlantic to the Mediterranean, the first keeping mainly to the lower hills and valleys, the second following the frontier crest as far as possible. For much of the way across the Basque country the two routes share common footpaths and enjoy huge vistas. In recent years they have become immensely popular among Europe's outdoor fraternity.

## Forêt d'Iraty

Predominantly beech and yew, this is one of the great forests of the Pyrenees. It sprawls over both sides of the international frontier and is managed by joint communities from the upper Nive valley and the Soule. In the past large quantities of timber from the forest were sent to the coast to be used in the manufacture of ships' oars, and in the 17th century fears of deforestation had reached Paris. As a result, Louis XIV's finance minister, Colbert, sent a forester to check on its condition. Today the abundant beeches are interspersed with open pastures. Many footpaths and tracks wind through the forest, and alongside the road between Burdincurutcheta and Bagargui picnic areas have been set aside. At the summit of Col Bagargui there are tourist facilities.

## St Jean-Pied-de-Port

Once the capital of Basse-Navarre, this small and pretty town on the River Nive makes a perfect base from which to explore the surrounding countryside and is very popular among trout anglers. As its name suggests, St Jean lies at the foot of a *port*, or pass – that of Roncesvalles, otherwise known as the Ibañeta, which was crossed in the Middle Ages by thousands of pilgrims from all over Europe *en route* to the tomb of St James the Apostle in Compostela. St Jean-Pied-de-Port was a regrouping centre and the last stopping-place before entering Spain, and as large groups of pilgrims descended on the town bells rang out as if to warn the housekeepers of the refuge in the Rue de la Citadelle to prepare for an influx of visitors.

It is still possible to follow the pilgrims' route through the town today, entering by the Porte St-Jacques and leaving by the Porte d'Espagne. Cobbled streets lead past the church of Notre-Dame-du-Pont and across the old bridge over the Nive, which makes a focal point for picturesque views along the river.

The old town is contained within 15th-century fortifications, while the Citadelle, built on the orders of Richelieu in 1628, was redesigned by the military engineer and architect Vauban in 1685.

## Sommet d'Occabé

This broad, bald mountain top is, at 1,456m, the highest summit reached when travelling on foot from the Atlantic, and is crossed by the GR10. The summit is noted for its low, Iron Age circle of cromlechs, or standing stones, and may be gained by a little more than an hour's walk from Chalet Pedro, a restaurant near the Plateau d'Iraty, below Col de Burdincurutcheta.

The red sandstone church of Notre-Dame-du-Pont in St Jean-Pied-de-Port has a fine position by a bridge over the Nive, but has been heavily altered over the centuries.

# THE HIGH PYRENEES AND THEIR RESORTS

The thermal resorts of Barèges, Cauterets and Luz-St Sauveur line the edge of the Parc National des Pyrénées, providing access to some of the most stimulating scenery of this great mountain range. Barèges has the Massif de Néouvielle on its doorstep, while above Cauterets cascades pour from a trio of beautiful valleys. Beyond Luz the great cirques of Troumouse, Estaubé and Gavarnie have undisputed attractions all their own.

The Grande Cascade, a 400-m ribbon of tumbling water, adds to the already superb spectacle of the Cirque de Gavarnie

## Barèges

A winter-sports resort and centre for mountain activities in summer, Barèges is also the highest Pyrenean thermal spa. In 1787 Ramond de Carbonnières based himself there for several weeks, during which he made a number of explorations in the heart of the range, effectively heralding the advent of mountaineering in the region.

## Cauterets

Known to the Romans, a dozen sulphurated springs first brought Cauterets its fame, and through the centuries the number of illustrious visitors has included Gaston Fébus, who recovered his hearing there, Marguerite de Navarre, who wrote part of the *Heptaméron* while being treated for rheumatism, Georges Sand, Chateaubriand, Victor Hugo, Flaubert and Tennyson. Today the spa is enjoying something of a revival, while the fortunes of the town itself rely on the drawing power of the surrounding mountains, which attract visitors in both winter and summer. There is no shortage of excursions for motorist, pedestrian or athletic climber.

## Cirque de Gavarnie

Without question the Cirque de Gavarnie is the best-known feature of the Pyrenees, drawing tens of thousands of visitors each summer. Rising almost sheer from the valley floor to a summit ridge topping 3,000m, the limestone walls are divided by two main snow platforms. A long ribbon of waterfall showers from the upper crags of Marboré (3,248m), while across from it to the west the great gash of the Brèche de Roland, said to have been made by the sword of Charlemagne's nephew, provides access to the Ordesa canyon in Spain.

The village of Gavarnie is a whimsical place of hotels, restaurants and postcard and trinket stands. Its streets are crowded with ponies and donkeys, which are employed to convey visitors up the valley to the Hôtellerie du Cirque for a close view of the Grande Cascade and the mountain walls towering dramatically overhead.

The fit walker and the experienced climber will both find an enormous choice of challenges in the Pyrenees.

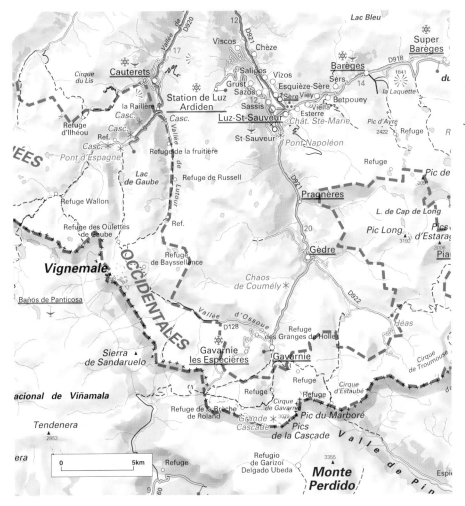

Comité Département al
du Tourisme des
Hautes-Pyrénées
11 Rue Gaston Manent
65000 Tarbes
Tel: 05 62 56 70 65
www.cg65.fr

**Touring:**
AA Road Map France
series 5: Aquitaine

Luz itself is more interesting than the spa and occupies a basin at the junction of two valleys. Its 12th-century church was fortified by the Hospitallers of St John in the 14th century as a defence against marauders from Spain; it has an impressive Romanesque doorway, two square towers and a crenellated wall. The nearby Maison du Parc houses a number of displays detailing the natural history of the Parc National des Pyrénées. Above the town stand the ruins of the Château Ste-Marie, which once has an important role as the principal stronghold of the valley of Barèges.

## Parc National des Pyrénées

Created in 1967, the Parc National des Pyrénées stretches from the Aspe valley in the west to the Massif de Néouvielle in the east and, butting against the Spanish frontier, covers an area of almost 500 square km. Within its boundaries rise many of the finest individual peaks of the range: Pic du Midi d'Ossau, Balaïtous, Vignemale, Marboré and the cirques of Gavarnie, Estaubé and Troumouse. While tourist developments are permitted on the periphery, the park itself is protected as a sanctuary where the natural life and beauty of the mountains are preserved.

## Pont d'Espagne

At the road-head of Val de Jéret above Cauterets, Pont d'Espagne gives access to two major valleys worth exploring on foot.

The first of these is the Vallée du Marcadau, in whose upper reaches gentle pastures lead to a wonderland of mountain lakes and inviting peaks; the second is the Vallée de Gaube, with the popular Lac de Gaube a short walk from the road. The head of the valley leading to the lake is blocked by the savage north face of the Vignemale, at 3,289m the highest peak on the border with Spain.

## Cirque de Troumouse

Reached from Gèdre by way of the hamlet of Héas, the Cirque de Troumouse is larger than the Cirque d'Estaubé and the Cirque de Gavarnie to the west. It is a superb 10-km wall of mountains with rough pastures and a scattering of tiny lakes trapped beneath. A steeply climbing toll road, offering fine views, winds into the mouth of the cirque from Héas.

## Luz-St Sauveur

Luz and St Sauveur are divided by the Gave de Pau, a mountain stream that has carved a deep defile between them. St Sauveur is a thermal spa, a single street of tall buildings. The lower part of the avenue is named after the Duchesse de Berry, wife of the second son of Charles X, the upper part after the Empress Eugénie, who spent two months there in 1859 with Napoleon III. To commemorate the imperial couple's sojourn, the single-span Pont Napoléon was built across the gorge above St Sauveur.

*Luz-St Sauveur's church was built in the 12th century and fortified two hundred years later to keep out invaders from the other side of the Pyrenees.*

**LOURDES**
More than four million people a year visit Lourdes, the majority of them pilgrims bound for the grotto where Bernadette Soubirous had the first of her visions of the Virgin in 1858. Many are invalids hoping to join the list of the faithful who have been cured during their visit.

Lourdes is now the site of the world's greatest pilgrimage. Because the extravagant Basilique du Rosaire was unable to contain the crowds, another, underground and large enough to hold a congregation of 20,000, was consecrated in 1958.

# THE CERDAGNE

The Cerdagne is the only broad, flat-bottomed valley in the Pyrenees. Half French, half Spanish, this high plain is a sun-trap enjoying almost 3,000 hours of sunshine a year. Formerly the basin of a glacial lake, this fertile region is protected from northerly winds by the Carlit mountains, and walled in to the south by the Puigmal range. Virtually lacking in humidity, the air is dry and bracing.

**Comité Département al du Tourisme des Pyrénées-Orientales**
16 Avenue des Palmiers - BP 540
66005 Perpignan Cedex
Tel: 04 68 51 52 53
www.cg66.fr

**Touring:**
AA Road Map France series 6: Midi-Pyrénées

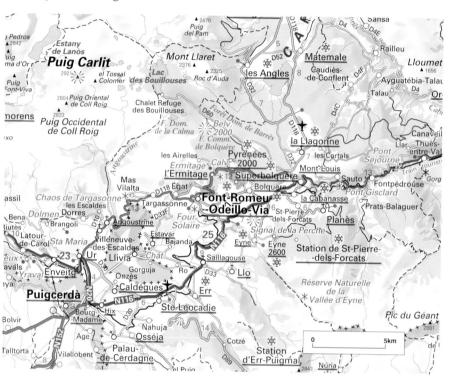

*Alpine plants adorn the quiet meadows of the Eyne valley, a beautiful, secluded part of the Cerdagne.*

## Bourg-Madame

Formerly called La Guinguette, this small frontier village changed its name in honour of the Duchess of Angoulême, daughter of Louis XVI, after she and her husband passed through in 1815. Across the Sègre, which marks the frontier, stands Puigcerdà.

## Col de la Perche

Of modest altitude (1,581m), Col de la Perche, on the N116 west of Mont-Louis, nonetheless enjoys a magnificent panorama; to the east the deep valley of the Têt, with Mont-Louis commanding it, to the west the broad Cerdagne from the Carlit massif to Sierra del Cadi in Spain. Sweeping from the col to Cambras d'Azé, the countryside has a moorland-like aspect, but below are lush pastures and fields under cultivation. Nearby Signal de la Perche (1621m) or Perche Belvédère, on the side road (D33) that leads to Eyne and Llo, extends the view even farther and is worth the diversion.

## Eyne

The village nestles against the hills, its soft, sand-coloured stone glowing in the sunlight. At first glance it appears not to belong to this century, a small, shy hill village linked with nearby Llo by a scenically delightful narrow road. In the church, Notre-Dame-du-Remède is worshipped as a deliverer from ill health. Behind, the Eyne valley is noted for its wealth of plants while Col de Nuria at its head is one of the most important migration routes in the Pyrenees. In the autumn a magnificent variety of birds crosses the mountains there, heading south.

## Font-Romeu

This 'Pilgrim's Fountain' has changed from its original role as a place of pilgrimage to one of the most popular and best equipped of Pyrenean ski resorts.

**THE LITTLE YELLOW TRAIN**

Between Villefranche-de-Conflent and Latour-de-Carol, the *Petit Train Jaune* links Perpignan with the main Paris-Toulouse-Barcelona railway.

This once-essential local service run by the SNCF is now very much a tourist attraction, a romantic 'runaway train' decked out in yellow with red trim. Unlike standard state railway services, the *Petit Train Jaune* allows passengers who wish to board it at a minor station to wave it down. Similarly, those who need to disembark at a minor stop must sit in the front carriage and inform the driver as their destination approaches.

Along the Cerdagne the railway picks its way easily from village to village, but the route through the steep Têt valley is spectacular, crossing suspension bridges and viaducts that span deep defiles.

## SOLAR POWER

Just above Odeillo, near Font-Romeu, stands an astonishing piece of engineering work built by the Centre National de la Recherche Scientifique. It is the Four Solaire, a solar furnace in which almost 10,000 small mirrors, fixed to a concave surface and directed by moveable reflectors, managed to

concentrate the sun's rays into the centre of a huge dish where temperatures in excess of 3,500°C were achieved. Today the centre is privately owned but may be visited; demonstrations show how the heat generated can be used to fire pottery or melt metal.

Set high above the Cerdagne, with a superb outlook and a reputation as the sunniest place in France, it is very much a resort in the modern idiom but, despite the variety of its buildings, not even winter snow can hide its architectural shortcomings. The most prominent of its many hotels is the large and imposing Grand, built just before World War I broke out, and consequently it was several years before it was put to use. Athletes used Font-Romeu for altitude training in preparation for the Mexico Olympics of 1968.

## Lac des Bouillouses

This high, dammed lake on the eastern edge of the Carlit massif is fed by the Têt, which rises on the slopes of Pic Péric. Forests clothe the rocky shores, but above them wild landscapes of stone and water make this a delightful region for walking.

## Llivia

The former Roman capital of the region, known then as Julia Livia, is one of the anomalies of France: a Spanish enclave surrounded by French territory. Under the Treaty of the Pyrenees of 1659 it was agreed by delegates from both sides that 33 villages in the Cerdagne would be ceded to France, but a year later it was pointed out that Llivia was in fact a town and therefore should remain a Spanish possession. Agreement was eventually reached on the assurance that it would never be fortified, and that the

connecting road be considered neutral territory. Llivia today has narrow alleyways, a 15th-century fortified church, the Torre de Bernat adjoining it, and the municipal museum opposite.

## Llo

The village blends into the shape and texture of the hills among which it sits. It has one of the finest Romanesque churches in the district, and a ruined tower standing above it. The church's eye-catching doorway has two pairs of pillars that are accompanied by detailed carvings depicting grotesque faces and other subjects. Behind the village stretch the Gorges du Sègre, or Gorges du Llo.

## Mont-Louis

Fortified by Vauban following the Treaty of the Pyrenees and named after Louis XIV, this small military town is a sturdy place contained within low, moat-ringed walls. No longer a resort, it has the air of a garrison, heavy and masculine, but trees have been planted to soften the approach, and the views it commands over a wide territory include Cambras d'Azé and neighbouring mountains on the south side of the Cerdagne. The citadel at the top end of the town houses commandos who use the surrounding countryside for exercises. Near the citadel stands a memorial to Emmanuel Brousse, one-time Deputy for the *département*.

*The Cerdagne is a high-lying plain blessed by abundant sunshine and sheltered by mountains to both north and south.*

*The church at Llo has a fine open belfry with three bays, but the carved doorway attracts the most attention. Hideous faces, shells and patterns, all skilfully executed, decorated the arch and the jambs.*

# PROVENCE AND THE CÔTE D'AZUR

For many visitors the south of France means the adjacent regions of Provence and the Côte d'Azur, even though these account for only about half of the country's Mediterranean coast.

So many have praised the Provençal light that their adulation has become almost a commonplace. But this remarkable light is not all that makes Provence special, for it also has Roman and medieval antiquities, the Camargue and its world-famous herbs. Provence is a region of wide vistas that are dominated by low scrub of one of two forms. Where original forests have been thinned there is the *maquis*, a scrub formed of tree-heather, strawberry trees, juniper, myrtle, broom, cistus and turpentine trees. Larger tracts of open land exist where the underlying rock is so close to the surface that trees were unable to gain enough purchase, so that there was never a forest to thin. Here there is the *garrigue*, a mix of aromatic herbs, kermes oak, gorse and ling heather.

In contrast to Provence, which represents an older way of life, provincial southern France, the Côte d'Azur, is modern living epitomised. The coast, especially from Cannes to the Italian border, seems to be one long promenade running between a line of luxurious high-rise hotels on the landward side and a marina full of expensive boats on the seaward. But that is not a criticism; it is just a fact, and should not deter you, for the Côte d'Azur is a wonderful area, with sea the colour of its name and ancient ports as picturesque as you could hope for.

Inland from the coast the picturesque qualities are maintained, with pretty hill villages set on the flanks of the Haute-Provence peaks. Here are the lavender fields that provide the raw material for Grasse's perfume industry, and here too the stupendous Grand Canyon du Verdon, one of the natural wonders of France (and Europe). The hills of Haute-Provence lie within the borders of the Parc National du Mercantour, an area of high peaks that includes at its eastern end the valley of Merveilles and Mont Bégo, one of the world's finest sites for Bronze Age art. The area is also home to most of Europe's mountain animals.

Birds, rather than animals, are the main attraction of the Camargue, and include flamingos, one of Europe's most exotic avian residents. Close to the Camargue are Marseille and Toulon, neither of which can be described in detail here. Toulon is a naval port with fine museums on the history of the French Navy. Marseille is France's second city and a major port. Its history is fascinating, and the Musée des Docks Romains explores the first port, the Musée de la Marine its later development.

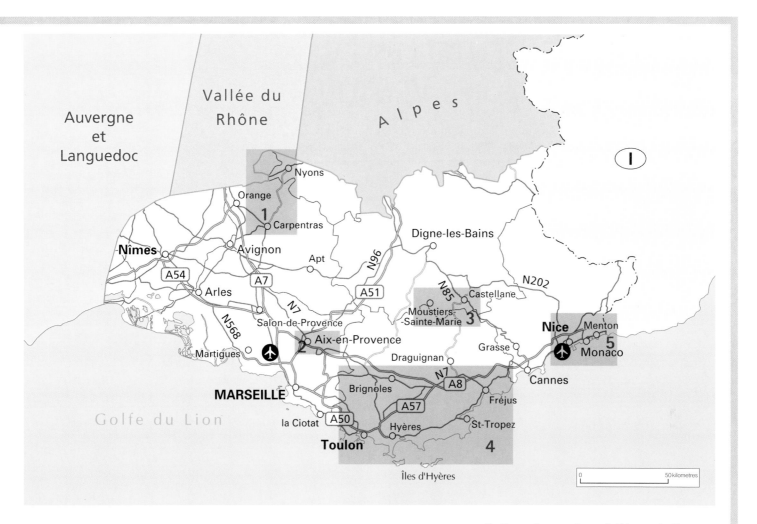

Auvergne
et
Languedoc

Vallée du
Rhône

A l p e s

I

The Roman theatre at Orange (left) has survived in splendid condition and is still used today

Sweet chestnut on the Massif des Maures (below)

An ornate tiled cupola decorates Menton's 17th-century harbourside fortifications (right).

Provence is renowned the world over for its herbs (centre right).

Like many coastal towns on the Côte d'Azur, Menton (above) combines the role of fishing port with that of smart holiday resort.

# THE DENTELLES DE MONTMIRAIL AND MONT VENTOUX

As the Rhône flows down towards Provence it swings westward, avoiding the Roman town of Orange. To the east of Orange are the low, attractive hill ranges of the Dentelles de Montmirail and Mont Ventoux with their vineyards, while to the north, Nyons is a centre for olive oil.

## Carpentras

Set at the fringe of the pastoral land at the southern edge of the Dentelles de Montmirail and Mont Ventoux, Carpentras is both the market town for the local market gardens and a light-industrial town. Of chief interest here is the Cathédrale St-Siffrein, a 15th-century Gothic edifice entered through the Porte Juive (in the Flamboyant Gothic style). The door was thus named because it was through it that Jews converted to Christianity went for their baptism. Carpentras once had a thriving Jewish community and until the Revolution there was a ghetto of about 1,200 Jews. The synagogue is the oldest in France, dating from the 15th century. Visitors can view its ground-floor baths and kosher bakery, as well as the first-floor temple.

*The limestone hills of the Dentelles de Montmirail (top) continue to attract walkers and climbers, as well as artists and nature lovers.*

*The presence of the Romans in Provence is recalled by a carving near the cathedral in Carpentras (above).*

To the west of the cathedral, in Boulevard Albin-Durand, is a museum complex that includes local paintings and objects with regional associations. There is also a collection of rare books, not open to the public.

## Dentelles de Montmirail

Geologically, the Dentelles are the last section of the Ventoux ridge. They would be rounded hills, covered in vineyards and topped with pine and oak woods, had not folding of the earth's crust pushed up the limestone rock into a jagged line of points like the edge of lace, from which the range gets its name. The peaks are beloved of rock climbers and those seeking a hard day on difficult terrain. The best approach is from Suzette on the eastern side or Gigondas to the west.

Below the Dentelles lie a string of charming wine villages. Séguret nestles below a sheet of rock and would be worth a visit for the views alone. However, among its further attractions are the steep streets with their old houses, a 12th-century church, a 15th-century fountain and a ruined castle.

From Séguret a road skirts the base of Montmirail to reach Gigondas, whose Grenache is reckoned to be second only to Châteauneuf-du-Pape as a red wine of quality. From the village a road climbs up to the Col du Cayron, which lies in the heart of the Dentelles.

## Mazan

Of particular interest in this village are a set of Roman sarcophagi that make up a wall of the cemetery, and the chapel of Notre-Dame de Pareloup, Our Lady Protectress against Wolves, half buried in the same cemetery. The chapel was built in the 12th century to protect the buried from being eaten by demons disguised as wolves.

## MONT VENTOUX

In geological terms Mont Ventoux is the westernmost ridge of the Alps. Its high point (1,909m) is laid bare of vegetation by the scouring of the wind, which seems to blow constantly. In Provençal the peak's name is *Ventour*, meaning Windy Mountain.

The mountainside is clothed in pine, oak and beech woods, but these soon give way to broom, and finally to a few alpine flowers. On the summit there are a weather observatory, a TV mast and a radar station. The view from the top is a 360-degree panorama, and an orientation panel helps to identify the Lubéron hills, the Alpilles and the Montagne Ste Victoire. In summer you

**Comité Départemental du Tourisme du Vaucluse**

12 Rue du Collège-de-la-Croix – BP 147
84008 Avignon Cedex
Tel: 04 90 80 47 00
www.provenceguide.com

**Comité Départemental du Tourisme de la Drôme**

8 Rue Baudin
26000 Valence
Tel: 04 75 82 19 26
www.drometourisme.com

**Touring:**

AA Road Map France series 15: Provence & Côte d'Azur

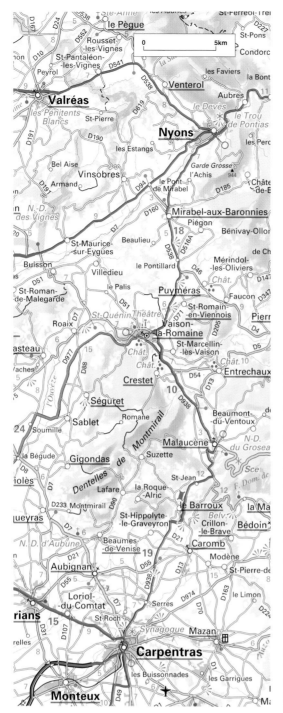

can walk along the bare limestone ridge, following in the footsteps of the Italian poet Petrarch, whose ascent of the peak in 1336 is the first recorded conquest of it.

Because of its shape, Mont Ventoux has always attracted competitive cycling. It was used as a hill-trials course for over 70 years until 1973, and frequently features as a climb in the Tour de France. It was on the flank of Mont Ventoux that the English cyclist Tommy Simpson became the race's only fatality.

You can cross Mont Ventoux by car by driving east from Malaucène on the D974. The return journey along the southern flank of the mountain allows a visit to Le Barroux, where there is a restored Renaissance château.

## Nyons

The town of Nyons is in Drôme rather than Provence, yet its climate and appearance are Provençal and it makes a good introduction to the South. It is popular as a summer and winter retreat. In winter the surrounding shrub-dotted hills give protection from the *mistral*, while in summer a cooling breeze, the *pontias*, blows down the Eygues valley and keeps the occasionally searing heat at bay. The name of the river is sometimes written as Aigues, but both words simply mean water.

At the northern end of the town arcaded streets lead into the Quartier des Forts, built in medieval times. The 13th-century Tour

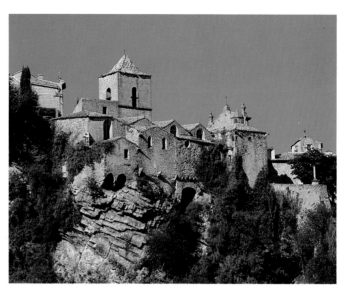

Randonne encloses a tiny chapel. Take the beautiful, covered Rue des Grands Forts to reach an old gateway that is most of what remains of the town's fortifications. The old bridge over the river, with its single 40-m arch, dates from the 14th century.

## Vaison-la-Romaine

The suffix to this town's name is a clue to its Roman ancestry and to its Roman site, which includes the remains of houses, shops, a basilica, a colonnaded street and even a theatre. But there is more to Vaison-la-Romaine than its Roman past. Notre-Dame-de-Nazareth is a superb 13th-century cathedral in the simple but elegant Provençal Romanesque style. Inside there is the sarcophagus of St Quentin, the 6th-century bishop of Vaison-la-Romaine. It is set before the bishop's throne in an apse of exceptional beauty.

On the other side of the River Ouvèze a steep road leads to the upper town, which is dominated by a ruined castle of the Counts of Toulouse. This part of the town is well worth seeing. There is a fountain at the centre of Place du Vieux-Marché, and narrow alleys lead off the square in apparently haphazard fashion. Many of the tall houses have ornate wrought-iron gates.

*Although Vaison-la-Romaine has Roman remains, the medieval town, including the 13th-century cathedral, is no less impressive.*

*It is worth seeing one of the olive-oil mills that are open to visitors in Nyons. Here you will find the local speciality: black olives pickled in brine.*

# AVIGNON AND ARLES

## Arles

The site that is now occupied by Arles was first settled by Celtic-Ligurian peoples, though it is to the Greeks that the name is owed. Aptly they called their settlement Arelate, the 'town in the marsh'. Later the town became the most important Roman settlement in southern France. In medieval times Arles was caught up in the strife between the Holy Roman Empire and France, and when it was finally absorbed into France it entered a decline. For centuries the Rhône ensured a certain level of commercial activity, but the coming of the railways put an end to even that trade.

By 1888 Arles was an historically interesting place, a little down on its luck perhaps, but still blessed with pure Provençal light. In February of that year Vincent Van Gogh took rooms in Place Lamartine.

Van Gogh spent only 15 months at Arles and yet in that time produced almost 200 canvases, half of them local

landscapes, with around 50 portraits and 40 still lifes or interiors. This period in Arles was one of the most creative of his life, and yet there is almost

*Around the Place de la République in Arles (above) can be seen, from left to right, the town hall, the church of St-Trophime and the library.*
*Arles commemorates Van Gogh in simple style (left).*

To the west of Marseille lies the Camargue, one of the most remarkable areas in Europe, a salt marsh with an almost African bird life. On the northern edge of the Camargue, where the Rhône enters the salt-marshes, is Arles, the artistic centre of Provence and the town most closely associated with the painter Vincent Van Gogh. North again, through an area sandwiched between the Rhône and the hills of the Alpilles and rich in history, is Avignon, the seat of medieval popes.

nothing in the town to remind the visitor of his presence. *The Yellow House* where he roomed in Place Lamartine was destroyed by bombing in 1944 and the café of *Café Terrace at Night* is now a furniture shop. The Pont de Langlois, the famous drawbridge, still stands, but it is in a different spot, reconstructed after its demolition in 1926. Yet no one who has seen the works of Van Gogh can be unmoved by

Arles. In the surrounding fields grew the artist's *Sunflowers*; the *Alyscamps* are still here, and much that must have inspired him remains: the church of St-Trophime, with its Gothic, rib-vaulted cloisters; the cobbled, stepped back streets; the river bank.

While he was staying at Arles Van Gogh sold not one painting. Indeed he had to barter several for food, and it is said that one masterpiece was found years later boarding up the broken window of an outhouse. It is ironic therefore that Arles does not have a museum of his work – for the simple reason that it cannot afford to buy the work needed to fill it. Instead it has the Espace Van-Gogh, where the artist was treated in 1889, and the Fondation Vincent Van Gogh, whose permanent collection of works pays homage.

## Avignon

In 1309 the French Pope Clement V moved the papal seat from Rome to Avignon. Even now there is a difference of opinion among academics about the reasons behind this move. Most believe that Clement retreated among his own countrymen when internal strife in Italy and the threat of invasion from the east made Rome an insecure papal capital. Others believe that the move was a virtual kidnap by Philippe IV, who was anxious to control the Papacy in order to stop mutterings about his expansionist policies and the horrifying cruelty of the Albignesian Crusade against the Cathars in southern France. Whatever the reason the town of Avignon, then just a crossing point on the Rhône, was thrust on to the turbulent centre stage of medieval politics.

Clement V remained in Avignon throughout his papacy, as did his successors until 1377.

During the early years of the Avignon Popes, and particularly in the case of Clement V, it does appear that they were virtual prisoners in their palace, though towards the end of their stay their position was clearly not that of captives. When the Great Schism of 1378–1417 occurred and an *antipape* was elected in opposition to the one in Rome, it was to Avignon that the former, favoured by France, Spain and Northern Italy, retreated. By then the Papal State owned Avignon and the surrounding area, a situation that lasted until the late 18th century, when the Papal State was annexed by France.

In Avignon the Popes occupied the Palais des Papes, a huge and impressive, if

*The Avignon Popes of the 14th and early 15th centuries occupied a fortress-like palace (above). Avignon's light still attracts artists (above right). The Pont St-Bénézet in Avignon (right) has undergone much rebuilding over the centuries. The dancing of the nursery song took place beneath the bridge*

somewhat austere, building of pale grey stone. More fortress than mansion, the palace mirrors the insecurities the occupiers must have felt, with its soaring walls, towers and battlements. It covers a hectare, with a myriad of rooms leading off from the central Great Courtyard. The rooms themselves are mostly bare of furniture – though this

merely adds to the stern grandeur of the huge Great Hall – but some are sumptuously decorated with frescoes, notably the Pope's Bedroom. Beside the

palace is the Petit Palais, which now houses a museum of medieval art.

Elsewhere in the town there are fine museums set in a street plan that successfully integrates narrow alleys and wide, airy boulevards. From the Palais des Papes a narrow enclosed series of alleys spirals down to the Pont St-Bénézet. The bridge, made famous by the nursery song, was built in the later 12th century, but time and floods have reduced it to half its original length, so that it now stops forlornly in the middle of the Rhône. But the song should read not 'sur le pont', but 'sous le pont', for the dancing took place on a now long disappeared island surrounding the central pier of the bridge.

Avignon is also famous for its annual July festival of drama, dance and music, which, like Edinburgh, has both an official programme and a 'fringe'.

## Camargue Wildlife

Just north of Arles the Rhône splits into the Grand Rhône and the Petit Rhône. These rivers, flowing almost at right angles to each other, below Arles form with the coastline a triangular delta that has been semi-flooded to form a flat salt-marsh interspersed with wider expanses of brackish lagoons. Within this area, the Parc Naturel Régional de Camargue, the bird life is unique in Europe: flamingos

flock and nest – the only place in Europe where they do so – vultures soar overhead and egrets stand erect among the reeds. There are avocets and stilts, storks and herons, bee-eaters, rollers and hoopoes, and turtles swim in the waters.

Small black Camargue bulls live semi-wild among the reed margins. Each year they are herded by *gardians*, gaucho-like cowboys who ride white horses, herds of which also roam freely among the marshes.

*A little egret, one of the Camargue's inhabitants.*

The bulls fight in the Provençal bullfights held at Arles and Nîmes. These differ from the Spanish variety in that the bull lives on to fight again another day.

# AROUND AIX-EN PROVENCE

Only a few kilometres north of Marseille lies a town that could hardly be more different. While Marseille is big and impersonal, crowded and noisy, Aix-en-Provence is small and quiet, a sedate university town where there is always time for a coffee and some lazy exploration.

**Comité Départementale des Bouches-du-Rhône**
Le Montsequieu, 13 Rue Roux-de-Brignoles
13006 Marseille
Tel: 04 91 13 84 13
www.visitprovence.com

**Touring:**
AA Road Map France series 15: Provence & Côte d'Azur

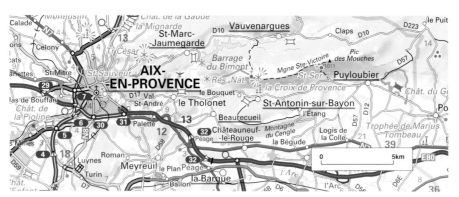

## Aix-en-Provence

Although Aix was the seat of the dukes of Provence, it had an unremarkable history until the 15th century, when the dukedom passed to René (1409–80), who was also King of Sicily and Duke of Anjou. René was a committed 'green' at a time when such concerns were viewed with suspicion if thought about at all. In addition he was a patron of the arts, a linguist, a mathematician and a lawyer. He was also a rather incompetent ruler, but that seems to have been overlooked. René is credited with bringing the muscat grape to Provence, from Sicily, and with importing the first silkworms. A statue of him can be seen at the end of Cours Mirabeau, the finest boulevard in Aix. But the visitor will also notice frequent reference to René in shop, café and restaurant names, for Aix is very fond of its eccentric ruler.

Cours Mirabeau is named after a citizen of the town at the time of the Revolution, an ugly man of ugly habits who, nonetheless, was a superb orator, and beloved of the common folk. The boulevard is wide and airy, each pavement planted with a double row of plane trees that offer welcome shade from the summer sun. In the centre of the boulevard is a moss-encrusted hot-water fountain, supplied by the same source that

the Romans tapped in 122 BC. The water is a brew of mineral salts and is mildly radioactive; it reaches the surface at 36ºC.

The north side of Cours Mirabeau is lined with cafés, restaurants, bookshops and shops selling *calissons* (see facing page), while the south side is more formal, with the occasional elegant mansion from the 17th century, its façade enriched with caryatids and wrought iron.

Vieil Aix, the city's oldest and most charming section, lies between Cours Mirabeau and the cathedral. Some of the streets here are pedestrian-only and are lined with smart fashion shops, antique dealers and shops selling Provençal handcrafts. To get a real flavour of the old town, follow Rue Roumer from Cours Mirabeau and turn right into Rue Espariat. Here the Hôtel Boyer d'Éguilles houses the Muséum d'Histoire Naturelle, which, among many other things, has a collection of dinosaur eggs unearthed on the Montagne Ste Victoire. Thousands of eggs were discovered, and to date no satisfactory explanation has been found as to why they failed to hatch.

Rue Espariat leads into Place d'Albertas, the most delightful of the little squares old Aix, cobbled, and with elegant terraced houses around a central fountain. Close by is Place des Prêcheurs, where a food market is held on Tuesday, Thursday and Saturday mornings. North again are the Tour de l'Horloge (Clock Tower) and the Cathédrale

*The ornate 16th-century Tour de l'Horloge, with its bell in a wrought-iron cage, stands next to the town hall in Aix-en-Provence.*

## CÉZANNE

Paul Cézanne was born in Aix in 1839, at 28 Rue de l'Opéra. He was baptised in the chapel of Ste-Marie-Madeleine in the same year, and attended a primary school in Rue des Épinaux from 1844 until 1849. The family moved to 14 Rue Mathéron and Paul attended the Collège Bourbon – now the Lycée Mignet – in Rue Cardinale, where he was a pupil at the same time as Émile Zola. Cézanne's father, a well-to-do man, acquired an estate about 4km southwest of Aix called Jas de Bouffan; this is now home to the Vasarely Foundation, showing the work of the Hungaro-French geometric artist. In 1859 Cézanne went to Paris intending to study law. There, however, he decided to fulfil his dream of becoming a painter. He left Paris in 1881,

*A wealth of brightly coloured vegetables and fruits adorn street markets, like this one in Aix, all over Provence.*

*The Montagne Ste Victoire is probably the most familiar natural landmark in Provence. Cézanne, who was particularly fond of it, painted it many times (see picture below).*

disillusioned by what he saw as the limitations of Impressionism, but also by the public reaction to his Impressionist friends, whose work he believed to be critical to the development of art. Back in Aix, he rented rooms in several locations, most importantly in the Château Noir, on the D17 to the west of the town. When his mother died in 1897, Cézanne had a house with a studio built, surrounded by a garden, at number 9 in the avenue that now bears his name. The studio is now the Atelier Paul Cézanne, a museum devoted to the artist's work.

Cézanne was a modest man, but clear about his own position in art. 'A painter like me,' he said, 'there's only one every other century.' His ideal was to create strictly harmonious pictures, for he admired greatly the balance of the great classical artists.

He imposed this balance on his landscapes, creating paintings that appear to be patchworks or mosaics, blocks of colour which complement each other in addition to portraying the subject.

St-Sauveur, two of Aix's landmarks. The first dates from the 16th century, but the lower statues of Night and Day are modern. The wooden statuettes of the four seasons are each visible for three months at a time. The cathedral has a 5th-century baptistery, and work from many different architectural periods is incorporated in this impressive 16th-century Gothic building.

South of Cours Mirabeau is another attractive old neighbourhood, the Quartier Mazarin, smaller and more restrained than Vieil Aix. Beyond the Musée Paul-Arbaud, which houses a collection of local pottery and books on Provence, the Fontaine des Quatre Dauphins stands in the square of the same name. At the head of Rue Cardinale, which leads off the square, is the Musée Granet, which has important works by French, Italian, Flemish and Dutch artists as well as a separate gallery of paintings by Cézanne.

## Montagne Ste Victoire

When the Romans moved into this part of Provence they discovered the hot springs that still feed the fountain in Cours Mirabeau, and founded Aquae Sextiae

Saluviorum – the future Aix – around them in 122 BC. Twenty years later, Roman historians record, a band of Teutonic barbarians invaded the area and were confronted by a Roman army on the hillside to the east of the town. In the battle 100,000 barbarians are said to have been killed and the same number captured. The mountain above the battlefield was called Victory to commemorate the slaughter.

The mountain was beloved of Cézanne, and a visit to it can feel like a pilgrimage. Those willing to punish themselves in true medieval pilgrim fashion can climb up to the Croix-de-Provence, on the highest peak of the long ridge. Starting from Les Cabassols, on the D10, this route involves a 550-m climb and takes about two and a half hours. The reward is a close-up sight of the summit cross and a breathtaking view.

## Vauvenargues

This pretty village is famous for its Renaissance château, which was inherited by Pablo Picasso in 1958 and is where he died in 1973. Picasso is buried in the château's extensive park, but neither park nor château is open to the public.

### PROVENÇAL SWEETS

So much has been written on Provençal cooking, particularly on *bouillabaisse* and *aïoli*, that other specialities of the region are sometimes overlooked. One of these is sweets, and at Aix one of the most famous is made. These are *calissons*, small, diamond-shaped biscuits that are made of iced almond paste.

You could also try crystallised fruit or jam from the small town of Apt; or the preserved melon from Avignon. Carpentras is famous for its *berlingots*, caramel sweets, while Sault, on Mont Ventoux, produces a nougat made from honey that is every bit as delicious as the more famous sweet from Montélimar. Montélimar nougat started as a local, home-made sweet, but is now a full-scale industry. The nougat is a blend of almonds and honey, but the detailed recipes of the different manufacturers are closely guarded secrets. Tarascon, between Avignon and Arles, specialises in chocolates called *tartarinades*.

Elsewhere, do not turn down the chance of sampling *beignets de fleurs d'acacia*, a pancake flavoured with acacia blossom, or a *torta bléa*, a cake made with raisins and crushed pine kernels.

# THE VERDON GORGE

The River Verdon is a long tributary of the Durance, and would be pleasing but hardly remarkable were it not for the deep gorge it has cut into the limestone plateau of Haute-Provence between the villages of Castellane and Moustiers-Ste-Marie. The Grand Canyon du Verdon is one of the natural wonders of Europe, and is scattered with spectacular viewpoints.

**Comité Département al du Tourisme des Alpes de Haute-Provence**
19 Rue du Docteur
Honnorat – BP 170
04005 Digne-les Bains
Cedex
Tel: 04 92 31 57 29
www.alpes-haute-provence.com

**Touring:**
AA Road Map France
series 15: Provence &
Côte d'Azur

*Opinions differ, but it is believed that the remarkable Grand Canyon du Verdon – 20km long and 800m deep in places – was cut either while the limestone plateau was being raised or while the local sea level was falling.*

## Aiguines

This tiny village, at the start of the road known as the Corniche Sublime, is delightfully set among cypresses and has a 17th-century château. There is also a small craft museum, exhibiting wood carvings.

## Bargème

Bargème is a typical Provençal village and can only be visited on foot. Visitors should park below the village and enter it through a gate. There is a Romanesque church, and excellent views can be had from the ruins of the medieval castle.

## Castellane

When he landed close to Antibes from Elba on 1 March 1815, Napoleon Bonaparte knew he would not receive a universal welcome from the French. He was disappointed, however, to be rejected by the garrison at Antibes, and, learning that he could expect no better treatment in the Rhône valley, he decided to strike inland, intending to reach the Durance valley and to use that to penetrate the French heartland. He and his followers headed towards Grasse, continuing on a difficult path to Séranon. To cross the River Verdon they made for the village of Castellane. Support grew, and when Napoleon reached Grenoble on 7 March he was met by shouts of 'Long live the Emperor'.

In Castellane, Napoleon stopped for lunch at 34 Rue Nationale, the road that forms, with Place Marcel Suavaire, the centre of this charming old village. Close by is the picturesque 14th-century clock tower set above one of the ancient gateways into the village. To the north there remains a section of the old ramparts.

Dominating Castellane is a huge cuboid limestone block topped by the chapel of Notre-Dame-du-Roc, a viewpoint which is reached via a steep, narrow track marked by the Stations of the Cross.

### THE SENTIER MARTEL

The Verdon Gorge was first explored by the renowned French speleologist Édouard-Alfred Martel (1859–1938), and a footpath through it has been named in his honour: the Sentier Martel. The ends of this path are reached by others that go down the steep rock face at the Point Sublime, or at the Chalet de la Maline on the Route des Crêtes. Walking the path will take not less than six or seven hours, and because of the stops that will certainly be made, it is best to set aside a whole day.

Walkers on the route will find seven tunnels but only the first two reached from the Point Sublime should be entered. All the tunnels were made as part of an aborted scheme to dam the Gorge and the remainder are partially collapsed and very dangerous. The walker must also keep to the marked path: the level of the Verdon can rise suddenly and swiftly as upstream sluices are operated, and if you are caught off the path at an awkward point it could be very dangerous.

Walkers must be well equipped: warm and waterproof gear should be carried, boots with ankle support worn, and a head torch is essential. There is no drinking water along the route (despite the river's proximity) so water as well as food must be carried. Walkers should also obtain a map or guide, both of which are available locally, before setting out on this long and challenging route.

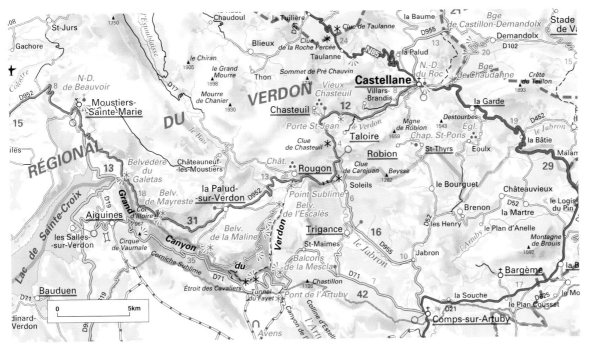

## HILL VILLAGES

In the high hills of Haute-Provence there is a series of villages as characteristic of the area as the resort towns are of the Côte d'Azur. These are the *villages perchés* (perched villages), sometimes called *nids d'aigles* (eagles' nests). The villages performed the same function as the walled towns of the plains and valleys, or even of the hill-forts of an earlier age, being refuges from marauders. Some of the villages are so close to the coast that they may even have been used as a refuge from seaborne pirates.

Many of the villages are piled up in a remarkable but very picturesque way. In the main, however, problems connected with access and water made them less favoured by the inhabitants than by visitors, and may of the least accessible gradually fell into disrepair. Recently there has been a revival in their fortunes, with craftsmen and city-dwellers restoring the houses and

## Grand Canyon du Verdon

Though Europe cannot match Arizona's Grand Canyon, the Verdon Gorge, which shares the name, is spectacular in its own right. Over millions of years the River Verdon has carved down into the limestone plateau. In principle the method of channelling is straightforward, yet the production of such a deep, clean-cut gorge is not fully understood, and experts disagree, because it requires a process that is both rapid – on geological rather than human timescale – and very corrosive.

Two roads run along the rim of the Canyon, each with numerous viewpoints. The southern route leaves the D952 a few kilometres south of Moustiers-Ste-Marie and goes down to the Lac de Ste Croix, and artificial lake feeding a hydro-electric power station, before rising to the rim of the Canyon. The road is called the Corniche Sublime, and passes several tiny stopping points before reaching the attractively situated Hotel Grand Canyon. Ahead now are the spectacular Tunnels de Fayet and a bridge over the River Artuby, before the high spot, the Balcons de la Mescla, is reached. 'Mescla' refers to the mixing of the Artuby and the Verdon hundreds of metres below.

*Moustiers-Ste-Marie has long been famed for its glazed pottery. Visitors can see a museum devoted to the craft and choose from a wide range of items of local pottery on sale in the village.*

To reach the Castellane road (at Pont-de-Soleils) the visitor can either take the longer route via Comps-sur-Artuby, or the short cut through Trigance. On the southern edge of the Canyon, going now from Castellane to Moustiers-Ste-Marie, the road first reaches the Point Sublime, which is considered to give the finest view. Park at the inn here and walk to the edge of the 180-m cliffs.

Further on, the Route des Crêtes leaves the D952, clinging closer to the rim and reaching the belvedere at Barre de l'Escalès, which is another famous viewpoint. the D952 is joined again at La Palud-sur-Verdon, several more excellent viewpoints being passed before Moustiers-Ste-Marie is eventually reached.

## Moustiers-Ste-Marie

The most surprising thing about Moustiers-Ste-Marie is the star hanging from a rusty chain that spans the gorge above the village. This was put up by a local knight to celebrate his release from captivity during the Crusades. The village beneath the star is noted for its pottery, which became famous in medieval times when a monk from Faenza in Italy brought the secret of the glaze with him to the monastery here. By the 18th century the potteries had ceased production, but the tradition was revived in the 20th century.

revitalising the communities. Bargème and Trigance (above), near the Grand Canyon du Verdon, are typical hill villages.

# VAR AND THE MASSIF DES MAURES

Sandwiched between the *départements* of Alpes Maritimes and Bouches-du-Rhône lies Var. Its coastline includes the extremes of Toulon, a heavily industrialised port, and glamorous St Tropez. There is much of interest to be found between the two, and the coast is backed for much of its length by the Massif des Maures, an extensive range of tree-covered hills.

## Bormes-les-Mimosas

Drive east on the N98 from Hyères to Le Lavandou as the sun is rising or setting and you will see Bormes-les-Mimosas at its best, picked out by low-angled light.

This charming hill village, alive with mimosa and camomile, offers excellent views from the ruined castle. It also has

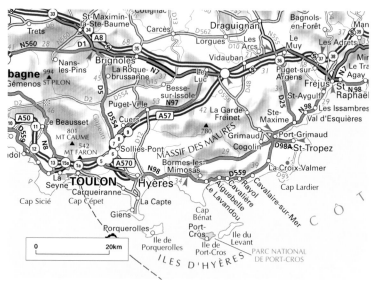

**Comité Département al du Tourisme du Var**
1, Boulevard Foch – BP 99
83003 Draguignan Cedex
Tel: 04 94 50 55 50
www.tourismevar.com

**Touring:**
AA Road Map France
series 15: Provence &
Côte d'Azur

an 18th-century church built in the Romanesque style and a museum of local art.

## Fréjus/St Raphaël

The two towns form a single conurbation, with Fréjus offering the inland, historical aspects and St Raphaël the beach resort. Fréjus was a Roman port and many sections of the Roman city can still be seen, but the harbour silted up after it was neglected, and efforts to revive the port were finally abandoned. The town's later history includes the construction of a fortified complex that takes in a small cathedral, cloisters, baptistery and a bishop's palace. The baptistery dates from the 4th or 5th century, and is therefore one of the oldest buildings in France.

St Raphaël is a sedate beach resort, a pleasant change, some might say, from

St Tropez and the livelier resorts to the east. Its clear waters make it a popular centre for scuba diving.

## Hyères

Hyères claims to be the oldest resort on the Côte d'Azur, and indeed in the 16th century Catherine de Medici considered building a royal villa here. Three hundred years later Queen Victoria visited the town, but ultimately its exposed winter position caused it to lose out to resorts further east. Tropical gardens are Hyères' pride: the Parc St-Bernard has a great number of tropical plants, as have the Jardins Olbius–Riquier, where there is also a fine collection of cacti. Even the wide, airy streets of the town are lined with plants.

## Le Lavandou and the Maures Coast

Le Lavandou is one of the discoveries of the Var coast, a Provençal fishing port that is still just that, despite an increase in tourism further east towards St Tropez. East of Le Lavandou there are several more charming spots, many with excellent beaches: St Clair, Cavalière, Le Rayol-Canadel-sur-Mer and Cavalaire-sur-Mer.

## Massif des Maures

The heavily forested Maures – the name derives from the Provençal word for a dark forest – are a rocky range of mountains created in the same geological upheaval that formed Corsica. Today there are vineyards in the lush hill valleys, and cork oaks are grown to provide the corks for the bottles. The range can be explored by a series of narrow, difficult roads with sudden

*The pretty village of Bormes-les-Mimosas benefits from a pleasant hillside setting with the sea in front and forest behind. Its three sandy bathing beaches and good-sized marina make it an attractive holiday resort.*

*Cork oaks abound in the densely wooded Massif des Maures, which stretches from Hyères to St Raphaël.*

## THE PORT-CROS NATIONAL PARK

Most of France's Parcs Nationaux are set in high, unspoilt country – the Cévennes, Vercors and so on. One exception is Port-Cros, which embraces several small islands and a marine nature reserve. The Ile de Port Cros can be reached by boat from Hyères, Port-de-Miramar (east of Hyères) or from the nearby Ile de Porquerolles. The Park was created in 1963 and protects a sub-sea forest of seaweeds and kelp, inhabited by sea urchins, octopus and a large number of different species of fish. An underwater path is marked out for visiting divers

On the island itself the vegetation can be divided into four distinct, and equally interesting, areas: the coast, the mountain slopes, the valleys and the high peak – not very high at 194m, but burned out by the sea and wind. The island is also famous for its reptiles, amphibians and butterflies.

The neighbouring Ile du Levant to the east and Ile de Porquerolles to the west, can also be explored. Levant has a single village, Héliopolis, which is used nowadays by naturists.

Ile de Porquerolles, the largest island, has a small holiday village. There are good walks from here to the lighthouse and the signal station, each of which gives a superb view. (Please note that no vehicles are allowed on the islands.)

viewpoints, reaching picturesque villages such as Collobrières, where the river is crossed by a humpback bridge.

## Ste Maxime

Across the bay from St Tropez lies Ste Maxime, a lively resort well sheltered from the *mistral*. There are fine beaches, shops, cafés and restaurants, enough entertainment at night to keep the most discerning visitor happy and an extraordinary museum of mechanical music, with old gramophones, music boxes and barrel organs.

## St-Maximin-la-Ste Baume

For 13 years after the Crucifixion, it is said, Mary Magdalene lived with the Virgin Mary. Then, with several others, she was set adrift on the Mediterranean in an open boat. The party survived the journey and came ashore at Stes Maries-de-la-Mer, and went their separate ways. So it was that Mary Magdalene found and occupied a cave high on the mountainside of St Pilon, on the Massif de la Ste Baume. There she lived for 30 years until, sensing her end, she came down to a village at the foot of the mountain to be blessed by St Maximin, Bishop of Aix.

A Provençal legend of long standing, the story goes on to tell that after Mary's death a church was raised over her sarcophagus, and that which contains the remains of St Maximin. Following a Saracen raid the remains were lost, but they were rediscovered in the 13th century. The fine

basilica in the town was then built to house the original sarcophagus and the bronze reliquary containing Mary's skull.

## St Tropez

It is difficult to separate the real St Tropez from the myth that surrounds it. Yet once the yachts, the topless stars-in-waiting and the dream-seeking crowds have all left, it is revealed as a charming little town, bathed in the pure light that attracted Matisse, Braque an others to the area in the days before its notoriety. Some of their work can be seen in the Musée de Peinture de L'Annonciade, but most visitors come to see the port, the little squares and the view across the bay.

## Toulon

France's second naval port was heavily bombed during World War II, its reconstruction creating a modern city, ideal for the shopper but with less to offer the committed tourist. The Tour Royale on the eastern harbour arm was built by Louis XII in the 16th century and has walls over 6m thick. It houses exhibits for which there was not room in the naval museum on the harbour's west side.

Toulon is a good starting-point for a visit to Mont Faron, reached by funivia or road from the north end of the town.

*The very name of St Tropez evokes the luxurious lifestyle associated with the Côte d'Azur as a whole. But alongside the glamorous resort an ordinary little fishing port gets on with its daily business.*

*Toulon's naval connections are evident all over the city, whose fine harbour is overlooked by hilltop forts*

# NICE TO MENTON

When the brilliant blue of the Mediterranean is seen from the high *corniches* that follow the coast between Nice and Menton, it is easy to understand why this stretch of coast, perhaps more than that to the west, is though of as the heart of the Côte d'Azur. This is a busy, densely populated coastline, a vibrant and colourful area that invigorates all the senses.

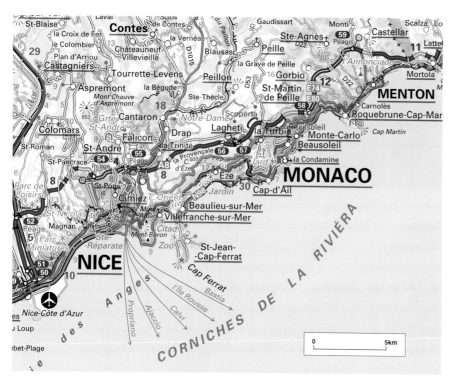

**Comité Regional du Tourisme de Riviera**
55, Promenade des Anglais – BP1 602
06011 Nice
Tel: 04 93 37 78 78
www.guideriviera.com

**Touring:**
AA Road Map France series 15: Provence & Côte d'Azur

## Beaulieu

Cap Ferrat is reached across a narrow neck of land, on the inland side of which is Beaulieu, a resort town grouped around the sheltered Baie des Fourmis.

Overlooking the bay is the curious Villa Kerylos, a faithful 20th-century reconstruction of a Greek villa.

## Cap Ferrat

Beyond the Mont Boron headland, Cap Ferrat thrusts out into the Mediterranean. At its southern point – Cap Ferrat itself, though that name is now more commonly applied to the whole peninsula – is a lighthouse where a climb up 164 steps reveals an awesome panorama.

On the Cap there is a zoo and the old fishing village of St Jean-Cap-Ferrat. No visitor should miss the Musée Ile de France, an Italianate villa which displays Flemish tapestries, Chinese porcelain and Impressionist paintings, including works by Monet and Renoir.

## Menton

Menton, which claims to be the warmest town on the Côte d'Azur and boasts citrus orchards that reinforce the claim, is a typically Italian town set down in France. The Jardin Biovès, at the western end of the Promenade du Soleil, is fringed with palm and lemon trees, and is the setting for the annual citrus festival in February, which uses over 100 tons of fruit as lavish decoratons. At the other end of the town the Colombières gardens have a splendid collection of Mediterranean shrubs and flowers.

Within the town itself the Musée Jean-Cocteau, at the southern corner of the port, has a good collection of the artist's work. Admirers of Cocteau should also see the Salle de Mariages, which he decorated with murals depicting, among other things, a traditional Menton fisherman and a girl in a Nice bonnet. Across the port from the Cocteau museum is the Jetée Impératrice Eugénie, with its fine statue by Volti.

## Monaco

Completely surrounded by France, the Principality of Monaco is a sovereign state of less than 200 hectares and with fewer than 25,000 inhabitants. Of these only about 4000 are genuine Monégasques, a population who preserve their own language, Monégasco, a French dialect. Monaco has its own car licence plates and stamps(though since the advent of the euro, no longer its own money) and everything the tourist needs.

*Hilly Menton gently echoes the mountains that lie behind it. The vantage point of the Jetée Impératrice Eugénie gives a good view of both the town and the peaks. Near by is Cap-Martin, another splendid viewpoint.*

*Villefranche-sur-Mer is a fishing port with the added attraction of the fine Citadelle, now a museum.*

*The Changing of the Guard outside Monaco's Palais du Prince preserves an ancient tradition much loved by visitors.*

The Principality comprises three separate 'towns': Monaco itself, with the Palais du Prince; La Condamine, the commercial centre; and Monte Carlo, with its casino, marina and exclusive hotels, shops and restaurants. For many it is Monte Carlo that is the draw, a fabled, glittering town. But it comes as a surprise to learn that the Casino – a sumptuous building that looks even better when floodlit – now provides only 3 per cent of Monaco's income. To appreciate Monte Carlo it is not necessary to be a big spender. The parks and gardens are beautiful, the seafront and views outstanding, while beyond the Grand Prix's hairpin bend the collection of dolls and automata in the National Museum is thought by many to be the world's best.

Monaco is more staid, though no less glamorous. The palace of the Grimaldi family – who have ruled the Principality since the 14th century – is both ornate and imposing. Visitors walk past the distinctive guards and below the fish-tailed battlements on a guided tour. Close by is the superb Jardin Exotique, with thousands of varieties of cacti and other succulents, and breathtaking views across to Monte Carlo. But no less fascinating is the Musée Océanographique, holding over 4,000 species of fish from all over the world.

## Nice

Nice is regarded by many, and certainly by the city itself, as the capital of the Côte d'Azur. It enjoys a beautiful setting, sheltered on its landward side by a ring of low hills and on its seaward side by the headlands that enclose a semicircular section of the Baie des Anges. Travellers arriving by air will be treated to breathtaking views of the coast on landing, and will be astonished by how close they are to the city, for the airport is right by the seafront.

The seafront road is the Promenade des Anglais. Its name recalls the efforts of the 19th-century British community, who built the earliest road, in order to provide better access to the water.

Nice is divided into two by the River Paillon, though for much of its journey through the city this flows beneath the buildings. To the east of the river is the old quarter. Until 1860 Nice was Italian – Antonio Garibaldi, the hero of the Italian Risorgimento, was born here – and that ancestry is reflected in the buildings close to the old port. The port, and the older, Italianate, quarter are overlooked by the 'castle', which is no more than a wide, flat-topped hill once occupied by a fortress that was demolished in the early 18th century. In the old quarter below is the Palais Lascaris, built in Genoese style by a 17th-century Count of Ventimiglia, and furnished in the grand Italian tradition.

Nice is rich in art collections – Duffy, Chagall and Matisse each have a museum, and as well as the Musée des Beaux Arts which houses mainly 18th and 19th-century works, there is a museum of naïve art and a new Museum of Contemporary Art.

## Villefranche-sur-Mer

Nestling on the island flank of Mont Boron, and protected by Cap Ferrat, is Villefranche-sur-Mer, a delightful old fishing and trading port. The port was guarded by the Citadelle, built in the mid-16th century by a Duke of Savoy. The castle was built after the Congress of Nice, held in 1538 in an effort to bring peace between Charles V, Emperor of the Holy Roman Empire, and François I of France.

### NICE CARNIVAL

Exactly when the first Carnival took place in Nice is debatable. Certainly it was held in the 14th century, and there is evidence for its having taken place at least two centuries earlier. Probably it was a pagan springtime rite even earlier still. After the Restoration, in 1814, the Carnival fell into decline and would probably have disappeared altogether had not Nice's Russian community shown an interest in reviving it 50 years later. Then, in 1873, the Nice painter, Alexis Massa, restored the Carnival to its present form. The Carnival, or Mardi Gras, occupies the two weeks before Lent.

*The Russian Orthodox Cathedral in Nice was consecrated in 1912. This magnificent building is constructed of red brick faced with grey marble and is topped by six onion domes.*

# INDEX

# ACKNOWLEGDEMENTS

The Automobile Association would like to thank the following photographers, libraries and associations for their assistance in the preparation of this book.

J ALLAN CASH PHOTOLIBRARY 17t Vitré Castle, 17bl Combourg Castle, 27t Dinard, 27b St Malo, 61r Chenonceaux, 101l Pilat Dunes, 121t View from Pug de Sancy, 121r Riom Virgin and Bird, 168/169 Basque Countryside, 168l Basque Houses, 172t Cirque de Gavarnie.

P ATTERBURY 39t Vimy.

BRIDGEMAN ART LIBRARY 183t Montagne
Ste-Victoire.

CHAMONIX TOURIST BOARD 145c Mont Blanc.

FRENCH PICTURE LIBRARY (BARRIE SMITH) 143l Chamonix, 153t Fishing, 174r Train, Cerdagne.

HAUTE SAVOIE 132 River Drance – Canoeist, 141t Lac d'Annecy.

LE STRADE AVEN ARMAND 129b Le Palmier.

J LLOYD 96b Cascades du Hérisson, 106t Marais, Poitevin, 126l Cévannes, 134l Lyon, silk weaving, 135t Tournon, 135r, Vivarais railway, 136t Aven d'Orgnac, 137 Belvédère de la Madeleine, 172b Climbers, 173l Luz-St Sauveur.

MARY EVANS PICTURE LIBRARY 145t Voegeli climbs Pic du Toedi.

JOHN MILLAR 122l Parc Régional des Volcans d'Auvergne, 146 L'Ecot, 147r Valé d'Avérole, 147b Bonneval Sur, Arc.

NATURE PHOTOGRAPHERS LTD 65tr Scarce Swallowtail Butterfly, 107 Mussels, 140r Alpine flowers, 174l Val d'Eyne, Alpine meadows.

OFFICE DÉPARTEMENTAL DE TOURISME DU DORDOGNE 154b Lascaux II Caves

PICTURES COLOUR LIBRARY 142l The Cerdagne , 175t Llo Carvings

SCOPE 131t Cheese.

SPECTRUM COLOUR LIBRARY 17bc Fougères Fortress, 128r Grottes des Demoiselles.

THE PHOTOGRAPHERS LIBRARY 122t Salers, 140l Annecy and town.

VLOO 41t Amiens Cathedral, 82b Farm in the Morvan, 145b Alpine sport.

WORLD PICTURES LTD 52b Strasbourg Old Town, 141b View across L'Annecy, 143r Mer de Glace.

ZEFA PICTURE LIBRARY (UK) LTD 9c Carnac Standing Stone, 9cb Finistère, 10 Carnac, 11t Quiberon, 12l Quimper Cathedral, 15r Crozon Coast, 43c Reims Cathedral.

All remaining pictures are held in the Association's own library (AA PHOTO LIBRARY) with contributions from:

P Bennett, J Edmunson, P Enticknap, P Kenward, R Moore, D Noble, T Oliver, K Paterson, D Robertson, B Rieger , C Sawyer, M Short, B Smith, A Souter, R Strange, J A Tims, R Victor.

The publishers would like to acknowledge the facilities and assistance
provided to the authors by the following:

Aunis Nord Tourisme
Brittany Ferries
Toby Oliver of Brittany Ferries
Departmental Tourist Offices
The Ford Motor Company Limited
The French Government Tourist Office
Novatel
P & O Ferries
Véronique Seban of the Côte d'Azur tourist office